THE
LOGIC
OF
SURVEY
ANALYSIS

THE LOGIC OF SURVEY ANALYSIS

Morris Rosenberg

Basic Books, Inc., Publishers

New York   London

To Florence and Paul

Foreword

PAUL F. LAZARSFELD

The history of *surveys* can be divided into three phases. Up to about 1930, the term connoted the collection of factual information which would help to improve social conditions. Then about this time two new ideas were introduced: sampling techniques and the measurement of attitudes. For some years the notion of surveys was associated with studies of public opinion, employee morale, and consumer preferences.

The third period might be dated from the appearance of "The American Soldier"[1] after World War II. In this work, a large body of data was made coherent and meaningful by careful statistical analysis. "Survey analysis" now took on a broader connotation. It became the language of empirical social research, possessing its own rules for forming basic concepts and combining them into meaningful propositions.

In recent years, a number of important books have appeared elaborating and refining this new language. Hyman[2] summarized the general principles; Hirschi and Selvin[3] showed how they could be applied in delinquency research; Galtung[4] incorporated survey research into a more general logic of social inquiry; Glock[5] and his collaborators demonstrated the scope of its application. Survey analysis yielded rich findings in a wide range of fields.

This literature showed the fruitfulness of the new development. But one difficulty remained. It was necessary to have a certain amount of practical experience with survey work in order really to appreciate the generalizations. This was true not only for students but also for teachers who had not had the opportunity to learn the trade in the small number of centers where appropriate training was available. What was still lacking was a text which would link the general principles of survey analysis to the rapidly increasing number of concrete applications. This gap has now been filled by the present book.

First of all, the reader will be struck by the large number of examples assembled from a variety of sources, many of which are not easily accessible. More important, perhaps, he will be helped by the concreteness of specific distinctions which go well beyond the system available until now. It is the purpose of this foreword to share with the reader my understanding of Dr. Rosenberg's intentions.

The author starts out (as does the general literature) from the idea that the relations between two variables can be qualified by the introduction of one or more additional variables. But he then spends three chapters discussing the various kinds of such "test variables" which can be drawn upon. His distinctions are fortunate combinations of logic and psychology; and, by psychology, we mean a concern with the situation in which the survey analyst is likely to find himself. As a typical example, consider what the author calls "component variables." It is frequently the case that we must work with data which come to us from the social bookkeeping practices of modern society (for instance, age or occupation); we may then examine the relations of these characteristics to the attitudes and behavior patterns in which we are interested. Unfortunately, we also often end there. And yet the more sophisticated analysts will want to know *what it is* in a special age or occupational group which accounts for the empirical relations discovered. Rosenberg shows by what techniques the necessary specification can be achieved. In the process, he makes clear that quite different components in this complex classification might be operative, depending upon the subject matter with which we deal. And, implicitly, his analysis also points to the relationship between empirical research and various sociological and psychological theories.

After the author has discussed the various types of test variables, he turns around and raises a question which could be considered the other side of the coin: What kind of statistical patterns result from this process of elaboration? The next three chapters of the text are given to this topic. What happens when we maintain the distinction between the original independent variables and the test variables as against when we treat them asymmetrically—one of the distinctions, incidentally, which Rosenberg stresses in his first chapter. In the first case, one arrives at "conditional relations," to which Rosenberg devotes two chapters. It is again the richness of his examples and the subtleties of his distinctions which make this section especially useful. After all, the nature of the relations between variables among subsets is one of the main logical contributions of survey analysis. The more one understands what they contribute and how they are different from partial correlations, the better will one have grasped the whole purpose of this book.

The author shows how such conditional relations can refute initial interpretations, reinforce them, or lead to revisions. Special attention should be drawn to the last section of Chapter 5, where the test variable has implications for the time element: the age of people, for instance, or the length of time they have been serving in the army. In such cases, even a cross-sectional survey, taken at one time only, can yield information which approaches the study of change and processes.

What the author calls "conjoint influences," in the next chapter, is the same matter seen under a different aspect. Nothing can be added here to the explication by Rosenberg. One should notice that the author assembles here a number of examples which are still very difficult to find. These are cases in which one of the variables characterizes collectives, not individuals. Survey analysis has sometimes been blamed for being too narrow because it neglects the social context within which people act. The use of "collective variables" in survey analysis clarifies greatly its relation to what one might call general sociology.

The last two chapters summarize the main ideas in the light of some case studies. (For some readers, it might be advantageous to start with these two chapters to get a general idea of what this book is driving at; then they will all the more appreciate the details of the main text.) Especially recommended is the example of the "younger-minority boys," the boys who have a majority of older sisters. The reason for the higher self-esteem of these boys is traced in a series of ingenious cross-tabulations.

The final chapter faces head-on some of the main issues confronting empirical social research. Do we always have to follow the traditional idea that all we do is test hypotheses thought of in advance? Rosenberg asserts that often the *unexpected* findings, if pursued by proper analysis, can be most rewarding. There can be little doubt that he is right. This, of course, raises the question as to what is meant by a proper "pursuit of an idea"? Accepting this challenge, the book closes with a careful discussion of the nature of evidence in empirical social research.

There is a story about an English duke who was once asked by a visitor how he kept the lawn of his castle so smooth and green. The duke answered that it was very simple: you just water, weed, and roll it daily, and in a few hundred years you have a perfect lawn. The range and wealth of Rosenberg's presentation is probably explained in a similar way: his collection and systematization of the pertinent literature from twenty-five years of practical survey work. We all owe him a debt for it.

September 1968

NOTES

1. Samuel A. Stouffer et al., *The American Soldier: Adjustment during Army Life*, Vol. I, and *The American Soldier: Combat and Its Aftermath*, Vol. II (Princeton: Princeton University Press, 1949).
2. Herbert H. Hyman, *Survey Design and Analysis* (Glencoe, Ill.: The Free Press, 1955).
3. Travis Hirschi and Hanan C. Selvin, *Delinquency Research* (New York: The Free Press, A Division of the Macmillan Company, 1967).
4. Johan Galtung, *Theory and Methods of Social Research* (New York: Columbia University Press, 1967).
5. Charles Y. Glock, ed., *Survey Research in the Social Sciences* (New York: Russell Sage Foundation, 1967).

Preface

During the past generation the sample survey has been transformed from a brash, struggling, uncertain youngster into a mature, secure member of the establishment. The survey is now accepted as a fundamental instrument of sociological research.

In the course of its transformation from a state of youthful rebellion to one of bourgeois respectability, its rationale has been more clearly explicated, its procedures codified, and its techniques sharpened. The principles and practices of survey research are now widely transmitted from one intellectual generation to the next. But one of the most striking characteristics of contemporary social research education is the sharp imbalance between the emphasis on research design and data collection, on the one hand, and data analysis, on the other. Despite its legitimate family position, data analysis is treated as the proverbial neglected stepchild.

Yet the importance of data analysis is self-evident. Good data are important, but what is done with them is equally so. The data must be viewed within the framework of a certain logic. It is the explication of this logic—the *reasoning* behind the analytic operation—which is the central concern of this book.

The title of this book, *The Logic of Survey Analysis,* serves as much to delimit its focus as to express its characteristic emphasis. It focuses on the *logic,* rather than on the mechanics or statistics, of research procedures; on the *survey,* rather than on experimental, sociometric, or similar techniques; and on *analysis,* rather than on the various problems of research design, data collection, or data processing.

While many ideas on data analysis are the common property of the field, each author inevitably brings to bear a certain distinctive approach and perspective. Perhaps the flavor of what is to come is best given by pointing to certain emphases or orientations which guide this work.

The first is a stress upon the *substantive and theoretical significance* of survey data. It may be argued, of course, that this issue need not concern the methodologist or the scientific instrument maker. A microscope, after all, may be used to look at microbes or at pictures of Mickey Mouse. Similarly, it may be contended that the principles of data analysis apply equally to the study of people's taste in candy and to their alienation from society, and that the analytic principles can probably be more clearly illustrated in the former case.

The value of a research instrument, however, is ultimately dependent on what one is able to learn by using it. The sociologist searches for theoretically meaningful generalizations about the nature of social life. Hence, the present work attempts to show, wherever possible, how the general methodological principles enunciated may be brought to bear on issues of theoretical relevance. Its sole concern is to suggest how data analysis procedures may enrich, enliven, and fortify our understanding of sociological and social psychological phenomena.

A second emphasis is on *explication*. Part of the task of the methodologist is to make explicit certain procedures which are implicit in the work of the practicing investigator. The point is not to tell the researcher something he does not know, but to make him more clearly aware of what he does know. In so doing, it is possible to alert him to theoretic and analytic potentialities in his data which he might otherwise overlook.

A third emphasis is on the *actual process of data analysis*. Research procedures in principle are very different from those in practice. The student reading a published report will usually have an erroneous notion of how the research actually went on, and is likely to be dismayed to find that his own research does not correspond to the neat, compartmentalized principles he has learned. By seeking to communicate the actual process of data analysis, we hope to assuage the student's uneasiness that his research has not proceeded in accord with a strictly proper plan and at the same time stimulate in him greater flexibility in handling his data.

Finally, a stress in this work has been on *simplicity*. Since our interest is in the *logic* of survey analysis, this logic is more likely to be clear when more sophisticated procedures are omitted. Once the logic is clearly understood, there should be little difficulty in introducing techniques of greater complexity and power.

The goal of simplicity has been sought in three ways. The first, and most central, has been to confine the discussion basically to one innocent question: *Given a relationship between two variables, what can be learned by introducing a third variable into the analysis?* For example, one might find that city dwellers are more anomic than rural residents. How can one's understanding of this relationship be enhanced by introducing another variable—say, class, sex, or religion—into the analysis? Hopefully it will be shown that much richness and depth of understanding can be gained by this approach.

Secondly, statistical simplicity has generally been followed. No knowledge of statistics beyond the ability to add up to 100 per cent is required to follow the discussion. Many investigators will prefer to use more exact and powerful statistics, such as standardization, partial correlation, multiple correlation, etc., rather than the primitive subgroup classification which will be generally employed. But the principles discussed apply irrespective of the statistics used.

A third simplifying procedure has been to bypass many issues which are integral and essential aspects of data analysis, for example, the relationship of concepts to indices, contextual analysis, measurement, etc. Satisfactory data analysis is not possible without mastery of many of these topics; they are omitted solely because they outstrip the scope of this work.

Finally, there has been an attempt to sharpen the various points by means of abundant concrete illustrations. However clearly enunciated an abstract principle may be, it is always made more vivid, meaningful, and compelling by rooting it in actual research. Perhaps this is the place to enter an apology for using so many examples from the author's own research. The reason, obviously, is that these are the examples which spring most readily to mind, not that they are the best examples of research. Also, on occasion, examples were used which fell short of the highest statistical requirements if they represented pointed illustrations of the idea under discussion. It must be stressed that an example is only an example, and must be subordinated to the general principle it is designed to exemplify.

The theme of this book can be stated concisely: it deals with the analytic procedure which has come to be known as *elaboration*. In most research, one begins with an hypothesis concerning the relationship between two variables. On the basis of certain theoretical reasoning, one might predict that Negroes are more alienated than whites, that women are more politically apathetic than men, or that social class is positively associated with political conservatism. Such hypotheses are almost invariably predictions concerning the relationship between two variables.

The analyst interested in understanding the meaning of such relationships is usually impelled to ask two questions: "why," and "under what conditions." These questions, often enough, are answered on the basis of informed speculation. Elaboration does not dispense with informed speculation; rather, it exposes such speculation to systematic test. Theoretical acumen, creative imagination, and sound reason are thus indispensable elements of good survey analysis. Elaboration enables the analyst to *test* his reasoning, and at the same time serves as an instrument of discovery.

Before one can undertake the procedure of elaboration, however, one must first consider what the relationship may *mean*. Chapter 1 thus considers the *range of possible meanings* which a relationship between two variables may have. Chapters 2 to 4, dealing with test factors, focus on *why* the relationship exists. Chapters 5 and 6, dealing with conditional relationships, examine the question: *under what conditions* does the relationship appear? Chapter 7 examines the issue of *conjoint influence*. The concluding two chapters, dealing with "the strategy of survey analysis," consider some general issues underlying the approach to, and treatment of, survey data.

As one pores over the research literature, one is struck by the wide variation in the quality of analysis, ranging from the incisive and inspired to the fuzzy and pedestrian. To an important extent, no doubt, good analysis is an "art," a matter of ingenuity, inspiration, and insight; these qualities cannot be conveyed by cold analytical principles.

Art it surely is, but to aver that art cannot be taught is to hasten the demise of schools of music, of drama, journalism, etc. To be sure, no one can teach an analyst imagination or flair, but one can at least suggest certain principles which direct his attention to areas he might otherwise overlook and to meanings which may enrich his own analysis. The analyst's imagination is thus offered increased scope at the same time that it is subjected to firmer discipline.

It is a pleasure to express my gratitude to the many people kind enough to help me. My chief intellectual debt is to my teacher, collaborator, and friend, Paul F. Lazarsfeld; indeed, this book is fundamentally an exposition, extension, and exemplification of Lazarsfeld's approach to survey data analysis. In this area, as in so many other areas of social science methodology, Lazarsfeld's work has been fundamental; the sum of his contributions is monumental.

I also wish to thank John Campbell, Melvin Kohn, and Leonard Pearlin, my good friends and colleagues in the Laboratory of Socio-environmental Studies, National Institute of Mental Health. Their careful readings and creative observations represented constructive criticism at its best. I am indebted, too, to Edward A. Suchman, Robert Dubin, Frank Furstenberg, and Albert Gollin, who were kind enough to offer critical evaluations of the manuscript.

Roberta G. Simmons is the author of Appendix A. She undertook this task at my suggestion, and her contribution is deeply appreciated. Fredrica M. Levin was also extremely helpful at the final stages of this work.

Finally, I would like to thank Erma Jean Surman for typing the various drafts of the manuscript. It is indeed rare that the skills of secretary and research assistant are so felicitously joined.

MORRIS ROSENBERG

Bethesda, Maryland
September 1968

Contents

THE
LOGIC
OF
SURVEY
ANALYSIS

CHAPTER 1

The
Meaning
of
Relationships

The first step in the analysis of survey data is to examine the relationship between two variables. Such a relationship, however, may have many different meanings. In a formal sense there are three possible meanings which a relationship between two variables may have:[1] (1) *Neither* variable may influence the other; such relationships are termed *symmetrical*. (2) *Both* variables may influence one another; these are *reciprocal* relationships. (3) *One* of the variables may influence the other; the term *asymmetrical* is applied to this type of relationship. It is useful to consider some of the different types of symmetrical, reciprocal, and asymmetrical relationships appearing in research.

Symmetrical Relationships

A symmetrical relationship, as noted, assumes that neither variable is due to the other. We may find, for example, that people who do well on verbal tests also do well on mathematics tests. But we would not assume that the mathematical ability is responsible for the verbal ability, or vice versa. It is a matter of indifference whether we say that people who are high on verbal skills tend to be high on mathematical skills or that people who are high on mathematical skills tend to be high on verbal skills.

Symmetrical relationships, while generally of lesser theoretical significance than asymmetrical relationships, are often valuable in understanding social processes. It is thus relevant to consider five types of symmetrical relationships.

The first and most obvious type of symmetrical relationship is one in which both variables are viewed as *alternative indicators of the same concept*. One finds, for example, that there is a relationship between palmar perspiration and heart pounding. Both these symptoms may be interpreted as signs of anxiety; neither variable would be viewed as the cause of the other. Similarly, if there is an association between contributing to the community chest and freedom in lending money to friends, this relationship might be interpreted as one between alternative expressions of the disposition of generosity. If one finds an association between the statements, "I seldom feel blue," and "I often feel depressed and discouraged," one is almost certain that this relationship is due to the fact that these are alternative symptoms of depression.

It is obvious in such cases that it makes no difference how one phrases the relationship. One might say that people whose palms perspire are more likely to experience heart pounding or that people who experience heart pounding are more likely to have palmar perspiration. There is no logical reason for assigning priority to either symptom.[2]

A second type of symmetrical relationship is one in which the two variables are *effects of a common cause*. The presence of a relationship between hay fever and the size of the corn crop does not mean that one causes the other. It simply means that the same favorable climatic conditions that promote corn production also promote the growth of ragweed. Similarly, one generally finds a relationship, among nations, between the level of medical practice and the frequency of

4

air travel. But it is not that medicine keeps pilots alive or that airplanes enable doctors to travel more quickly. Both are consequences of the conditions which have produced the scientific and technological revolutions of recent times, revolutions which find expression in diverse aspects of human behavior.

It is conventional to describe relationships between variables which are consequences of a common cause as "spurious," and to dismiss the result as trivial or meaningless. This conclusion is not invariably justified. For example, it is implicit in Durkheim's analysis that societies which have a restitutive form of justice will be characterized by a high level of egoism in the population.[3] There is no reason to believe, however, that the form of justice is responsible for the level of egoism or that the level of egoism has influenced the nature of the legal system. Durkheim suggests that each of these social phenomena is an outgrowth of the division of labor. To understand this fact is surely to have an improved understanding of these social phenomena.

Such relationships may thus point to the diversity of consequences of some common cause. The relationship is, however, symmetrical, since neither variable is essentially responsible for the other.

A third type of symmetrical relationship is one involving the *functional interdependence* of the elements of a unit.[4] Thus, there is a correlation between the presence of a heart and the presence of lungs: where one is found, the other appears; where one is absent, so is the other. This relationship is based on the fact that the various parts of the total organism perform distinctive functions, thus enabling the unit to survive. But one organ does not "cause" the other, although all the parts are dependent on one another in order for each to perform its task.

The concept of "bureaucracy" is a case in point. One might find, for example, that organizations characterized by formal, abstract, impersonal rules tend to have an elaborate system of hierarchical ranks. It is not that the rules or the ranks cause one another, but that both are indispensable elements in the functioning of the total system.

A closely related type of symmetrical relationship is one in which elements are associated as *parts of a common "system" or "complex."*

They are not, however, functionally interdependent, for the elements are often arbitrary. There may be an association between joining the country club and attending the opera. Both practices are elements of a class "style of life," encompassing a variety of interests, attitudes, values, and behavior which develop out of communicative interaction. But these practices are not indispensable for the unit; they may easily be supplanted by other practices; they are dependent solely upon acceptance by the relevant group.

Such relationships are especially characteristic of cultural practices. Where one finds hamburgers, one also tends to find hot dogs; people who eat lasagna are more likely to eat minestrone; the public burning of blankets is associated with the public destruction of coppers. Such associations shed light on the elements of a whole which hang together for arbitrary reasons. There is, of course, no causal link between the two variables.

Occasional ambiguity arises in deciding whether a relationship is functional or reflects parts of a larger complex. In a sense, both represent the "organismic-holistic" approach. A functional relationship, however, implies an entity in which the various parts play a role indispensable to the operation of the totality. The human body, a machine, a group, an organization all illustrate a functional interrelationship of parts.

A "joint complex," on the other hand, reflects a series of elements that hang together for essentially normative reasons. The elements are, however, socially relevant, and it is important to know what they are. That people who drink martinis tend to patronize concert halls reflects no interdependence between these two practices (such practices might change without doing violence to the complex), but simply indicates that these are components of a certain "style of life." The sociologist is necessarily interested in such life styles or cultural complexes, and such symmetrical relationships may thus be of great interest.

Finally, of course, some symmetrical associations are simply *fortuitous*. The fact that there is an association between proportion of orientals and consumption of rice is simply an accident of history and geography. The fact that there is a rough chronological relationship between rock 'n' roll music and the onset of the space age does not mean that one is in any sense responsible for the other or that they both are associated with a common source (although the imaginative thinker may be capable of establishing such a link). There may be a temptation to see in such correlations the subtle hand of causation or association with a common variable, but one must always acknowledge the possibility of coincidence. The child who has misbehaved and who later accidentally stubs his toe may interpret this sequence of events as divine retribution, but whether it is causal or coincidental remains an imponderable.

It is important to be explicit about the interpretation of a symmetrical relationship, for such interpretations are often susceptible of further test. For example, if one interprets a relationship as reflecting an association between two indicators of a common concept, this assumption can often be tested through scaling techniques, factor analysis, or other internal consistency procedures. If, on the other hand, one interprets the relationship as representing two separate consequences of a common cause, then this assumption can often be tested through control on a test factor (to be discussed in Chapter 2). Similarly, finding that there is a relationship between two indicators of a common concept sheds light on the range and diversity of manifestations of a phenomenon. The finding that two consequences are attributable to a common cause can tell us something about the importance of that cause in accounting for a wide range of social phenomena. The finding that a relationship is based on the functional contribution of two elements to a social unit may often shed light on the structure and operation of the unit. Finally, if a relationship represents the concordance of elements in a system or complex, then it may be of considerable descriptive value in clarifying the nature of the complex.

While symmetrical relationships may not generally match the theoretical significance of asymmetrical relationships in social research, they nonetheless often make important contributions to understanding. It would thus represent a theoretical loss to present such findings simply as descriptive results without attempting to interpret them. The interpretation would ordinarily suggest, however, that elaboration is *not* a useful next step.

Reciprocal Relationships

One frequently encounters relationships in social research in which it is not immediately possible to specify which is the independent (causal) and which the dependent (effect) variable, but in which causal forces are nonetheless in operation. This is the case in which the two variables are reciprocal, interacting, and mutually reinforcing; one might describe this pattern as one of "alternating asymmetry."

Probably the classical illustration of a reciprocal relationship is that between the temperature and the thermostat. The temperature influences the action of the thermostat, and the thermostat influences the temperature in the room, in an endless cyclical process. The *present* relationship is due to the mutual effects of both variables; each is cause and each is effect. The engineering concepts "feedback" and "servomechanisms" illustrate this type of relationship.

Such reciprocal relationships are extremely common in survey research. One finds, for example, that Republicans tend to be exposed to Republican communications and Democrats to Democratic communications. It is apparent that the causal influence between exposure and political affiliation operates in both directions. Republican convictions cause one to select Republican messages, and Republican messages reinforce one's Republican convictions. Again, one might find a relationship between alienation and low social status. Low status may alienate one from the societal value system, and alienation may cause behavior which results in low status. Similarly, one may find a relationship between investments and profits. A company which makes profits increases its investments, which increases its profits, which increases its investments. The elucidation of such mutually reinforcing processes may contribute substantially to the understanding of social phenomena.

We have described this pattern of asymmetry as alternating because, as Blalock notes:

Probably most persons agree that *A* cannot be a cause of *B* and *B* simultaneously a cause of *A*. Yet we may wish to speak of *X* and *Y* being

"mutual causes," or we allow for "reciprocal" causation.
mean would be something like this: a change in X produ
Y, which in turn produces a further change in X at some la
produces a still further change in Y, and so on. Symbolica

$$X_{t_0} \to Y_{t_1} \longrightarrow X_{t_2} \longrightarrow Y_{t_3} \longrightarrow X_{t_4} \longrightarrow \ldots$$

An increase in the level of unemployment might lead to fewer retail sales at a somewhat later time. This, in turn, could lead to further unemployment, and so on.[5]

The reciprocal type of relationship thus stands somewhere between the symmetrical and the asymmetrical types. It is symmetrical in the sense that one cannot say which variable is cause and which effect, which independent and which dependent. At the same time it is asymmetrical in the sense that each variable is continuously affecting the other. In such cases, of course, one might speculate as to a "primal cause," but it is an open question whether this can be considered the independent variable. For example, one may find a relationship between a husband's hostility toward his wife and her hostility toward him. Perhaps his hostility has caused him to behave disagreeably toward her; this behavior arouses her hostility, which causes her to respond with equal unpleasantness, which increases his hostility, etc. One might say that the primal cause was his original hostility. But after this has been going on for some time, it is no longer the original cause, but the unpleasant behavior of each toward the other, which arouses their mutual hostility. The relationship is one of alternating asymmetry. It is sufficient to know that the chicken and egg are responsible for one another without confronting the problem of which came first.[6]

Asymmetrical Relationships

The core of sociological analysis is to be found in the asymmetrical relationship. In this type of relationship, we postulate that one variable (the independent variable) is essentially "responsible for" another (the dependent variable). If younger people go to the movies more, it is apparent that it is some aspect of their age which is responsible for the movie attendance, since there is no way in which going to the movies can make one young. Asymmetrical relationships thus propel one into the vital scientific area of causal analysis.[7]

Thus far we have used the concept of causation rather loosely, employing it in its common-sense meaning of one variable being "responsible for" another. Causation, however, has a more restricted meaning. We speak of a cause when an external influence produces a change in some unit. The term "produces" is crucial in this definition, for it implies that an efficient, external agent exercises an isolable power on the unit. Causes have properties of uniqueness, isolability, productiveness, invariability, unidirectionality, etc.,[8] which are by no means characteristic of many asymmetrical relationships in social science.

It is generally assumed that causal analysis is the basic approach of the scientific method. This is a misconception. The scientist is interested in explanation and understanding (as well as prediction and control); causation is only one of several ways of producing this explanation and understanding.

Bunge notes: ". . . There are many ways of understanding, that is, of answering why-questions, the disclosure of causes being but one of such ways. . . . Causality is not a sufficient condition for understanding reality, although it is quite often a component of scientific explanation. . . . Scientific explanation is, in short, explanation by laws—not necessarily explanation by causes."[9] One need merely note such formulae as "energy equals one-half of mass times the square of velocity," or "electrical resistance equals current divided by pressure," to recognize that these noncausal statements (neither side of the equation "causes" the other) are of enormous scientific value.

Causation, in fact, is but one type of *determination*.[10] Determination involves a *necessary connection* between two variables; a causal relationship represents but one among a much larger number of types of necessary connections among variables.[11]

Since the material available to the survey analyst is a correlation, on what basis does he decide which is the determining (independent) variable and which the determined (dependent) variable? The key criterion for understanding the direction of determination appears to be *susceptibility to influence*. If one finds a relationship between sex and political interest, it is obvious that one's level of political interest cannot determine one's sex; the influence can only be in the other direction. If older people are politically more conservative, their conservatism surely did not make them old; it can only be that their age, in some sense, is responsible for their conservatism.

Two factors are basically involved in deciding on the direction of influence of the variables: (1) the time order, and (2) the fixity or alterability of the variables.

The importance of the time sequence has been universally emphasized. Since something that happened later cannot be responsible for what happened earlier, it follows that the variable which is temporally prior must always be the determinant or independent variable. If one finds a relationship between the way children have been toilet-trained and their adult personalities, the adult personalities cannot be responsible for the toilet-training experiences. "If, for instance, we relate length of engagement with subsequent marital happiness, the length of engagement comes earlier in the time order. If we relate parole breaking to some conditions of a criminal's adolescence, the latter again is prior in the time sequence."[12]

The time factor, while important, is not an infallible guide in determining the direction of determination. If someone is born both Negro and poor, and remains that way throughout his life, neither variable has temporal priority. Yet there is no doubt whatever that race is the determining variable. It is not that race came first, in the temporal sense, but that race is not subject to change, whereas income is. Similarly, if one finds a relationship between education and television viewing, it is difficult to establish any temporal priority; during the years of education one watched television, and during the years of watching television one went to school. Time thus does not tell the tale. Yet the direction of determination is clear. It is easy to see how level of education may determine one's preference for certain kinds of programs, but it is much less likely that preference for certain kinds of programs will importantly determine one's educational level.

These observations suggest the second criterion of determinacy, namely, the *fixity, permanence,* or *alterability* of the variables. Sociology employs a number of such fixed variables, for example, sex, race, birth order, national origin. The variable of age, while not unchangeable, is not subject to influence by any power. Similarly, if Negroes are more alienated than whites,[13] it is evident that the alienation cannot be responsible for the race. If Italians feel they have less control over their government than Americans,[14] the attitudes toward the government cannot be responsible for their nationality. Race and national origins are fixed, uninfluenceable properties.

Certain important sociological variables are relatively, but not absolutely, fixed properties of the individual. Social class, religion, and rural-urban residence are of this nature. As a consequence, some element of reciprocity may enter into an asymmetrical relationship; that is, the dependent variable may have some influence on the independent variable. For example, consider the relationship between social class and organizational membership. While one's social class generally determines one's organizational membership, it is possible that some people may join organizations to "meet the right people" and thereby achieve acceptance into the higher reaches of the status system. Or consider the well-documented relationship between religion and political affiliation. While religion must generally be considered the determinant, it is conceivable that a man might change his religion to agree with his political affiliation (an ambitious Protestant running for office in a heavily Catholic neighborhood might "convert").

Does this mean that if it is at all possible for the dependent variable to influence the independent variable, then one can no longer treat the relationship as asymmetrical? This appears to be the position taken by Srole and his colleagues,[15] who argue that only the unalterable variables—age, sex, parental socio-economic status, etc.—can be treated as independent determinants of mental health, whereas no direction of determination can be made for the *relatively* fixed variables, in which some element of reciprocity is possible.

Such a position strikes us as excessively rigid. Survey research must allow for *the dominant direction of influence* of variables. If one finds that a man's religion is related to his mental health, one may reasonably suggest that religion is the dominant influence, although there undoubtedly are cases in which a man's mental health may cause him to change his religion. Similarly, the fact that joining an organization may help one to rise in the status hierarchy should not blind one to the fact that it is the social class which overwhelmingly is responsible for the organizational membership.

The failure to accept this view is actually seen by some as a drawback to the causal principle. According to Bunge:

A severe shortcoming of the strict doctrine of causality is that it disregards the fact that all known actions are accompanied or followed by reactions, that is, that the effect always reacts back on the input unless the latter has ceased to exist. However, an examination of real processes suggests that there are often *predominantly* (though not exclusively) unidirectional C $\longrightarrow$ E (cause leads to effect) actions. Causality may be a good approximation in cases of extreme asymmetry of the cause and the effect, that is, when there is a strong dependence of the effect upon the cause, with a negligible reaction of the output upon the input—and, of course, whenever the cause has ceased existing.[16]

Needless to say, the analyst must give due consideration to the possibility of reciprocal interaction in his interpretation. The decision regarding the dominant direction of influence may either be made on the basis of panel data or on logical or theoretical grounds. So long as the dominant direction of influence can be specified and defended, it is legitimate to interpret one's relationships as asymmetrical and determinative.

Types of asymmetrical relationships

Unless one is engaged in purely descriptive research, the analyst wishes to interpret his relationship in order to reveal its theoretical implications. The particular interpretation he applies to his data will, as we shall see, have important implications for his further data analysis. It is thus worth considering the types of asymmetrical relationships which the sociologist is likely to encounter in his research.

One type of relationship involves an association between *a stimulus and a response*. This would be the most directly causal type of determinant. One might examine the effect of rainfall on the price of wheat, or the threat of war on civilian morale. Such relationships may be mediate or immediate (and they are rarely perfect), but they refer to the influence of some external stimulus upon a particular response.

In order to infer a stimulus-response relationship, it is essential that those exposed to the stimulus and those not exposed are reasonably comparable in other respects. For example, a study was conducted in England to determine the effects of television on children.[17] One might, for example, compare the study habits of children who did or did not have television sets in the home, but this would be questionable since these homes might differ in ways other than the possession of a set. In the early 1950's, however, some British communities had television stations and others did not. The investigators thus took the TV owners in the community with TV reception and matched them on age, socio-economic status, and sex with children in the community without reception. This procedure enabled them to test the effects of television on the children.

The stimulus-response type of relationship encounters peculiar difficulties in social research because of the principle of selectivity. One could not, for example, compare the attitudes of those who have or have not seen a specific film and attribute the difference to the effect of the film, since those who have chosen to see the film may differ in their initial attitudes from those who have not. Some years ago, for example, Hollywood produced an anti-prejudice film entitled "Gentleman's Agreement." If one had studied the prejudice levels of those who had or had not seen the movie, one could not attribute the difference to the film, since it is likely that unprejudiced people sought it out and prejudiced people avoided it. If, however, there is a basis for believing that the two comparison groups are approximately equivalent, or if panel data are available, then it is possible to interpret the relationship as reflecting an association between a stimulus and a response.

Another type of asymmetrical relationship involves an association between *a disposition and a response*. A disposition refers not to a state or condition of the individual, but to a tendency to respond in a certain way under designated circumstances.[18] For example, when we characterize a rubber band as "elastic" or sugar as "soluble," we mean that they are capable of being stretched or dissolved, not that they actually are stretched or dissolved. Similarly, when we characterize a man as a "liberal," we do not mean that he is manifesting liberal inclinations at any particular moment, but that he *would* respond liberally if the appropriate circumstances arose.

Such dispositions, it may be noted, are not "stimuli," in the sense of some external force impinging on an object and producing a certain effect. It is not that some people hear a lecture and others do not, but that some people *have* a certain attitude, trait, or personality quality and others do not. Under certain circumstances, the disposition will give rise to the behavior.

Along with "properties" (to be discussed shortly), dispositions constitute the main type of concepts employed in research. These include: *attitudes* (toward liberalism, toward economic systems, toward political candidates); *abilities* (musical skill, artistic talent, athletic prowess); *reflexes* (eye-blink, Babinski reflex, heat or cold sensitivity); *habits* (brushing teeth, eating at a certain time, watching a recurrent television program); *values* (belief in democracy, equality, success); *drives* (sex, food, belongingness, self-actualization); *"personality traits"* (authoritarianism, compulsiveness, depression); or "powers" or "tendencies" generally.

A very prominent type of research analysis thus considers the relationship between a disposition, as the independent variable, and behavior (verbal or otherwise), as the dependent variable. One might, for example, find a relationship between liberalism and vote, prejudice and discrimination, extraversion and joining groups, intelligence and test performance, valuation of success and striving for good grades, etc. Such relationships tend to be unidirectional and asymmetrical.

Most relationships between dispositions and responses are fairly straightforward. There is, however, a special type of disposition-response relationship which appears to be a partial redundancy, but which is often enlightening and theoretically fruitful. This is the case of a relationship between a broad variable and a more specific variable which is encompassed by it. One would probably find, for example, that authoritarianism (measured, let us say, by the F-scale)[19] is associated with inordinate respect for power. Since the concept of authoritarianism includes, as one of its several elements (or part of its syndrome) attitudes toward power, one would say that the association is due to a larger concept embracing a smaller one.

Or consider the following example. One finds an association between a generalized attitude of misanthropy (distrust of people) and attitudes toward certain specific aspects of the democratic process, for example, the beliefs that the mass of the people are capable of reaching rational political decisions, that political figures are responsive to the will of the people, that people must be restrained by law, etc.[20] While there may be an element of tautology in such a relationship, the result is by no means trivial or irrelevant. If a person has a general disdain or hatred of human nature, then, when confronted with those aspects of a political system which presuppose certain qualities of human nature, he will tend to respond in terms of his general attitude. Thus, the democratic ideology is based on certain fundamental assumptions of man—that man is generally rational, that his elected representatives are responsive to him, that he is capable of guiding his own political destiny without degenerating into anarchy, chaos or ineffectuality. A man's basic attitude toward human nature may thus meaningfully bear on his attitudes toward a political system insofar as the general attitude is implicated in the political attitude. Otherwise expressed, the political attitude is a specific expression of the general attitude.

Similarly, Lott and Lott show that the California E (ethnocentrism) scale is related to the "judgments about the relative superiority of one's own country as compared with another."[21] The broader disposition thus helps one to understand the specific expression of it.

A third type of asymmetrical relationship is one involving a *property*[22] of the individual, as the independent variable, and a disposition or act, as the dependent variable. A property may be distinguished from a disposition in being a relatively perduring characteristic which is not dependent upon circumstances for its activation. In the realm of objects, we might say that solubility is a disposition of a lump of sugar, but its shape, size, weight, and color are its properties. Size and shape are not qualities that an object "can be" or "tends to be"; they refer to what an object "is."

So it is when one studies people. Such qualities as sex, race, religion, rural-urban residence, age, marital status, nationality, hair color, eye color, etc., may be thought of as properties of the individual. A person is a male, a white man, an American, a first child, irrespective of what he does or what happens to him. This is quite different from calling a man "politically liberal." He is "liberal" in the sense that he carries around in him this potential or tendency which may or may not be activated, but not as a firm property, such as his sex, size, nationality, etc.

The relationship between a property and a disposition or act is probably the central type of relationship in social research. The relationships between race and alienation, region of country and voting behavior, age and conservatism, class and anomie, religion and authoritarianism, sex and vote—all these are examples of the relationships of properties, as independent variables, and dispositions or behavior, as dependent variables.

As we observed earlier, the reason properties will almost invariably be treated as the determinant factors in such relationships is that they are either strongly or absolutely resistant to influence. It may be noted, however, that they are "determinants" in a rather different sense from a precise stimulus. To say that a particular political speech makes one more Democratic is surely different from saying that "Catholicism" makes one more Democratic.

A fourth type of asymmetrical relationship is one in which the independent variable is essentially a *necessary precondition* for a given effect. For example, one may find a relationship between a nation's level of technological development and the possession of nuclear weaponry. The technological development does not "cause" the nuclear weaponry; it only makes it possible. Some technologically advanced nations do not possess atomic bombs. Technology is thus a necessary, but not a sufficient, condition for creating the dependent variable. It is not causal in the sense of "forcing" or "producing" the result.

Similarly, it is generally true that there is a relationship between a free and mobile labor force and a particular stage of capitalist development. Marx believed that a free labor force was an essential condition for the development of capitalism—capitalism could not develop without it—but was not solely responsible for capitalism. Marx interpreted such diverse events as the enclosure movement in England and the Civil War in America as events establishing the free labor precondition for capitalism.

A fifth type of asymmetrical relationship is one involving an *immanent* relationship between the two variables. Such a relationship derives from the fact that qualities inherent in the nature of an organism give rise to certain consequences. For example, the sociologist of organization would probably find a relationship between size of bureaucracy and amount of red tape; he would not say that the bureaucracy causes the red tape but that red tape is immanent in bureaucracy. It is inherent in the nature of bureaucracy that it establishes abstract, impersonal rules which cannot adequately adapt to the diverse concrete situations which fall under its rubric. It is also inevitable in the nature of authority and tenure that the bureaucrat will tend to become more concerned with strict adherence to the rules than with effecting the purposes for which the rules were designed. Hence, the phenomenon of red tape. It is not that one factor causes the other, but that the dependent variable arises out of the independent variable.

Michels' contention that organization leads to oligarchy implies a similar determinative sequence.[23] Michels' reasoning, briefly stated, is as follows: Many organizations, such as socialist political parties or labor unions, are created under the aegis of the democratic ideology. The membership bands together, democratically choosing its leaders. In the course of time, however, the leadership develops specialized and expert knowledge of their jobs as, say, union leaders. They also lose their original skills as plumbers and cigar makers, which increases their desire to remain union leaders. At the same time, the membership develops feelings of familiarity with, and respect for, the leadership, and accepts their decisions. Eventually, the membership becomes uninterested and apathetic, thus making it easier for the leaders to maintain their positions.

On the basis of this analysis, Michels erected his "iron law of oligarchy." All organizations originally motivated by a democratic impulse eventually degenerate into oligarchies. It is not that the nature of the organization "causes" oligarchy, but that the democratic organization inevitably becomes *oligarchical*. One may say that oligarchy is immanent in organization.

A sixth type of asymmetrical relationship is one involving an association between *ends* and *means*. The relationship is interpreted as

purposive; it is based on the fact that the means contribute to the
Thus, to cite Bunge's example, there is a relationship between
building of nests by birds and the survival of the young; the nest
building is a means for insuring that survival.[24] Similarly, there is a
relationship between standardization in industry and production costs.
Standardization is a means of reducing costs.

This type of relationship appears with considerable frequency in
social science. One might find, for example, that there is a relationship between hard work and success, amount of studying and school
grades, national aggressive aims and expansion of military forces,
investment and profits, care for personal appearance and marriage
rate, and so on. In each case, the means serve the end.

Since such relationships are viewed as purposive, the question arises:
In whose mind does the purpose reside? Thus, the bird builds her nest
on the basis of instinct, not with the conscious purpose of insuring the
survival of the species. People who are hard-working may end up
successful, even if this was not their particular goal. On the other
hand, a nation with expansionist aims will intentionally enlarge its
military establishment, just as a student who aspires to be accepted
by the college of his choice may decide to concentrate on his school-
work. In some cases, then, the purpose may be in the mind of the
actor, whereas in other cases it is inferred by the analyst.

This leads to the problem of whether the ends determine the means
or whether the means determine the ends. Both are possible: a person
with a goal will select the means best suited to attain it; conversely,
certain behavior may lead to certain ends. How, then, can one decide
whether it is the ends or the means which is the independent variable?

One rule of thumb is that if the purpose resides in the mind of the
actor, then the ends determine the means. Man can plan, and he
selects his behavior in accord with its contribution to his goals. It is
the goal of increased profit that induces the businessman to invest; he
would not do so otherwise. On the other hand, if the purpose resides
in the mind of the investigator, then the means determine the ends
and are the independent variables. The ascetic, this-worldly, work-
dedicated orientation of the early Calvinist was a response to the
unbearable uncertainty posed by the riddle of salvation, but it was

rowth of capitalism. In this case the means gave

the foregoing discussion that there are many
relationships. Hence, when a survey analyst
relationship, his first task is to assign meaning
..., and to do so as explicitly as possible. For one thing, the particular meaning he assigns to the relationship generally determines the next step in his analysis. For another, the theoretical contribution of the finding will depend on the framework within which it is viewed. The first question he must pose, then, is: Is the relationship to be viewed as symmetrical, reciprocal, or asymmetrical; if asymmetrical, which is the independent (determinative) variable and which the dependent (effect) variable?

As we have observed, symmetrical relationships may contribute importantly to scientific understanding in showing that the variables may be indicators of a common concept, in showing the related consequences of a common cause, in revealing the functional relationships among variables, and in showing the concordance of elements in a social complex. Similarly, the understanding of reciprocal relationships is of great value in clarifying the dynamic nature of social processes. Finally, asymmetrical relationships may be enlightening in revealing how stimuli may effect responses, how dispositions may influence behavior, how properties may influence dispositions or behavior, how necessary preconditions may be responsible for consequences, how variables may be immanent in structures, and how ends and means are associated. Each type of interpretation makes its distinctive contribution to the understanding of social phenomena, and all should be given due consideration in the analysis of survey data.

While symmetrical, reciprocal, and asymmetrical relationships all have theoretical significance, the process of elaboration, which is the focus of this book, is undertaken only with *asymmetrical relationships*. The type of asymmetrical relationship most commonly investigated in sociology is one between a *property,* as the independent variable, and a *disposition or act,* as the dependent variable. The relationships between race and vote, age and mental health, class and self-values are illustrative. Once the decision is made that the relationship is asymmetrical, one then introduces a third variable into this two-variable relationship in order to understand it better. It is to this process of elaboration that we now turn.

NOTES

1. Hubert M. Blalock, Jr., *Causal Inference in Nonexperimental Research* (Chapel Hill: University of North Carolina Press, 1961).
2. It is often possible to test the assumption that both variables are indicators of the same concept, through methods of internal consistency, scaling (Guttman, Likert, and Thurstone scales), factor analysis, etc. Such symmetrical relationships may thus represent a first step toward the clarification of dimensions and the improvement of measurement.
3. Emile Durkheim, *The Division of Labor in Society*, trans. George Simpson (Glencoe, Ill.: The Free Press, 1947).
4. Robert K. Merton, *Social Theory and Social Structure* (Glencoe, Ill.: The Free Press, 1949), chap. 1; Kingsley Davis, "The Myth of Functional Analysis," *American Sociological Review*, XXIV (December 1959), 757–782.
5. Blalock, *op. cit.*, pp. 56–57. (Reprinted by permission of the University of North Carolina Press.)
6. It is important to know, of course, whether each variable *equally* affects the other or whether one variable has the more important influence. Fortunately, this issue can be solved through panel analysis. See, for example, the discussion of mutual interactions in Paul F. Lazarsfeld, "The Use of Panels in Social Research," *American Philosophical Society Proceedings*, XCII (1948), 405–410; Morris Rosenberg and Wagner Thielens, "The Panel Study," in Marie Jahoda, Morton Deutsch, and Stuart Cook, eds., *Research Methods in Social Relations* (New York: Dryden Press, 1951), Vol. II, 587–609; and Donald C. Pelz and Frank M. Andrews, "Detecting Causal Priorities in Panel Study Data," *American Sociological Review*, XXIX (December 1964), 836–848.
7. Attempts have been made by Blalock, *op. cit.*, and Herbert A. Simon, *Models of Men* (New York: John Wiley & Sons, Inc., 1957) to establish the direction of causal relationships by means of statistical models. By examining the fit of the empirical data to alternative models, one is in a position to establish causal priorities among variables. This is a promising method, but the statistical principles are too advanced for the present discussion. The panel technique, through the study of temporal sequences or mutual interaction analysis, also helps one to deal with the causal problem.
8. Mario Bunge, *Causality* (Cambridge: Harvard University Press, 1959), part III.

9. *Ibid.*, pp. 305–306.

10. *Ibid.*, Part I.

11. In social science, it must be noted, such determination is virtually never invariable. Relationships are based on statistical trends, so that the relationships reflect tendencies. The independent variable, then, is one which "tends to determine" the dependent variable; the former might be said to "influence" the latter. Ernest Nagel, *The Structure of Science* (New York: Harcourt, Brace, and World, Inc., 1961), pp. 505–509, has noted that one reason social science deals with statistical relationships whereas physical science deals with absolute laws is that the social science laws are stated as though applicable to real situations rather than ideal ones. In order to apply to the real world, for example, the law of falling bodies would have to be stated in statistical terms since the law holds only in a vacuum, which never occurs in the real world (cited in Blalock, *op. cit.*, pp. 16–17).

12. Paul F. Lazarsfeld, "Interpretation of Statistical Relations as a Research Operation," in Paul F. Lazarsfeld and Morris Rosenberg, eds., *The Language of Social Research* (Glencoe, Ill.: The Free Press, 1955), p. 120.

13. Russell Middleton, "Alienation, Race, and Education," *American Sociological Review*, XXVIII (December 1963), 973–977.

14. Gabriel Almond and Sidney Verba, *The Civic Culture* (Princeton: Princeton University Press, 1963), chap. 4.

15. Leo Srole et al., *Mental Health in the Metropolis* (New York: McGraw-Hill Book Company, 1962), p. 20.

16. Bunge, *op. cit.*, p. 170.

17. Hilde Himmelweit, A. N. Oppenheim, and Pamela Vince, *Television and the Child* (New York: Oxford University Press, 1958).

18. Carl G. Hempel, *Fundamentals of Concept Formation in Empirical Science,* International Library of Unified Science (Chicago: University of Chicago Press, 1952), Vol. II, No. 7; David Weissman, *Dispositional Properties* (Carbondale: Southern Illinois University Press), 1965.

19. T. W. Adorno et al., *The Authoritarian Personality* (New York: Harper & Row, Publishers, Inc., 1950), chap. 7.

20. Morris Rosenberg, "Misanthropy and Political Ideology," *American Sociological Review,* XXI (December 1956), 690–695.

21. Albert J. Lott and Bernice E. Lott, "Ethnocentrism and Space Superiority Judgments Following Cosmonaut and Astronaut Flights," *Public Opinion Quarterly,* XXVII (Winter 1963), 608.

22. Weissman, *op. cit.*

23. Robert Michels, *Political Parties* (Glencoe, Ill.: The Free Press, 1949).

24. Bunge, *op. cit.*, p. 19.

CHAPTER 2

Extraneous
and
Component
Variables

The reason why sociology tends to focus on asymmetrical relationships and, in particular, on the relationship between properties and dispositions or behavior is rooted in the nature of its subject matter. The sociologist is characteristically interested in the relationship of social experience to individual mental processes and acts. He thus tends to select as his independent variable certain groups, collectivities, or social categories and chooses as his dependent variable socially relevant opinions, attitudes, values, or actions. Thus he may ask: Are workers more alienated than middle-class people? Do Catholics vote Democratic more than Protestants? Are older people more prejudiced than younger people? Are small town youngsters less likely to go on to college than city dwellers? And so on.

Given proper sample and research design, the analyst may be able to provide correct answers to these questions. But these results are essentially descriptive. They may show that Catholics vote Democratic more than Protestants do, but they do not indicate *why* this is so. While it is valuable to explain such a relationship on the basis of informed speculation, it is still more valuable to subject this speculation to systematic test. The most important systematic way of examining the relationship between two variables is to introduce a third variable, called a test factor, into the analysis. This is what is meant by the process of *elaboration.*

The test factor, it should be stressed, is introduced solely for the purpose of increasing one's understanding of the original two-variable relationship. The aim of the analysis is to determine whether the relationship between X (the independent variable) and Y (the dependent variable) is due to Z (the test factor).

But what is meant by saying that the relationship is "due to" Z, or that Z is "responsible for" or the "determinant of" the relationship between X and Y? In the present discussion, these terms have a rather definite meaning. To say that the relationship between X and Y is due to Z is to mean that *were it not for Z,* there would be *no* relationship between X and Y. The statement, "Catholics have lower suicide rates because they are more integrated," must be translated as, "Were Catholics not more integrated, they would not have lower suicide rates." Similarly, "Lower-class people have higher rates of schizophrenia because they are more socially isolated," is translated as, "Were lower class people not more socially isolated, they would not have higher rates of schizophrenia."

The procedural aspect of the key phrase "were it not for" is to *control on,* or *hold constant,* the test factor, thereby eliminating its influence on the relationship. Let us consider how one "holds constant" a test factor by means of the technique of *subgroup classification.*[1] (If the reader is totally unfamiliar with survey data, it is suggested that he turn to Appendix A, "Basic Principles of Table Reading," by Roberta G. Simmons.)

Assume we begin with the finding that older people are more likely than younger people to listen to religious programs on the radio[2] (Table 2–1). In considering why this may be so, we suggest that perhaps this is due to the factor of education. Translated: were older people not more poorly educated, then they would not be more likely to listen to religious programs.

The task, then, is to eliminate the influence of education. This can be done simply by comparing older and younger people of *equal education.* Thus, one compares the listening habits of *well-educated*

Table 2–1

*Age and Listening to Religious Programs**

Listen to Religious Programs	Young Listeners	Old Listeners
Yes	17%	26%
No	83	74
Total per cent	100	100

* Paul F. Lazarsfeld and Morris Rosenberg, eds., *The Language of Social Research* (Glencoe, Ill.: The Free Press, 1955), p. 117, Table 4 (abridged and adapted). (Reprinted with permission of The Macmillan Company. Copyright 1955 by The Free Press, A Corporation.)

and *poorly educated* old and young people. Table 2–2 shows the results.

We see that among the well-educated, older people are hardly more likely to listen to religious programs, and the same is true among poorly educated people. Thus, were it not for education, there would be almost no relationship between age and listening. These data thus point to the following conclusion: older people are more likely to listen to religious programs because older people are generally more poorly educated and poorly educated people are more likely to listen to religious programs.

This analytic process may be expressed more generally by means of technical terminology. Typically one begins with a relationship between an independent variable (age) and a dependent variable (religious program listening). One then seeks to explain this relationship by introducing an explanatory variable, called a test factor (education). The method used is to *stratify* on the test factor and to

Table 2–2

*Age and Listening to Religious Programs, by Education**

Listen to Religious Programs	HIGH EDUCATION		LOW EDUCATION	
	Young	Old	Young	Old
Yes	9%	11%	29%	32%
No	91	89	71	68
Total per cent	100	100	100	100

* Paul F. Lazarsfeld and Morris Rosenberg, eds., *The Language of Social Research* (Glencoe, Ill.: The Free Press, 1955), p. 117, Table 4 (abridged and adapted). (Reprinted with permission of The Macmillan Company. Copyright 1955 by The Free Press, A Corporation.)

examine the contingent associations. "Stratification" means that we have broken the test factor into its component categories. In this case it is highly educated and poorly educated; in other cases it might be men and women, or Catholics, Protestants, and Jews, or upper, middle, and lower classes, etc.

The process of stratification creates "contingent associations." In Table 2–2, two contingent associations appear. The first is the association between age and program listening among the well-educated; the second is the association between age and listening among the poorly educated. If the test factor has more categories (say, grammar school education, high school education, college education, and post-graduate education) then there will be more contingent associations— one for each category. If the relationship between age and listening disappears within each contingent association, then we can say that the relationship is due to the test factor (education).

In order to understand the relationship between two variables, then, it is necessary to introduce additional variables into the analysis. But which variables should these be? In order to answer this question, it is necessary to digress momentarily to discuss a peculiar but decisive characteristic of sociological variables, namely, the fact that they are "block-booked."

The concept of block-booking is drawn from the field of mass communications research. At an earlier period in the history of the film industry, it was customary for film producers to rent films to exhibitors en masse, for example, in blocks of five. Thus an exhibitor had the option of renting or not renting a block of five films, but could not choose among them. If the block contained, say, one highly desirable film, one fairly desirable film, and three undesirable films, the exhibitor was compelled to take the undesirable films in order to obtain the desirable ones.

Human beings (or other sociological units) are similarly "block-booked." Each man (or group, or region) may be characterized in terms of a number of dimensions. When we describe a man in terms of certain characteristics, we are at the same time describing him in terms of other characteristics.

Let us say that we find that blue-collar workers are more alienated than white-collar workers. But blue-collar workers differ from white-collar workers in many ways other than in the type of work they do. They tend to be more poorly educated; they are more likely to be Catholic; they are more likely to be liberal on economic issues and illiberal on social issues; they are less likely to engage in abstract modes of thought; they are less likely to have high IQ's; they are more likely to come from large families; and so on.

"Blue-collar," then, means a great many things. When we try to explain why blue-collar workers are more alienated, then, we do so by giving consideration to these other factors associated with the status of blue-collar worker. It is these "block-booked," or associated, characteristics which enable us to understand why blue-collar workers are more alienated. The aim of the analysis is to ascertain *what there is* about being a blue-collar worker which accounts for the relationship with alienation.

Block-booking is the central fact of survey analysis. One cannot properly understand the relationship between an independent and a dependent variable without taking account of the fact that other variables are associated with them. These associated variables become the "test factors."

But not all test factors have the same meaning, serve the same theoretical purpose, or have the same statistical properties. At least six types of test factors may be distinguished: extraneous variables, component variables, intervening variables, antecedent variables, suppressor variables, and distorter variables. The purpose of this discussion is to suggest how these types of test factors enable one to achieve sounder, more precise, and more meaningful interpretations of two-variable relationships.

Extraneous Variables

When a research investigator discovers a relationship between two variables, the first question he implicitly asks is: "Is it real?" Knowing that sociological variables are "block-booked," he is concerned to know whether there is an *inherent link* between the independent and dependent variables or whether it is based on an accidental connection with some associated variable. In short, he must guard against what are called "spurious relationships."

Strictly speaking, there is no such thing as a spurious relationship; there are only spurious interpretations. It is customary to use the term "spurious relationship," however, to refer to a case in which there is no meaningful or inherent link between the two variables; the relationship is due solely to the fact that each of the variables happens accidentally to be associated with some other variable. It is a relationship which, on the surface, appears to be *asymmetrical* but which, on closer analysis, turns out to be *symmetrical* (for example, two indicators of the same concept, two consequences of the same cause, two elements of a functional unity, two manifestations of a joint complex, or two factors fortuitously associated).

The point is obvious when one considers gross examples. A common favorite is the finding that in Sweden there is a relationship between the number of storks in an area and the number of children born in the area.[3] One calls this relationship spurious, even though there is nothing spurious about the relationship; what is spurious is the *interpretation* that the storks bring the babies.

Or one finds that the death rate among people in hospitals is higher than that among people of comparable age outside of hospitals. This hardly justifies the conclusion that hospitals are inimical to health and length of life. Again, one finds that there is a positive association between the number of firemen at a fire and the amount of damage done. But this does not mean that the firemen did the damage.

In the above examples, the reason for the original relationship is always some associated third variable. The reason for the relationship between number of storks and number of babies is rural-urban location. Most storks are found in rural areas and the rural birth rate is higher than the urban birth rate. Similarly, the reason for the relationship between the number of firemen and the amount of the damage is the size of the fire. Large fires call forth more firemen and also cause more damage.

Unless one guards against such accidental associations, one is in danger of reaching erroneous and misleading conclusions. The significance of this point for sociological theory is apparent. Much ingenious and suggestive speculation, leading to important theoretical conclusions, may be advanced to explain certain empirical relationships, when the truth of the matter lies in the fact that an accidental link binds the independent and dependent variables. Without such a check, there may enter into the body of sociological theory ideas which are erroneous but which may exert a wide influence in the field.

No one, of course, will be deceived by the examples cited above. But let us consider some more serious illustrations. In each case we start with a relationship between two variables, we speculate on the meaning of this relationship, and we find that our interpretations are erroneous and misleading by virtue of our failure to take account of extraneous variables.[4]

Example A

A striking example of the theoretical importance of considering control variables appears in a study by Goldhamer and Marshall. In their book, *Psychosis and Civilization*,[5] they undertook to examine the widely held assumption that rates of psychosis had increased over the last century. And, in fact, the data did show a striking and consistent rise. It would not be difficult to suggest some of the changing conditions of life which created intensified stress and which might be responsible for mental breakdown: the increased mobility aspirations which were largely frustrated; the shift from the farm to the city, substituting the isolation and anonymity of urban living for the social integration of rural life; the breakdown in the stabilizing force of religion; the heightened competitiveness of economic life; the development of urban slums; the increased anomie of a swiftly changing and socially mobile society; the breakdown of the stability of the family expressed in increased rates of divorce, etc. All these factors represented theoretical bases for accounting for the observed rise in the rate of psychosis.

Goldhamer and Marshall noted that the increased rates of hospitalization for psychosis between 1845 and 1945, however, failed to take account of the factor of *age*. If one examined the rates of psychosis within each age category, one found (with the exception of those over 50) that *there was virtually no change over the century-long period.* The relationship was largely a spurious one.

How did age produce this misleading interpretation? The most common psychosis of advanced age is senile dementia; this is primarily an organic (rather than a functional) psychosis and is more often due to physiological degeneration than to psychological stress. Now, the advances in medicine during the period 1845–1945 had produced an increase in average length of life of the population. Hence, the proportion of old people in the population was much greater in the later period, thus producing a very large *number* of people with senile dementia. There has also been "an increased tendency to hospitalize persons suffering from the mental diseases of the senium."[6] Hence, the higher total rate of psychosis in 1945 was largely a reflection of the changing age distribution of the population and a tendency to hospitalize older people, not a reflection of increased societal stress (except perhaps among older people).

This is a striking illustration of how an elaborate and sophisticated theoretical structure might have been constructed to account for a relationship which was, in fact, completely misleading by virtue of the failure to take account of an extraneous variable.

Example B

Assume that a research study finds that older people read fewer books than younger people. What accounts for this relationship? One might reason that increasing age is often associated with a degeneration of eyesight and that these visual difficulties discourage reading among the elderly. One might further speculate that increasing age tends to produce a boredom with fiction and a general flagging of intellectual interests, thus producing a disinclination to read. These reasons appear to make sense and the data may be interpreted as supporting certain assumptions about the effects of aging.

There would thus appear to be an "inherent link" between age and book readership. In fact, however, it may be an "accidental link." When people who are now older were growing up, advanced education was much less widespread. It may thus be that the reason older people now read less is that, as a group, they are less well educated and that people with poorer education are less interested in books. In this case, age in itself would have no effect on book reading. The relationship would be entirely due to the fact that both age and book reading happen to be associated with education.

Example C

In a well-known study of the relationship between occupational structure and child-rearing practices, Miller and Swanson[7] suggested that location in the economic system would create a family integration setting which would influence the choice of child-rearing practices. The hypothesis was that the *entrepreneurial* families would emphasize self-control and an active and independent approach to the world, whereas *bureaucratic* families would stress an accommodating and adjustive way of life. This hypothesis was clearly supported by the data.

This significant theoretical contribution was, however, questioned by Lawrence Haber.[8] Haber noted that in the 1930's child-care advice, guided by the theory of behaviorism, stressed restriction and control, whereas in the 1940's, under the influence of Dewey and others, more permissive practices were the vogue. This raised the possibility that the differences in child-rearing practices in bureaucratic and entrepreneurial families were not an outcome of occupational and technological imperatives but were a reflection of the patterns current at different times.

In the Miller and Swanson study, respondents were classified as entrepreneurial if the husband was self-employed, if most of his income came from profits, fees, or commissions, if he worked in an organization with few levels of supervision, and if he (or his wife) was born on a farm or outside the United States. Others were classified as bureaucratic. But, argued Haber, these groups also tended to differ in *age*. "In the United States, foreign-born adults are as a group older than native-born adults; self-employed men are on the average older than salaried men; managers, owners and proprietors tend to be older than professionals."[9] In other words, the entrepreneurial group tends to be older than the bureaucratic group, a fact confirmed by Miller and Swanson's data. Haber thus concluded:

Given the age differences between the middle-class entrepreneurial mothers, a larger proportion of the entrepreneurial mothers than of the bureaucratic mothers would have reared their children during the early 1930's. Based on a median age of 23 years at the time of the birth of the first child, the proportion of women actively engaged in child care by 1937 is greater among entrepreneurial mothers than bureaucratic mothers. Under the influence of the advice and child care practices available as parental role models, proportionately more of the entrepreneurial group would have adopted the type of child-rearing current at the time. We would expect that the children of the entrepreneurial families have been raised in a substantially different climate of opinion from the bureaucratic families, who were proportionately more exposed to the advice and practices of the 1940's.

One would expect that the older, entrepreneurial population would be more likely than the younger, more recent parents in the bureaucratic group to have engaged in scheduled feeding, early control over elimination and masturbation and to have demanded more independence and self-control.[10]

The failure to take account of the extraneous variable of age may thus create a radically misleading theoretical interpretation. The profound significance of such test factors for theoretical understanding is thus evident.

To summarize: whenever we find a relationship between two variables, we attempt to make sense of it by suggesting how the independent variable exercises some influence on the dependent variable. The danger always lurks, however, that we are being misled. There may, in fact, be no "inherent link" between the two variables but simply a common association with a third variable. In other words, a relationship which appears to be asymmetrical may, in fact, be symmetrical.

The method of determining whether one has made a misleading interpretation is to control on the test factor. If, when the influence of the extraneous test factor is held constant, one finds that the relationship disappears, then it may be concluded that the relationship is due to the extraneous variable. If one is to avoid drawing erroneous or misleading conclusions from data, therefore, it is essential to guard against such accidental links.

Support of an interpretation

Just as test factors may be introduced to show that highly plausible interpretations are actually misleading, so may they provide evidence that highly dubious interpretations are actually sound. An investigation of the relationship between parental interest and adolescent self-esteem[11] affords a case in point.

In this study, adolescents were requested to think back to the period when they were about 10 or 11 years old and were asked, "During this period (age 10 or 11) did your mother know who most of your friends were?" Table 2–3 shows that the more friends known by the mother, according to the respondent's report, the larger the proportion with high self-esteem.

Table 2–3

*Reports of Mother's Knowledge of Child's Friends and Subject's Self-Esteem**

	"During This Period (Age 10 or 11) Did Your Mother Know Who Most of Your Friends Were?"		
Respondent's Self-Esteem	All or Most	Some or None	Don't Know or Can't Remember
High	46%	32%	27%
Medium	23	25	38
Low	30	43	35
Total per cent	100	100	100
Number	(1407)	(133)	(26)

* Morris Rosenberg, "Parental Interest and Children's Self-Conceptions," *Sociometry*, XXVI (March 1963), p. 38, Table 1 (adapted). (Reprinted with permission of the American Sociological Association.)

However, one is immediately suspicious of such a finding. It is entirely possible that the child who dislikes, or gets on poorly with, his mother will "remember" her as showing little interest in, or knowledge of, people who were important to him at an earlier age. In this case, the relationship might simply reflect the fact that adolescents with

Table 2–4

Reports of Mother's Knowledge of Child's Friends and Subject's Self-Esteem, by Identification with Parents*

	Student Currently Identifies Chiefly With . . .					
	MOTHER		FATHER		BOTH EQUALLY	
			Mother knew friends . . .			
Respondent's Self-Esteem	All or Most	Some or None	All or Most	Some or None	All or Most	Some or None
High	43%	32%	39%	27%	52%	39%
Medium	23	22	29	33	22	29
Low	34	45	32	40	26	32
Total						
per cent	100	100	100	100	100	100
Number	(381)	(40)	(185)	(15)	(407)	(31)

* Morris Rosenberg, "Parental Interest and Children's Self-Conceptions," *Sociometry*, XXVI (March 1963), p. 40, Table 3. (Reprinted with permission of the American Sociological Association.)

unfavorable attitudes toward their mothers say that their mothers did not know their friends, and these people also tend to have low self-esteem. The task, then, is to control an unfavorable attitude toward mothers in order to see whether the relationship then vanishes.

One question which partly reflects the student's present attitude toward his mother is, "When your parents disagree, whose side are you usually on—your mother's or your father's?" Table 2–4 shows that whether the adolescent says he is usually on his mother's side or usually on his father's side, or identifies with both equally, those who say that their mothers knew few of their friends are less likely to have high self-esteem than those who say she knew many. It is thus questionable whether the original relationship is due to the respondents' dislike of their mothers, since the difference obtains among those who do or do not identify with their mothers in this situation.

But perhaps it is not the respondent's *present* identification with the mother, but his past reactions to her, which are crucial. In other words, the adolescent may remember disliking his mother when he was 10 or 11 and may thus assume that she knew nothing of his friends at that time. In order to examine this point, respondents were asked, "When you were about 10 or 11 years old, to whom were you most likely to talk about personal things?" Table 2–5 shows that whether the child said he confided mostly in his mother, in some

Table 2–5

*Reports of Mother's Knowledge of Child's Friends and Subject's Self-Esteem, by Tendency to Confide in Others**

	Most Likely to Talk About Personal Things to . . .					
	MOTHER		OTHER PERSON		NO ONE OR CAN'T REMEMBER	
			Mother Knew Friends . . .			
Respondent's Self-Esteem	All or Most	Some or None	All or Most	Some or None	All or Most	Some or None
High	51%	39%	41%	35%	46%	29%
Medium	23	32	26	20	21	30
Low	26	29	33	45	34	41
Total						
per cent	100	100	100	100	100	100
Number	(540)	(41)	(537)	(55)	(195)	(27)

* Morris Rosenberg, "Parental Interest and Children's Self-Conceptions," *Sociometry*, XXVI (March 1963), p. 39, Table 2. (Reprinted with permission of the American Sociological Association.)

other person, or in no one, those who said their mothers knew most of their friends tended to have higher self-esteem than those who said their mothers knew few of their friends. The result is thus not due to a negative attitude toward the mother during this earlier period under consideration.

But a third possibility must also be considered. It may not be the child's attitude toward his mother in general, but his recollection of how she behaved toward his *friends* in particular, that colors his recollection of whether she knew his friends. If he recalls her as being unpleasant toward his friends, he might assume that she took little interest in knowing who they were. After the adolescents indicated whether their mothers knew most of their friends, they were asked, "How did she usually act toward them?" Table 2–6 shows that *irrespective of whether the students said their mothers were friendly or not friendly,* those who said their mothers knew most of their friends had higher self-esteem than those who said their mothers knew few of their friends. Their recollection of whether their mothers knew their friends is, then, not simply a reflection of their favorable or unfavorable memories of their mothers' behavior toward their friends.

We thus see that irrespective of whether the adolescent says he did or did not chiefly confide in his mother at an earlier time; irrespec-

Table 2–6

Reports of Mother's Knowledge of Child's Friends and Subject's Self-Esteem, by Mother's Behavior Toward Friends*

	How Mother Acted Toward Child's Friends . . .					
	VERY FRIENDLY		FAIRLY FRIENDLY		NOT FRIENDLY	
	Mother Knew Child's Friends . . .					
Respondent's Self-Esteem	All or Most	Some or None	All or Most	Some or None	All or Most	Some or None
High	48%	34%	45%	33%	32%	21%
Medium	23	24	26	28	29	26
Low	29	41	29	39	40	53
Total						
per cent	100	100	100	100	100	100
Number	(1091)	(58)	(259)	(51)	(38)	(19)

* Morris Rosenberg, "Parental Interest and Children's Self-Conceptions," *Sociometry*, XXVI (March 1963), p. 40, Table 4. (Reprinted with permission of the American Sociological Association.)

tive of whether he identifies with her, with his father, or with both equally at the present time; and irrespective of whether he says she was friendly or unfriendly to his mates, the student who reports that his mother knew most of his friends tends to have higher self-esteem than the one who reports that she knew few. It is likely, then, that the reported differential knowledge of friends does not simply reflect the student's biased perception of, or attitudes toward, the mother.

These three controls, of course, do not firmly establish that the report of mother's knowledge of friends is not contaminated with an associated variable, but they add to one's confidence in the measure. There is now stronger reason to believe that the answers reflect mothers' knowledge rather than the biased perception of the respondent.

Sometimes a very simple control may afford decisive support for a theory. For example, it was Durkheim's contention that in periods of national crisis, the collective sentiments were stimulated, the collective passions excited, and the level of social integration enhanced, thus leading to a reduction in suicide.[12] As an illustration of national crises, he considered great national wars. He showed that in various European countries the outbreak of war was very consistently followed by an appreciable decline in the suicide rate. But, Durkheim suggested, the relationship between war and suicide might be misleading because it was so difficult to keep track of suicides in the field of battle. How could this be checked? Very simply. Durkheim examined the suicide rates for *women* and found that these rates also declined during the war crises.[13] In effect, Durkheim examined the relationship of war crises to suicide controlling on sex. Since the relationship still obtained, confidence in his interpretation was enhanced.

We thus see that one special virtue of introducing test factors is to *increase* one's confidence that the observed relationship is a true one. This is of particular value when the relationship deals with obviously and grossly contaminated variables. Without the crucial test, a broad shadow of doubt may continue to hang over the interpretation.

Limitations on controls

The introduction of controls thus has a positive role to play in interpretation by increasing one's confidence that there is a meaningful and inherent link between the two variables. But how much confidence can one have? After all, one may establish that the relationship is not due to a particular extraneous variable, but this does not mean that it may not be due to a different extraneous variable. The procedure, then, is to control on these other relevant extraneous variables and see whether the relationship continues to obtain. Each time that one controls on a relevant variable and finds that the relationship remains, one's confidence that the relationship is real increases and the danger of misleading interpretations decreases.

It is never possible, however, to be absolutely certain that the relationship is not misleading. Each variable is block-booked with so many others that there is no foolproof assurance that some extraneous factor which has not been considered may not actually be responsible for the relationship. One can only be certain that the relationship is real if one has controlled on all extraneous variables, which is obviously impossible.

The problem is a serious one, but some of the implicit solutions adopted to deal with it are indefensible. One erroneous solution is to reason that if one cannot have complete confidence that the relationship is real, however many controls one introduces, then there is no point in introducing controls at all. But this argument overlooks the fact that much of science—particularly social science—is built upon degrees of confidence rather than certainty regarding one's conclusions. If one result may occur 1 in 10 times by statistical chance and another 1 in 1,000 times, we do not simply dismiss both findings on the grounds that they may be attributable to sampling variation. On the contrary, we have greater confidence that the latter result is not a reflection of sampling accident. Similarly (other things equal), we have greater confidence that a relationship is real if we have controlled on relevant variables than if we have not.

The second erroneous solution is to suggest that since one can never be certain that one's interpretation is not faulty by virtue of failure to consider an extraneous variable, then it is best not to interpret the relationship at all. One may be satisfied simply to report the descriptive result. To those who wish to understand social phenomena rather than simply to describe them, however, such a solution is totally unsatisfactory. It involves the abandonment of any hope for the development of a theoretically-based empirical social science.

A third erroneous procedure sometimes adopted by research workers is to introduce certain control variables routinely. They may automatically control on social class, sex, age, and perhaps one or two other variables. Such a rote procedure affords little confidence that one has not overlooked some essential variable.

On what bases, then, are decisions to introduce controls made? The first point is that one must consider whether the control variable is *relevant* or is otherwise implicated in the result. This is a logical, not a statistical, operation. If, for example, one finds a relationship between social class and size of income-tax payments, this relationship is obviously not due to child-rearing practices, recreational patterns, or speech mannerisms. It is logically senseless to control on these variables since they obviously cannot explain the relationship.

In cases of this sort, however, what is logically senseless to one man may not be so to another. In doubtful cases—where it is not perfectly apparent that the potential test factor is not implicated, or where positive empirical evidence that it is not is available—the cautious procedure is to introduce the controls. Nevertheless, this logical procedure will effectively eliminate the need to introduce a large number of control variables.

An equally important consideration is this: before one introduces a control variable, one must have some idea of the relationship of the test factor to the independent and dependent variables. This point is frequently overlooked by those who routinely or automatically introduce standard controls. If the test factor is not associated statistically *both* with the independent *and* the dependent variables, then it cannot be responsible for the relationship.

Assume, for example, that the research worker finds a relationship between social class and mental illness. He then considers whether this relationship may be misleading. His reflection might proceed as follows: "I know that Protestants are more likely to be middle or upper class and Catholics are more likely to be working class. Perhaps it is not "lower classness" that is responsible for the mental illness but the fact that lower class people are more likely to be Catholic and that something about Catholicism is conducive to mental illness. I will therefore control on religion to see if the relationship between social class and mental illness disappears." But this researcher may know that Catholics do *not* have higher rates of mental illness. Therefore, the higher working-class rates cannot be due to the fact that they are more likely to be Catholics. *There is thus no need to control on religion.* In this case the test factor (religion) is related to the independent variable (class) but is not related to the dependent variable (mental illness). One cannot say that lower-class people have higher rates of mental illness because they are more likely to be Catholic if one knows that Catholics do not have higher mental illness rates

The same consideration applies to the connection between the test factor and the independent variable. Assume we find that Democrats are more strongly opposed to the legal desegregation of private clubs. One might then reason: "Perhaps Democrats are more authoritarian and authoritarians are more likely to oppose desegregation. I can check this hypothesis by controlling on authoritarianism." But if one has positive evidence that Democrats are *not* more authoritarian, then this cannot be the explanation. There is no need to control on this variable.

In sum, if the purpose is to guard against a misleading interpretation, then the test factor is introduced only if (1) there is a theoretical or empirically based reason for assuming that it accounts for the relationship, and (2) there is no evidence indicating that it is *not* related both to the independent and dependent variables. These considerations mitigate the problem of having to "control on everything."

From the foregoing discussion, it is plain that consideration of extraneous variables may have important theoretical consequences. If, for example, one attempts to interpret a relationship between an independent and a dependent variable without introducing test factors, one's explanation is often in the realm of "plausibility" and the confidence that can be placed in it is dependent upon the analyst's intellectual acuity, theoretical sophistication, and knowledge of the field. If, however, one introduces a test factor, then one is in a position to select from between alternative kinds of interpretation, depending upon whether the relationship does or does not vanish. One is then guided not solely by one's reasoning, but one's reasoning is forced in the direction dictated by the pattern of the data. Other things equal, speculation which is disciplined and guided by the pattern of the data will tend to be more compelling.

A central theoretical contribution of taking account of extraneous variables is that it guards against the erroneous or misleading interpretation. While essentially a "cautious" contribution, and thus not very striking, it may be just as important for the total field that erroneous generalizations are abandoned, that blind alleys are avoided, as that more positive contributions are made. Especially in sociology, where post-factum explanations are all too easily available to account for findings, this contribution is especially valuable.

Component Variables

One problem still confronting social science, as Merton[14] notes, is the presence of propositions which are true but unspecific. Certain propositions are on such a broad level of generality that they do little to advance understanding. Thus, one may hear the statement that "the social environment plays an important part in attitude formation" or that "personality structure is an important determinant of social behavior." It would be incredible for anyone to deny these propositions, but no one is substantially enlightened thereby. Needless to say, it is of utmost importance that social science go beyond the stage of propositions so broad that they have only the vaguest empirical referents.

The problem does not really lie at this level, however, since everyone is aware that one must specify what aspect of the social environment has what kind of effect on what sorts of attitudes. What is more serious, because it is less often recognized, is the failure to specify the decisive component of a complex or global independent variable.[15]

Consider, for example, the well-documented finding that lower-class people have higher rates of psychosis. The problem with this finding is that one does not know *what it is* about being a member of the lower class which accounts for the mental illness. Is it lack of money that creates mental illness? Is it low prestige? Is it poor education? Is it tedious and unrewarding work? Is it a pernicious style of life? And so on. Until we know precisely which aspect, or aspects, of social class are of decisive significance, our knowledge is limited. Certainly not all aspects of social class are relevant. For example, Warner[16] notes that "old family" is an aspect of social class, but it is hardly likely that being a member of an "old family" in itself insulates one against mental illness. Without such specifying variables, propositions continue to remain on an excessively general level.

Or consider the finding by Leighton et al.[17] that in Sterling County 45 per cent of the people in the depressed areas, compared with 20 per cent of the county as a whole, needed psychiatric treatment. But what is *in* a depressed area? Such areas are characterized by many broken homes, a high crime rate, much physical illness, poverty, rapid social change, etc. It is scientifically essential to know whether one of these factors, or several in combination, is decisively responsible for the high mental illness rate in the area.

The general point is that many of the global concepts with which the social researcher deals are composed of a number of subconcepts which enter into it. These are *components*. Education, income, occupation, family, etc., are all part of social class. Similarly, when we speak of an "authoritarian personality," we mean someone with a particular complex of characteristics: conventionalism, authoritarian submission, authoritarian aggression, anti-intraception, superstition and stereotypy, power and "toughness," destructiveness and cynicism, etc. If we find that authoritarians differ from others in some regard, we might still wish to know which of these subconcepts was most crucially implicated in the particular result.

A striking illustration of the specification of the component variable appears in a cross-national study of social class and child-rearing values conducted by Pearlin and Kohn.[18] Parents were asked to indicate which qualities they valued most highly in their 12-year-old children: that the child is honest, that he is happy, that he is obedient, that he has good manners, that he has self-control, that he is dependable, that he is popular, etc. Many social class differences appeared in the American study, but the most striking finding was the following: working-class parents were much more likely than middle-class parents to emphasize "that he obey his parents well," whereas middle-class parents were more likely to stress "that he has self-control." This was true of both fathers and mothers. It was interesting to find that when these questions were asked of parents in Turin, Italy, exactly the same kinds of relationships appeared: the working class was more likely to stress obedience, the middle class self-control. The relevant data appear in Table 2–7.

The consistency of these results in two quite different social environments is a fascinating finding and suggests that some element of social class is of such decisive significance that it overcomes cultural differences between these two societies. But what is this element of class? Can one assign it simply to norms, to arbitrary and traditional patterns of behavior which arise out of social interaction? Is it a reflection of general styles of life, including *Weltanschauungen,* characterizing the different classes? Does money enter into it, or education, or type of work, or social prestige, or aspiration level, or what? If we can say *what it is* about social class which gives rise to these differences, then our understanding will be considerably enhanced.

The investigators focused on the *occupational activities* in which the classes were characteristically engaged. The manual worker, they

Table 2-7

Proportion of Parents in Italy and the United States Selecting Each Characteristic as One of the Three Most Important, by Social Class*

| | Italy | | | | United States | | | |
| | FATHERS | | MOTHERS | | FATHERS | | MOTHERS | |
Child-rearing values	Middle Class	Working Class	Middle Class	Working Class	Middle Class	Working Class	Middle Class	Working Class
Obeys	31%	45%	36%	48%	13%	39%	20%	33%
Self-control	23	11	16	8	20	6	22	13
Number	(160)	(148)	(263)	(205)	(46)	(36)	(174)	(165)

* Leonard I. Pearlin and Melvin L. Kohn, "Social Class, Occupation, and Parental Values: A Cross-National Study," *American Sociological Review*, XXXI (August 1966), 470, Table 1 (abridged and adapted). (Reprinted with permission of the American Sociological Association.)

reasoned, tends to be more under the supervision of others. Charac-teristically, he must obey the orders of others and has relatively little opportunity for the exercise of initiative and independence. The middle-class person, on the other hand, is more self-directed; he is more likely to make independent decisions and to guide his activities (and those of others) in accord with his own reason and knowledge. The authors thus reasoned that "jobs that allow, and require, self-direction should lead to a high valuation of self-control; jobs that require following the directions established by someone in authority should lead to high valuation of obedience and low valuation of self-control."[19]

The investigators thus examined the relationship between class and child-rearing values controlling on the degree of supervision or in-dependence in work. Table 2–8 shows the results. Originally, we see, 52 per cent of the middle class and 35 per cent of the working

Table 2–8

*Proportions of Italian Fathers Valuing Self-Control and Obedience, by Social Class: Original Comparison and Comparison Standardized on Independence in Work**

Valuation of Self-Control and Obedience	ORIGINAL COMPARISON		STANDARDIZED COMPARISON	
	Middle Class	Working Class	Middle Class	Working Class
Value self-control †	52%	35%	41%	41%
Value neither self-control nor obedience	26	25	34	24
Value obedience ‡	22	40	25	35
Total per cent	100	100	100	100
Number	(144)	(141)	(144)	(141)

* Leonard I. Pearlin and Melvin L. Kohn, "Social Class, Occupation, and Parental Values: A Cross-National Study," *American Sociological Review*, XXXI (August 1966), 477, Table 8 (abridged and adapted). (Reprinted with permission of the American Sociological Association.)
† Value self-control highly or moderately.
‡ Value obedience highly or moderately and self-control not at all.

class value self-control. When degree of independence in work is con-trolled by means of standardization,[20] however, 41 per cent of each class value self-control; the difference has vanished. Originally, the difference in the valuation of obedience between the two classes is 18 per cent, but when occupational activity is controlled, the difference is 10 per cent; the difference has thus been reduced by nearly one-half, but still remains substantial.

These data thus suggest that the reason that middle-class people are more likely to value *self-control* in their children is rooted in the fact that they are more likely to be engaged in independent occupational activities. The reason working-class people emphasize *obedience* more is to an important extent based on their work, but other factors, still undetermined, also play a role. Such analysis tells us what it is about being a white-collar or a manual worker which is responsible for differences in child-rearing values.

Another example appears in the work of Durkheim.[21] Controlling on age, Durkheim finds that married people have lower suicide rates than unmarried people. After considering whether this may be due to differences in types of people who marry or do not, he concludes that it is not. It is thus something in the marital state itself which reduces the rate of suicide. But *what* about marital life does it? Let us follow Durkheim's reasoning:

> But interesting as this result [the lower suicide rate of married people] is, it must be further defined; for the family environment consists of different elements. For husband and wife alike the family includes 1) the wife or husband; 2) the children. Is the salutary effect of the family on the suicidal tendency due to the former or the latter? In other words, the family consists of two different associations: the conjugal group and the family group proper. These two societies have not the same origin, nor the same nature, nor consequently, in all probability the same effects.[22]

> During the years 1887–91, a million husbands without children accounted annually for 644 suicides. To know how much the marriage status, alone and without reference to the family, insures against suicide, one has only to compare this figure with that of unmarried men of the same average age. . . . A million unmarried men of that age have about 975 suicides. Now 644 is to 975 as 100 is to 150; that is, sterile husbands have a coefficient of preservation of only 1.5; they commit suicide only a third less often than unmarried men of the same age. Quite otherwise when they have children. A million husbands with children annually show during this period only 336 suicides. This number is to 975 as 100 is to 290; that

is, when marriage produces children the coefficient of preservation is almost doubled[23]

It thus does not appear to be marriage itself—with its sexual gratification, companionship, freedom from loneliness, etc.—which chiefly accounts for the lower suicide rates of married people, but *the presence of children,* producing a normatively controlled, socially integrated unit.

Durkheim thus enables us to understand *what about* marriage is largely responsible for the lower suicide rate. As soon as one asks which is the decisive element, one is confronted with alternative hypotheses. The test factor enables one to determine in a systematic way which hypothesis is correct.

One area of considerable theoretical interest in recent years has been the relationship between social class and authoritarianism. Much has been written about middle-class authoritarianism, indicating how middle-class family structure, influenced by occupational position, is conducive to the development of an authoritarian character structure.

Contrary to this theory, recent research has shown that working-class people are actually *more* authoritarian than middle-class people. Lipset has attempted to explain this result, arguing that "low education, low participation in political or voluntary organizations of any type, little reading, isolated occupations, economic insecurity, and authoritarian family patterns" are among the most significant factors in shaping the relative intolerance of the working class as compared with the middle class.[24]

These factors, in turn, lead to "greater suggestibility, absence of a sense of past and future, . . . inability to take a complex view, greater difficulty in abstracting from concrete experience, and lack of imagination." "All of these qualities," Lipset asserts, "are part of the complex psychological basis of authoritarianism."[25]

But, as Lipsitz points out: "Neither these studies nor Lipset's analysis, however, reveals the degree to which each of the many factors cited actually contributes to the greater authoritarianism of the working class."[26] In other words, which of the many aspects of working-class life cited by Lipset actually accounts for the authoritarianism? Is it the worker's low education? Is it his low organizational participation? Is it his isolated occupation? Is it his economic insecurity? Is it his authoritarian family structure? Or is it some other factor associated with working-class life which accounts for the observed results?

Lipsitz hypothesized that the crucial factor was *education*. Combining the responses to a number of authoritarianism items, he constructed an authoritarianism scale (A-scale). He then examined the relationship between class and authoritarianism, controlling on education. The results appear in Table 2–9.

Considering the results for the total sample (at the right side of Table 2–9), one finds that working-class people are 23.9 per cent more likely than middle-class people to have a high score on the authoritarianism scale. Within each of the educational groups, however, the difference between the two classes is 6.3, 12.6, and 11.8 per cent, respectively. Within each educational group, the difference is smaller than in the total group.

We thus see that the higher level of authoritarianism of working-class people is largely due to their lower educational level. The difference, to be sure, is not completely eliminated, thus indicating that certain factors other than education also play a role. But the data indicate that a major factor accounting for the relationship is education.

Originally, we see, Lipset suggests at least six factors which may be responsible for the result. Several of these are of a radically different order. By specifying the component variable, or at least a crucial component variable, we have a better understanding of precisely what factors are responsible. It becomes much less likely, for example, that the decisive factor is economic insecurity, isolated occupational patterns, or even authoritarian family patterns.

These observations issue in further consequences of theoretical relevance. *They suggest that the "same" variables are not always the same.* For example, one of the most powerful variables in sociological analysis is the concept of social class. With startling consistency, social class is found to be associated with the wide variety of dependent variables with which the sociologist is concerned. The power of social class as a determinant of attitudes and behavior is one of the best documented of sociological findings.

Social class, however, consists of a number of component elements.

Table 2–9

Social Class, Education and Response to Authoritarianism Questions in Three Surveys (Men Only)*

| | Per Cent Giving Authoritarianism Response | | | | | | | | |
| | 0–8 Years Education | | 9–12 Years Education | | 12 or more Years Education | | Total | |
	Middle Class	Working Class	Middle Class	Working Class	Middle Class	Working Class	Middle Class	Working Class
High on A-scale score	82.9	89.2	59.5	72.1	38.2	50.0	35.9	59.5
Percentage difference		6.3		12.6		11.8		23.6

* Lewis Lipsitz, "Working-Class Authoritarianism: A Re-Evaluation," *American Sociological Review*, XXX (February 1965), 106–108, Table 1 (abridged and adapted). (Reprinted with permission of the American Sociological Association.)

One cannot assume, therefore, that if social class is related to X and is also related to Y, then the same aspect of social class exercises the effective influence in both cases. Consider the following simple example: In the first case one finds a relationship between class and exposure to public affairs programs and in the second case a relationship between class and home ownership. *The same aspects of class may not be the effective influence in the two cases.* In the first case it may be level of *education* which is the crucial element in exposure to public affairs programs, whereas in the second case it may be *income* which affects home ownership. In both cases we say social class is responsible, but it may be different aspects of social class which produce the observed effect. If social class is related to self-esteem, perhaps it is *social prestige* which is the effective influence. If class is related to economic liberalism, perhaps it is *union membership*. If class is related to membership in certain groups, perhaps *old family* is responsible. If class is related to certain attitudes, perhaps *style of life* factors are centrally implicated.

Thus, although the same idea (social class), and perhaps even the identical empirical measure, may be involved in each of these relationships, this does not mean that the same effective influences are operating in each case. Indeed, if a variable is a very broad one, then it may achieve deceptive theoretical power, in the sense that if some of its components have little bearing on the dependent variable, other components have a great bearing. But such power, while useful for prediction, is not really an aid to understanding. The factor in class which influences one dependent variable may not be the same factor that influences another dependent variable. Unless one takes account of component or specifying variables, one is in danger of attributing excessive importance to a variable simply because it is broad and encompassing.

What is true of social class is equally true of many other sociological variables. Age reflects a social status, a characteristic set of experiences associated with an historical epoch, a state of health, a level of energy and alertness, a characteristic relationship to work, etc. Each of these factors may have a different effect upon different dependent variables, even though "age" is related to each. In each case the "same" independent variable is not necessarily the same.

Controlling on the global variable

Thus far we have considered the specification of the crucial component of a global concept, such as class, age, race, sex, nationality, etc. In effect, the relationship is based on the fact that the global concept "stands for" the specific element. But it is also the case that specific elements may "stand for" broader concepts. In other words, if we find that a specific independent variable appears to produce a certain effect on a dependent variable, we do not know whether it is this specific factor which is crucial or whether it is the broader concept which it reflects.

Let us seek to exemplify these two contrasting approaches. In the first case one selects as a test factor a component variable which is an expression, aspect, or element of the independent variable. Assume that we find that authoritarian personalities are more likely than democratic personalities to hold the view that the common man is so stupid and irrational that democracy is not a viable system. But authoritarianism is a complex syndrome consisting of a variety of symptoms: extrapunitiveness, a hierarchical view of the world, parental idealization, rigidity of thought, excessive impulse control, hostility, contempt for human nature, etc. While these characteristics hang together, and the total syndrome is associated with the dependent variable, not all the components enter into the causal relationship equally. This is one of the problems with many global or multifaceted concepts: so many things are contained within them that one does not know which one is most crucially implicated in the observed result.

Let us say that we then control on "faith in human nature" and find that the relationship vanishes. To know that faith in people is the decisive factor is to obtain a more exact understanding of what is going on. The fact that an authoritarian is dubious about the political rationality of the common man is not directly due to the fact that he idealizes his parents, or has excessive regard for authority, or has excessive impulse control, etc.; *it is most directly due to his low regard for human nature.* If one can specify that faith in human nature is crucial to belief in political rationality, then one's understanding is considerably enhanced. If, on the other hand, one wished to explain

Table 2–10

Occupational Identification and Vote*

Vote	White Collar	Labor
Democratic	38%	56%
Republican	62	44
Total per cent	100	100
Number	(204)	(309)

*Paul F. Lazarsfeld, Bernard Berelson, and Hazel Gaudet, *The People's Choice* (New York: Columbia University Press, 1948), p. 19, Chart 4 (abridged and adapted). (Reprinted with permission of the Columbia University Press.)

the relationship between authoritarianism and absence of guilt feelings, then faith in human nature might have nothing to do with it; a resistance to introspection and absence of intrapunitiveness might be the decisive elements.

Now let us consider the case in which one begins with a relationship between a component variable and a dependent variable, and then controls on the global concept of which the component is a part.

One finds, for example, a clear relationship between occupational background and voting. As Table 2–10 shows, 56 per cent of the respondents classified as labor, but only 38 per cent of those in the white-collar group, intended to vote Democratic. When one controls on socio-economic status, however, the relationship almost vanishes (Table 2–11).

Table 2–11

Occupational Identification and Vote, Controlling on Socio-Economic Level*

	SOCIO-ECONOMIC LEVEL							
	A + B		C +		C −		D	
Vote	White Collar	Labor	White Collar	Labor	White Collar	Labor	White Collar	Labor
Democratic	23%	25%	45%	50%	50%	59%	67%	69%
Republican	77	75	55	50	50	41	33	31
Total per cent	100	100	100	100	100	100	100	100
Number	(78)	(20)	(78)	(101)	(42)	(116)	(6)	(72)

* Paul F. Lazarsfeld, Bernard Berelson, and Hazel Gaudet, *The People's Choice* (New York: Columbia University Press, 1948), p. 19, Chart 4 (adapted). (Reprinted with permission of the Columbia University Press.)

In other words, if we find a relationship between occupational category and voting, we do not know whether it is something specific to occupation (for example, the influence of labor unions among manual workers) which accounts for the voting behavior, or whether occupation is an indicator of a broader style of life whose varied elements influence voting behavior. In the present case it turns out that it is the broader concept that is the paramount factor. Occupational status is associated with voting behavior because it is an indicator of socio-economic status.

Again, assume we were to find that people who favor Medicare are more likely to vote Democratic. We might reason that this result is due in part to the view that the Democratic Party favored Medicare. In fact, however, approval of Medicare may be a specific expression of a broader attitude of liberalism. If the relationship between attitudes toward Medicare and toward the Democratic Party vanished when liberalism was controlled, we would know that attitudes toward Medicare exercised no influence on voting independent of the broader attitude of liberalism of which it is a part.

NOTES

1. The techniques of standardization and partial correlation may also be employed to hold constant a test factor. For a simple method of computing standardizations, see Morris Rosenberg, "Test Factor Standardization as a Method of Interpretation," *Social Forces*, XLI (October 1962), 53–61. Partial correlation is a very powerful statistical procedure, but unfortunately is not suitable for many kinds of sociological data. Given appropriate data, any of the three procedures may be employed; the logic remains unchanged. While examples using standardization and partial correlation will be used on occasion in our discussion, most of the examples will be based on subgroup classification, since this method requires no knowledge of statistics, reveals conditional relationships, and demonstrates the logical principles most sharply.

2. Paul F. Lazarsfeld, "Interpretation of Statistical Relations as a Research Operation," in Paul F. Lazarsfeld and Morris Rosenberg, eds., *The Language of Social Research* (Glencoe, Ill.: The Free Press, 1955), p. 117.

3. Herbert Hyman, *Survey Design and Analysis* (Glencoe, Ill.: The Free Press, 1955), p. 285.
4. The terms "antecedent variable" [Patricia Kendall and Paul F. Lazarsfeld, "Problems of Survey Analysis," in R. K. Merton and P. F. Lazarsfeld, eds., *Continuities in Social Research: Studies in the Scope and Method of "The American Soldier"* (Glencoe, Ill.: The Free Press, 1950), pp. 156–157] and "invalidating factor" (Hyman, *op. cit.*, p. 247) have also been applied to this concept. Subsequent discussion will make clear why the term "extraneous variable" is preferred.
5. Herbert Goldhamer and Andrew W. Marshall, *Psychosis and Civilization* (Glencoe, Ill.: The Free Press, 1949).
6. *Ibid.*, p. 91.
7. Daniel R. Miller and Guy E. Swanson, *The Changing American Parent* (New York: John Wiley & Sons, Inc., 1958).
8. Lawrence D. Haber, "Age and Integration Setting: A Re-Appraisal of *The Changing American Parent*," *American Sociological Review*, XXVII (October 1962), 682–689.
9. *Ibid.*, p. 686.
10. *Ibid.*, p. 687. (Reprinted by permission of the American Sociological Association.)
11. Morris Rosenberg, "Parental Interest and Children's Self-Conceptions," *Sociometry*, XXVI (March 1963), 35–49.
12. Emile Durkheim, *Suicide,* trans. John A. Spaulding and George Simpson (Glencoe, Ill.: The Free Press, 1951), p. 205.
13. *Ibid.*
14. Robert K. Merton, *Social Theory and Social Structure* (Glencoe, Ill., The Free Press, 1949), pp. 83–96.
15. Hyman, *op. cit.*, chap. 6, describes such variables as "configurations."
16. W. Lloyd Warner and Paul S. Lunt, *The Social Life of a Modern Community* (New Haven: Yale University Press, 1941).
17. Dorothea C. Leighton et al., *The Character of Danger: Psychiatric Symptoms in Selected Communities* (New York: Basic Books, Inc., 1963).
18. Leonard I. Pearlin and Melvin L. Kohn, "Social Class, Occupation, and Parental Values: A Cross-National Study," *American Sociological Review*, XXXI (August 1966), 466–479.
19. *Ibid.*, p. 473.
20. The "standardized comparison" in Table 2–8 indicates what the child-rearing values of the classes would be if degree of supervision or independence in work were controlled or "held constant." The effect of controlling on independence in work is seen by comparing the original (uncontrolled) relationship with the standardized (controlled) relationship. A procedure for computing the standardized figures appears in Rosenberg, "Test Factor Standardization as a Method of Interpretation," *Social Forces*, XLI (October 1962), 53–61.
21. Durkheim, *op. cit.*, chap. 3.
22. *Ibid.*, p. 185.
23. *Ibid.*, p. 186. (Reprinted with permission of The Macmillan Company. Copyright 1951 by The Free Press, A Corporation.)
24. Quoted in Lewis Lipsitz, "Working-Class Authoritarianism: A Re-Evaluation," *American Sociological Review*, XXX (February 1965), 104.
25. *Ibid.*
26. *Ibid.*

Intervening
and
Antecedent
Variables

The purpose of introducing test factors, we have seen, is to aid in the meaningful interpretation of the relationship between two variables. One considers extraneous variables, for example, in order to guard against misleading interpretations which might derive from the assumption that an inherent link exists between the two variables. The examination of component variables enables one to obtain a more exact understanding of which element of a broad concept is decisive for the observed effect. Another theoretical advantage of test factors is that through the use of intervening and antecedent variables they may enable one to trace out causal sequences.

Intervening Variables

The logical status of an intervening variable is that it is viewed as a consequence of the independent variable and as a determinant of the dependent variable. The characteristics of this type of test factor may be highlighted by contrasting it with an extraneous variable. Consider the following two examples: Assume, in a Northeast sample of the population, we find that people who are devoutly religious are more likely to vote Democratic. In speculating on this finding, we hypothesize that the reason is that Catholics are more dedicated to religion and that Catholics traditionally vote Democratic. When we control on religious affiliation, we find that the relationship between religiosity and political affiliation disappears. We then rightly conclude that the relationship is "due to" religious affiliation or, more exactly, to the association of each of the variables to the test factor.

Now consider a second example. Assume that we find a relationship between rural-urban residence and a tendency to stress obedience as an important child-rearing value. We hypothesize that the reason rural people emphasize obedience is that rural life tends to emphasize traditional values and that this traditional emphasis will be fostered by unquestioning acceptance of social norms and rules which are best induced by stressing obedience in the child. When we control on the test factor of traditionalism, we find that the relationship between rural-urban residence and the "obedience" value disappears. We again correctly say that the relationship is "due to" the test factor, that is, to the fact that traditionalism is associated both with rural-urban residence and with the value of obedience.

Note the similarities in these two examples. In each case the relationship is "due to" the test factor. In each case the statistical procedure is identical: one finds a relationship between two variables, selects a test factor, stratifies the sample by the test factor, and finds that the relationship in each of the contingent associations vanishes (or is considerably reduced). In each case the test factor is statistically correlated with both the independent and the dependent variables. In the first case, however, the test factor is extraneous, whereas in the second case it is intervening.

The distinction between an extraneous and an intervening variable is a logical and theoretical issue, not a statistical one. It lies in the assumed causal relationship among variables. With an extraneous variable, it is assumed that there is no causal connection, no inherent or intrinsic link, between the independent and dependent variables. The association is entirely due to their independent association with a third variable.

The first example cited above illustrates such an extraneous variable. Membership in the Catholic religion involves a set of norms which includes a more intense dedication to religious values. It is also a long-standing tradition among Catholics to vote Democratic. But the religiosity did not cause the political affiliation. The relationship is entirely due to the fact that religiosity and political affiliation are independently associated with membership in the Catholic religion. Such relationships, in which there is no inherent link between the two variables, may be represented schematically as follows:

$$\text{Test factor} \overset{\displaystyle \nearrow \text{Independent variable}}{\searrow \text{Dependent variable}}$$

The test factor leads to the independent variable, and the test factor also leads to the dependent variable; the crucial point is that the independent variable does not lead to the dependent variable. The relationship is symmetrical; the variables are consequences of a common determinant.

The establishment of an intervening variable involves a different analytic process. In this case the test factor, rather than being independently related to the two variables, represents a factor *intervening* between the independent and the dependent variables. The matter may be represented schematically as follows:

Independent variable⟶ Test factor⟶ Dependent variable.

Consider the second example cited earlier. We noted a relationship between rural-urban residence and obedience values for children and introduced as a test factor "traditionalism." It turned out that the relationship disappeared when the test factor was introduced. In this case, however, it was reasoned that "traditionalism" was an intervening variable. Living in rural areas presumably results in the development of a traditionalistic society and traditionalism leads to an emphasis on obedience for children,

To establish a variable as intervening, it may be noted, requires the presence of *three asymmetrical relationships:* (1) the original relationship between the independent and dependent variables (rural-urban residence and stress on obedience); (2) a relationship between the independent variable (rural-urban residence) and the test factor (traditionalism), here serving as the *dependent* variable; and (3) a relationship between the test factor (traditionalism), here serving as the independent variable, and the dependent variable (stress on obedience).

These three asymmetrical relationships may involve a dominant, rather than an absolute, direction of influence. Rural-urban residence may be responsible for child-rearing values, but child-rearing values are not responsible for rural-urban residence. Rural-urban residence is usually responsible for traditionalism, although it is possible that some city traditionalists may move to the country. Finally, traditionalism leads to child-rearing values, since the influence will rarely be the reverse. So long as one can establish the dominant direction of influence in the three asymmetrical relationships, it is possible to characterize the test factor as intervening.

Let us begin with a simple example drawn from Zeisel.[1] In a study of factory absenteeism among female workers, it was found that married women had a higher rate of absenteeism than single women (Table 3–1).

The question is: What might be a consequence of marital status and a determinant of absenteeism? The fairly obvious explanation is amount of housework: married women tend to have more cooking, cleaning, etc., to do. If amount of housework is indeed the inter-

Table 3–1
Proportion of Working Days Absent*

	Married Women	Single Women
Absent	6.4%	2.3%
Working	93.6	97.7
Total per cent	100.0	100.0
Number	(6496)	(10,560)

* Hans Zeisel, *Say It With Figures* (revised 4th ed., New York: Harper and Row, Publishers, Inc., 1957), p. 196, Table IX-2. (Reprinted with permission of Harper and Row, Publishers, Inc.)

vening variable, then, if one controls on this variable, the relationship between marital status and absenteeism should vanish. This is the technical equivalent of saying that were it not for the factor of housework, married and single women would not have different absenteeism rates.

The results appear in Table 3–2. Among women with equal amounts of housework, there is now little difference in rates of absenteeism. To be sure, the difference is not completely eliminated, so that house-

Table 3–2

Proportion of Working Days Absent by Marital Status and Amount of Housework[*]

| | Amount of Housework | | | |
| | A GREAT DEAL | | LITTLE OR NONE | |
	Married Women	Single Women	Married Women	Single Women
Absent	7.0%	5.7%	2.2%	1.9%
Working	93.0	94.3	97.8	98.1
Total per cent	100.0	100.0	100.0	100.0
Number	(5680)	(1104)	(816)	(9126)

[*] Hans Zeisel, *Say It With Figures* (revised 4th ed., New York: Harper and Row, Publishers, Inc., 1957), p. 196, Table IX-3 (adapted). (Reprinted with permission of Harper and Row, Publishers, Inc.)

work cannot be considered the sole explanation, but it is plainly a major factor. Its logical status is also plain: it is an intervening variable—a consequence of marital status and a determinant of absenteeism.

Another example appears in a study of political behavior, *The People's Choice*.[2] The investigators were interested in examining the relationship between location in the stratification system and participation in the election. In examining this question, they found that better-educated people were somewhat more likely to vote than those who were poorly educated (Table 3–3).

The reason for the relationship, it was hypothesized, lay in the factor of political interest. Greater education, it was reasoned, would stimulate political interest, and this interest would inspire people to vote. If this were so, then the elimination of the influence of interest should eliminate the relationship between education and vote.

Table 3–3

*Education and Intention to Vote**

	Some High School	No High School
Will not vote	8%	14%
Will vote	92	86
Total per cent	100	100
Number	(1613)	(1199)

* Paul F. Lazarsfeld, Bernard Berelson, and Hazel Gaudet, *The People's Choice* (New York: Columbia University Press, 1948), p. 47, Chart 15 (adapted). (Reprinted with permission of the Columbia University Press.)

Table 3–4 shows that this is largely the case. Among those with equal interest, there is no consistent or substantial relationship between education and vote. The original relationship is explained by the factor of interest (although not very much is explained since the original relationship is only represented by a 6 per cent difference).

Nevertheless, it is clear that interest is an intervening variable. Diagrammatically,

Education⟶ Interest⟶ Vote.

The sequence is apparent. The social experience (education) gives rise to the subjective experience or attitude (political interest), and the subjective experience determines the behavior (voting). Three

Table 3–4

*Education and Intention to Vote, by Political Interest**

	Political Interest					
	GREAT		MEDIUM		LOW	
	Some High School	No High School	Some High School	No High School	Some High School	No High School
Will not vote	1%	2%	7%	10%	44%	41%
Will vote	99	98	93	90	56	59
Total per cent	100	100	100	100	100	100
Number	(495)	(285)	(986)	(669)	(132)	(245)

* Paul F. Larzarsfeld, Bernard Berelson, and Hazel Gaudet, *The People's Choice* (New York: Columbia University Press, 1948), p. 47, Chart 15 (adapted). (Reprinted with permission of the Columbia University Press.)

asymmetrical relationships (education and vote, education and interest, and interest and vote) are involved in this analysis.

A somewhat more complex illustration of an intervening variable comes from a study of adolescent self-esteem.[3] In this study, it is found that boys from higher social classes tend to have higher self-esteem. Social class is determined by the *father's* location in the social

Table 3–5

*Social Class and Self-Esteem, Among Boys**

Self-Esteem	SOCIAL CLASS		
	Upper	Middle	Lower
High	55%	47%	36%
Medium	17	25	26
Low	28	28	39
Total per cent	100	100	100
Number	(89)	(1383)	(168)

* Morris Rosenberg, *Society and the Adolescent Self-Image* (Princeton: Princeton University Press, 1965), p. 41, Table 2 (abridged). (Reprinted by permission of Princeton University Press.)

structure, as indexed by his education, occupation, and source of income. Our theoretical understanding of this finding would be enhanced if we could better understand how the *father's* socio-economic position would ultimately lead to a certain level of self-evaluation by the *son*.

One factor which may intervene is the pattern of *father-son interaction*. Are the father and the son close to one another? Does the father take an interest in his son, encourage him, help him? This type of interaction would be viewed as a reflection of social group norms. In other words, it is a sociological axiom that when people become group members, they tend to interact with other group members; this interaction leads to group norms—characteristic attitudes, values, practices, conceptions of right and wrong, etc. Even if they originally entered the group with these norms, the group interaction tends to solidify, crystallize, and stabilize the norms. One might thus speculate that membership in the higher class would lead to the adoption of the norm of close father-son relationships. And Table 3–6 supports this reasoning: 65 per cent of the upper-class members, but 28 per cent of the working-class members, reported close father-son relationships.

Table 3–6

Social Class and Closeness of Father-Son Relationships[*]

| Relationship with father | SOCIAL CLASS | | |
	Upper	Middle	Lower
Close	65%	40%	28%
Intermediate	19	37	40
Not close	15	24	32
Total per cent	100	100	100
Number	(26)	(365)	(50)

[*] Morris Rosenberg, *Society and the Adolescent Self-Image* (Princeton: Princeton University Press, 1965), p. 44, Table 4 (abridged). (Reprinted by permission of Princeton University Press.)

But it is also reasonable to assume that if a boy has a close relationship with his father—if he is helped and encouraged by him—this support from a significant other will tend to enhance his feeling of worth. The data[4] show that this is so. If the relationship of father's class and son's self-esteem is due to the closeness of the father-son relationship, then, when the factor of closeness is controlled, the relationship should vanish or be substantially reduced.

Table 3–7 confirms this expectation. Originally, we see, 13.4 per cent more of the upper-class boys than working-class boys had high self-esteem; controlling (by means of standardization) on closeness of father-son relationships, this difference reduces to 8.0 per cent.[5] At the low self-esteem end of the scale the change is still more dramatic. Originally the upper-class boys were less likely to have low self-esteem,

Table 3–7

Social Class and Self-Esteem: (A) Original Relationship and (B) Relationship Standardized on Closeness of Relationship with Father (Boys)[*]

| | (A) *Original Relationship* | | | (B) *Standardized Relationship* | | |
| | SOCIAL CLASS | | | SOCIAL CLASS | | |
Self-Esteem	Upper	Middle	Lower	Upper	Middle	Lower
High	54.2%	50.1%	40.8%	52.3%	50.1%	44.3%
Medium	12.5	22.0	18.4	7.5	21.9	19.5
Low	33.3	27.8	40.8	40.2	27.9	36.3
Total per cent	100.0	100.0	100.0	100.0	100.0	100.0
Number	(24)	(345)	(49)	(24)	(345)	(49)

[*] Morris Rosenberg, *Society and the Adolescent Self-Image* (Princeton: Princeton University Press, 1965), p. 46, Table 6. (Reprinted by permission of Princeton University Press.)

whereas the standardized table shows that they are slightly more likely to do so.

In other words, the reasoning would be that father's location in the social structure leads him to adopt (or to maintain) norms of interacting with his son, and that the nature of this interaction is such as to elevate his son's feeling of worth. This finding can be expressed interchangeably in substantive, general, and formal models:

1. Substantive: Father's class——→ Father-son relationship——→ Self-esteem.
2. General: Social position——→ Interaction norms——→ Attitude.
3. Formal: Independent variable——→ Intervening variable——→ Dependent variable.

It is plain that one's understanding of the meaning of the relationship between father's social class and son's self-esteem is enhanced by the examination of the intervening variable. Since the relationship does not disappear completely, however, we would conclude that father-son interaction is an important intervening variable, but not the sole intervening variable.

It is apparent that the specification of intervening variables contributes substantially to the deeper understanding of the relationship between two variables. Consider the following kinds of purely descriptive findings which have appeared in the empirical literature: Protestants have higher suicide rates than Catholics; lower-class people have higher rates of psychosis; rural or small-town students are less likely to go to college; children from broken homes are more likely to be delinquents; only children are more likely to achieve eminence; lower-class boys have lower self-esteem; and so on.

Such findings achieve fuller and deeper meaning when intervening variables are introduced to account for them. Thus Protestants are said to commit suicide more because they are less highly integrated, and integration is an insulator against suicide. Lower-class people are said to have higher rates of psychosis because they are more socially isolated, and social isolation is productive of mental illness. Children from broken homes are said to be more likely to be delinquent because they lack a father figure with whom to identify, and the absence of a father figure encourages delinquency. Upper-class boys are said to have higher self-esteem because they have close relationships with their fathers, and such close relationships are productive of high levels of self-acceptance. And so on. Schematically, such analyses would be represented as follows:

Independent Variable	*Intervening Variable*	*Dependent Variable*
Religion ——————→	Integration ——————————→	Suicide
Class ——————————→	Isolation ——————————→	Psychosis
Broken home ——————→	Absence of father figure ——→	Delinquency
Class ——————————→	Relationship with father ——→	Self-esteem

In the absence of a concern for such mediating or intervening mechanisms, one ends up with facts, but with incomplete understanding.

It may be useful to attempt to locate more explicitly the theoretical relevance of intervening variables. The viewpoint advanced here is that *any asymmetrical relationship between two variables is an abstraction from a never-ending causal chain.* The greater one's understanding of the links in this chain, the better one's understanding of the relationship. The intervening variable is one of these links.

The idea of a causal chain involves the assumption that any cause has itself been caused by some influence which preceded it, and that many effects become causes of other effects. For example, one may say that the current American political system has been heavily influenced by the political ideas and behavior of men at the time of the American Revolution, but these political ideas and behavior were themselves importantly determined by prior social and political events in England. Furthermore, reversing the chronological sequence, the current political system is certain to make its influence felt on future political systems. One need simply change one's perspective or anchorage point to convert a cause into an effect of a prior influence or an effect into a cause of a subsequent state. The causal link may be broad, spanning centuries, or it may be minute, linking highly continuous states or events.

When one performs a causal analysis of social events, then, one is essentially "tapping in" to an ongoing stream of events proceeding *seriatim,* and in great complexity, from cause to effect. Where one "taps in" is largely an arbitrary matter, dictated by the guiding interests of the investigator and, of course, the availability of the data. Different people may tap in at different "levels" and use these as points of departure for their independent variables.

Assume that one were able to establish a strict causal sequence, A, B, C, D, E. A would be a cause of B, but it would also be a cause of C. A has influenced B, and this change in B has affected C. Admittedly, the causal chain often becomes highly attenuated, but it still exists. One may, then, tap into this chain at any point, examining the causal relationship, between A and D, B and D, B and E, etc. In many cases of social research the causal gap between the independent and dependent variables is very wide; one is, in effect, examining the causal relationship between A and E.

Without wrestling a straw man, we would suggest that many implicit disputes are simply differences of the points at which one taps into the causal sequence. If a psychiatrist says that the cause of anxiety must be sought in the family, whereas the sociologist says it is to be found in social class, there is not necessarily any difference of opinion between them. We do not mean this in the simple sense that both factors may operate, but rather that both are parts of the same causal sequence. Social-class factors may have a bearing on the family, and the family in turn may generate anxiety in children. These are part of the same causal sequence.

Erich Fromm[6] has provided an interesting example. In discussing the question of socially necessary character types, he suggests certain social functions that must be performed and certain social values that must prevail. But he does not contend that social functions are immediately translatable or convertible into personality types. Personality is largely formed in the family. Fromm points out, however, that the family is a part of the broader social system, that it is influenced by social needs and values; as a result of this influence, it tends to socialize its children in such ways as to produce the required character types. He stipulates a direct causal sequence rather than alternative influences. To say that the family influences character structure in the children and that social needs influence this character structure are both true, not in the sense that each exercises an independent influence but that the first influences the second which influences the third. The failure to take due account of this point tends to occur when the investigator rigidly adheres to a particular level of analysis, having "tapped in" on the causal sequence at a certain point, and refuses to admit that other levels of analysis are relevant.

The road traveled from the independent variable to the dependent variable may thus pass many intellectual way stages en route, each leading to the next in an endless causal itinerary. When the survey analyst deals with intervening variables, then, he is essentially dealing with *an* intervening variable, not *the* intervening variable. The discovery of an intervening variable thus cannot serve as a complete explanation of the original relationship, but may serve as a *landmark* on the intellectual journey from cause to effect.

Consider, for example, the relationship between social class and participation in voluntary organizations: studies show that lower-class people join and participate less.[7] One line of reasoning would be as follows: lower-class people are less likely to aspire to prestigious occupations which require advanced education. They are thus likely to view the educational process as relatively worthless for the satisfaction of their pragmatic needs and to set a low evaluation on it. The middle-class man, on the other hand, is especially likely to seek in education the development of his verbal skills, since these are often essential for his occupational success. Since formal voluntary organizations often require a knowledge of parliamentary procedure, an ability to express oneself well, and training in the formulation of arguments, etc., the manual worker will feel uncomfortable and inept in such an environment and will tend to avoid these organizations. As such organizations become more heavily populated by middle-class people, the discomfort of the working class will be increased by the strangeness and unfamiliarity with other middle-class norms and patterns of thought and behavior. This downward spiral will eventually result in a low rate of membership and participation in voluntary organizations among manual workers.

This example illustrates the type of difficulty encountered by the sociologist in reasoning from his independent to his dependent variable. Obviously, there are many steps along the path, and many missteps are possible. One may believe that one is reasoning "in a straight line," but one would have a great deal more confidence that this were so if one's reasoning crossed an *established landmark* on the trail from A to E. It is easy to see how essential this landmark is in sustaining the entire thread of the argument. *Notice how completely the argument would fail if it were found that working-class members had as much verbal fluency as middle-class people.* If it were found that they did not, this would provide some level of support for one's line of reasoning, although much more, of course, would be required to sustain the argument.

Antecedent Variables

The theoretical purpose of introducing an antecedent variable is the same as that of introducing an intervening variable, namely, to trace out a causal sequence. But while the intervening variable is one which comes *between* the independent and dependent variables in a causal sequence, the antecedent variable is one which comes *before* the independent variable in the sequence. The antecedent variable is a true effective influence; it does not explain away the relationship between the independent and dependent variables but clarifies the influences which preceded this relationship.

Of what value is the study of antecedent variables? Assume we begin with the finding that the poorly educated have less political knowledge. Education is viewed as a cause of political knowledge, Diagrammatically,

Education———→ Political knowledge.

But what is the cause of education? This is the question that antecedent variable analysis is designed to answer. One might hypothesize that the father's social class is responsible for the individual's educational level. If this could be shown to be the case, then we would postulate that

Father's class———→ Education———→ Political knowledge.

We would now have a more complete understanding of the causal chain which eventuated in the observed behavior. This causal chain can be carried as far back as is theoretically meaningful. Each additional step advances our understanding of the social process.

In principle, of course, the causal sequence could be traced back endlessly. Krech and Crutchfield illustrate this point vividly:

Explanations may frequently deteriorate into an endless search for the "ultimate" or "first" cause. If it be said that Mr. Arbuthnot seeks membership in the country club because he sees it as a goal of social approval, it is then asked why he seeks that goal. If it is answered that this goal has arisen because of a need for personal security, it is then asked why that feeling of insecurity arose. If it is answered that the feeling of personal insecurity has arisen because of a socially embarrassing speech defect that Mr. Arbuthnot has acquired, it is then asked why that speech defect. The answer may be that the speech defect was a defense against a precocious younger brother. Thus, at this stage, we are to understand that Mr. Arbuthnot seeks membership in the country club because his younger brother was precocious! *But why stop here? The analysis can go as far as the ingenuity of the theorist will carry him, without ever reaching the ultimate, or first, cause.*[8]

But to abandon the quest for first causes does not mean that it is useless to seek *any* prior causes. A two-variable relationship is, after all, a truncated segment of an extended causal sequence, and any meaningful extension of that sequence can only enhance our understanding of the larger process.

Consider a hypothetical example adapted from Kendall and Lazarsfeld.[9] Although the authors presented this case as an illustration of intervening variable analysis, we have modified the presentation to illustrate an antecedent variable.

We begin with the following finding: a sample of soldiers who had friends or acquaintances who had been deferred during World War II were more likely to feel that they themselves should have been deferred. This finding is easily understood. One of a soldier's major anchorage points or reference groups is his friends and acquaintances. They are like him, and he compares himself with them. If they have been drafted, then he should be also; but if many of them have been deferred, then he may he resentful that he has not been deferred.

But one may wish to trace the causal sequence one step back to see if one can locate the conditions which provide a man with a friendship environment in which deferral is or is not a common phenomenon. Having friends who are or are not deferred is an interpersonal phenomenon, but as it stands the result implies that this interpersonal environment is idiosyncratic: some soldiers happen to have friends who are deferred and others not. But the interpersonal environment of friends' deferrals need not be accepted as an accidental phenomenon but may be traced to its roots in the social structure.

One antecedent variable which might be considered would be social class, particularly the educational component of class. Drafted soldiers tend to be young men, and the better educated are more recently out of school. The more poorly educated have been out of school longer, and many of them have obtained employment in war factories and have been deferred as essential workers. Hence, a poorly educated man who was drafted might be resentful because many of his friends were deferred (and were making good wages in factories), whereas the well-educated man, almost all of whose friends have also been drafted, would tend to feel that his induction was justified. (This situation occurred during World War II.)

The introduction of the antecedent variable thus adds depth to one's understanding. Expressing the matter more technically, structure (class or education) determines a man's interpersonal environment (possession of deferred friends and acquaintances) which determine his morale (belief that he should have been deferred). In methodological terminology, the antecedent variable leads to the independent variable which leads to the dependent variable.

How would one test whether education is in fact the antecedent variable? Given a logical basis for assuming this to be the case, there are three statistical requirements which must be satisfied:

1. All three variables—antecedent, independent, and dependent —must be related.
2. When the antecedent variable is controlled, the relationship between the independent and the dependent variable should *not* vanish.

3. When the independent variable is controlled, the relationship between the antecedent variable and the dependent variable *should* disappear.

The raw data for this hypothetical illustration appear in Table 3–8. This table examines the relationship between possession of deferred friends and the soldier's feeling that he should have been deferred, controlling on education. All the remaining five tables (Tables 3–9 to 3–13) are derived directly from this initial table; the reader will find it easy to recompute these figures to form the subsequent tables. At the same time, these raw figures may make clear the precise meaning of the subsequent tables.

Table 3–8

*Possession of Deferred Friends and Feeling That One Should Have Been Deferred, by Educational Level**

	HIGH EDUCATION		LOW EDUCATION	
	Friends or Acquaintances Deferred	No Friends or Acquaintances Deferred	Friends or Acquaintances Deferred	No Friends or Acquaintances Deferred
Volunteered or should not have been deferred	210	1346	939	371
Should have been deferred.	125	80	545	21
Total	335	1426	1484	392

* Patricia L. Kendall and Paul F. Lazarsfeld, "Problems of Survey Analysis," in R. K. Merton and P. F. Lazarsfeld, eds., *Continuities in Social Research: Studies in the Scope and Method of "The American Soldier"* (Glencoe, Ill.: The Free Press, 1950), p. 151, Table B (abridged and adapted). (Reprinted with permission of The Macmillan Company. Copyright 1950 by The Free Press, A Corporation.)

1. All three variables must be related: One begins, of course, with the knowledge that the independent variable is related to the dependent variable. Table 3–9 (which can be computed from Table 3–8) shows that this is so. Thirty-seven per cent of those whose friends had been deferred, but only 6 per cent of those whose friends had not, felt that they themselves should have been deferred.

But one must also ascertain whether the antecedent variable is related both to the independent and to the dependent variables. Table 3–10 shows the relationship between the antecedent variable (edu-

Table 3–9

Possession of Deferred Friends and Feeling
That One Should Have Been Deferred

	Friends or Acquaintances Deferred	No Friends or Acquaintances Deferred
Volunteered or should not have been deferred	63%	94%
Should have been deferred	37	6
Total per cent	100	100
Number	(1819)	(1818)

cation) and the independent variable (possession of deferred friends). The relationship is strong: 81 per cent of the well-educated, but only 21 per cent of the poorly educated, had no friends or acquaintances who had been deferred.

Finally, Table 3–11 shows that the antecedent variable (education) and the dependent variable (feeling that one should have been deferred) are associated. Thirty per cent of the poorly educated, but only 12 per cent of the well-educated, hold this view.

The first requirement for establishing an antecedent variable is thus satisfied: all three variables show an association with one another.

2. The relationship between the independent and dependent variable must *not* vanish when the antecedent variable is controlled: There appears to be a frequent misunderstanding about this point. The antecedent variable does not "account for" the independent-dependent variable relationship; it *precedes* it in the causal sequence. The fact that a prior influence affected an independent variable therefore does not mean that the independent variable does not affect the dependent variable.

Table 3–10

Education and Feeling That One Should Have Been Deferred

	High Education	Low Education
Friends or acquaintances deferred	19%	79%
No friends or acquaintances deferred	81	21
Total per cent	100	100
Number	(1761)	(1876)

Table 3–11

Education and Feeling That One Should Have Been Deferred

	High Education	Low Education
Volunteered or should not have been deferred	88%	70%
Should have been deferred	12	30
Total per cent	100	100
Number	(1761)	(1876)

Table 3–12 shows that when the antecedent variable (education) is controlled, the relationship between the independent and dependent variables persists. Among the well-educated, 37 per cent of those with deferred friends felt that they should have been deferred, compared with only six per cent of those without deferred friends, and virtually the same findings apply to the poorly educated. Had the relationship vanished, then education would have been an extraneous variable, not an antecedent variable.

3. Finally, the relationship between the antecedent and the dependent variable should vanish when the independent variable is controlled: Table 3–13 shows that this is what occurs. Among soldiers with an equal number of friends deferred, there is no association between educational level and the feeling that one should have been deferred. (Tables 3–9 to 3–13, it may be noted again, are all *directly derivable* from Table 3–8.)

Table 3–12

Possession of Deferred Friends and Feeling That One Should Have Been Deferred, by Educational Level

	HIGH EDUCATION		LOW EDUCATION	
	Friends or Acquaintances Deferred	No Friends or Acquaintances Deferred	Friends or Acquaintances Deferred	No Friends or Acquaintances Deferred
Volunteered or should not have been deferred	63%	94%	63%	95%
Should have been deferred	37	6	37	5
Total per cent	100	100	100	100
Number	(335)	(1426)	(1484)	(392)

Table 3–13

Education and Feeling That One Should Have Been
Deferred, by Possession of Deferred Friends

	Friends or Acquaintances Deferred		No Friends or Acquaintances Deferred	
	High Education	Low Education	High Education	Low Education
Volunteered or should not have been deferred	63%	63%	94%	95%
Should have been deferred	37	37	6	5
Total per cent	100	100	100	100
Number	(335)	(1484)	(1426)	(392)

The data thus suggest that education is a true antecedent variable preceding the relationship between possession of deferred friends and the feeling that one should have been deferred. It should be stressed that the satisfaction of the three statistical criteria do not prove that an hypothesized antecedent variable is a true one. That is a logical, not a statistical, question. If (to take an absurd example) one had postulated as an antecedent variable the personality quality of extroversion, then, even if all the statistical criteria were met, one would not accept it as an antecedent variable unless there were a logical reason for assuming that extroversion was responsible for the possession of deferred friends. The data are only necessary conditions for an interpretation; they are never sufficient in themselves.

The singular nature of the antecedent variable may stand out more sharply if contrasted with extraneous and intervening variables.

Extraneous and antecedent variables

In our earlier discussion we noted that a variable is considered extraneous if it is logically prior to both the independent and dependent variables and if, when it is controlled, the relationship cancels out. In this case, one concludes that both the independent and dependent variables are consequences of a common cause (the extraneous variable), not that they bear any inherent relationship to one another. One might represent the relationship as follows:

Possession of deferred friends
(Independent variable)

Education
(Extraneous variable)

Feeling one should be deferred
(Dependent variable)

The antecedent variable, on the other hand, is assumed to be directly responsible for the independent variable which, in turn, influences the dependent variable. Schematically, this sequence could be represented as follows:

Education$\longrightarrow$ Deferred friends$\longrightarrow$ Feeling should be deferred
(Antecedent)   (Independent)   (Dependent)

Assuming that there are logical grounds for considering the test factor either as extraneous or antecedent, the resolution regarding its nature is subject to a statistical test. If the test factor is extraneous, then the relationship between the independent and dependent variables will cancel out; if the test factor is antecedent, then it will not.

Intervening and antecedent variables

Although antecedent variable analysis is essentially a derivative of interevening variable analysis, these two types of variables may be differentiated both on logical and statistical grounds. The intervening variable comes *between* the independent and dependent variables, whereas the antecedent variable comes *before* the independent variable.

In the present example, one would hardly consider education an intervening variable between possession of deferred friends and feeling that one should have been deferred. Why? Because it is hard to imagine how having deferred friends could be responsible for one's level of education. On the other hand, one can easily see how educational level may determine one's possession of deferred friends. The direction of the asymmetrical relationship is the decisive factor.

The two types of variables are also differentiated on statistical grounds. If the test factor is intervening, then the relationship between the independent and dependent variables should vanish, whereas, if the test factor is antecedent, it should not.

In formal terms, then, the contrast between the intervening variable and the antecedent variable is as follows:

Schematic representation of intervening variable:
    Independent variable———→ Intervening variable———→ Dependent variable
Schematic representation of antecedent variable:
    Antecedent variable———→ Independent variable———→ Dependent variable

Antecedent variable analysis is simply a derivative of intervening variable analysis. If one has a relationship between B and C, and one wishes to determine whether A precedes it, one does so by determining whether B intervenes between A and C. In the final step, then, the antecedent variable is treated as the independent variable, and the original independent variable is treated as if it were the intervening variable.

The theoretical contributions of the intervening variable and the antecedent variable are the same. Both assume that the variables under examination are linked to one another in an endless causal sequence and that the task is to trace out the chain of causation. The intervening variable is a link located between the independent and dependent variables, whereas the antecedent variable is a link preceding the independent variable. Whether a variable is intervening or antecedent depends entirely on the points in the causal sequence into which one happens to tap.

The tracing out of such causal sequences is of great importance in the understanding of social phenomena. After reporting a relationship between two variables, for example, it is a common practice to reflect on why the relationship exists. The form that such speculation assumes frequently involves the assumption of an extended causal sequence, of which the reported empirical relationship forms a part. Thus Marx suggested that technological development would lead to the physical concentration of workers in factories, that this concentration would lead to class consciousness, that this class consciousness would create political action, that this political action would eventuate in revolution and the establishment of socialism, etc.[10] Michel's "iron law of oligarchy"[11] is a similar case in point: the workers select leaders to advance their economic and political interests; these leaders develop an expertise in political and economic matters, thus rendering themselves indispensable; this indispensability enables them to exercise absolute control over the workers' organizations, thus nullifying the principles of democracy and equality for which the workers' organizations were originally established, etc.

Beginning with a relationship between two variables, much informed and imaginative speculation may be applied to trace out the causal sequence of which it is a part. But it is still speculation, and confidence in it is dependent upon its logical and theoretical rigor. It is patently helpful to be able to trace out such causal sequences by means of systematic test. Through the introduction of test factors, a systematic test of assumed intervening variables and antecedent variables becomes possible. To the extent that the logical and statistical criteria are satisfied, confidence in the interpretation is enhanced. The advantage of such a procedure for theoretical understanding is self-evident.

Survey Approximations to Experimental Design

Extraneous, component, intervening, and antecedent variables thus make distinctive contributions to theory. The special theoretical merit of extraneous variables is that they guard against the danger of misleading and erroneous interpretations; the virtue of component variables is that they enable us to specify the crucial element of the global concept which is of decisive significance; and the merit of intervening and antecedent variables is that they enable us to trace out the causal sequence linking socially relevant variables. Each of these contributions may help to create more exact, more confident, and more fruitful data analyses.

One of the merits of these test factors is that they enable survey research to partake of some of the advantages of experimental design. Aside from mathematico-logical deductive systems, experimentation represents the strongest model of proof in science. Before we consider how test factors enable one to approximate the virtues of the experiment, it is necessary to consider some of the characteristics of survey relationships.

In Chapter I, we pointed out that there are a number of different types of asymmetrical relationships with which the survey researcher may deal—stimulus-response, disposition-response, property-disposition, immanent, precondition-effect, and means-ends. We observed that the type of asymmetrical relationship which has been of greatest interest to the sociologist is that between properties, as independent variables, and dispositions or behavior, as dependent variables. Although this is but one among many types of possible relationships, we shall see why it is important to highlight some of the characteristics distinctive of this type of relationship.

A "property" is a relatively perduring characteristic of the individual which is not dependent upon circumstances for its activation.[12] The major sociological properties of an individual are social groups, collectivities, or categories, such as sex, age, race, religion, class, nationality, region, marital status, birth order, etc. A disposition, on the other hand, is a potential or tendency of the individual which may be activated under particular circumstances. Opinions, attitudes, values, abilities, habits, personality qualities, or "powers" generally are dispositions, in the sense that they only find expression under the impetus of certain stimuli or in the presence of certain conditions.

Thus, the sociologist is likely to examine relationships such as those between race and alienation, religion and suicide, rural-urban residence and occupational aspirations, sex and political interest, nationality and self-esteem, etc. Some of these properties, we have noted, are absolutely fixed and unalterable, and others are relatively so. The sociologist is thus usually justified in treating them, as he does, as independent variables.

The reason for the focus on properties (variously called demographic characteristics, background characteristics, or face-sheet data) is rooted in the sociological emphasis. The sociological social psychologist is primarily concerned with the relevance of groups, collectivities, or social categories[13] for individual personality, cognitive and affective structures, and behavior. This is not, of course, the sociologist's exclusive, but rather his dominant, interest.

Leaving aside test factors for the moment, it is useful to compare a property-disposition relationship,[14] as it appears in a survey study, with a stimulus-response relationship, as it appears in an experimental design.

The essential rationale for the experimental design appears in John Stuart Mill's "Method of Difference," which stipulates: "If an instance in which the phenomenon under investigation occurs, and an instance in which it does not occur, have every circumstance in common save one, that one occurring only in the former; the circumstance in which alone the two instances differ is . . . the cause . . . of the phenomenon."[15] An experimenter might thus take two matched groups of people, expose one of these groups to a stimulus, and then observe how these groups differ on the effect variable; the difference would then be attributed to the stimulus. In Mill's terms, the two groups have every circumstance in common except one, namely, the stimulus. This method is characteristic of the "after-only" design of experimentation[16] and is especially relevant here because it yields results most comparable to the type of relationship which appears in survey studies.

For example, during World War II, an attempt was made to determine the effect of certain communications on soldiers' opinions and attitudes. One communication presented was a film entitled "The Battle of Britain," which dealt with the "British resistance to German air attacks on England during the fall of 1940," and told of "the almost superhuman efforts of the British people and of the RAF and to the unwillingness of the British to give up even in the face of apparently hopeless odds."[17] In order to study the impact of this film, two matched groups were selected: an experimental group, which was shown the film; and a comparable control group, which was not.

When these soldiers were asked, "What do you think is probably the real reason why the Nazis did not invade and conquer Britain after the fall of France?" 70 per cent of the film group, but only 48 per cent of the control group, said, "The Nazis tried and would have succeeded except for the determined resistance of the British." Similarly, when asked, "In your opinion who gave the Nazis their first real defeat?" 43 per cent of the film group, but only 20 per cent of the control group, answered, "the British Royal Air Force."[18] Since, in accordance with Mill's canon of difference, the two groups were essentially alike in all respects but one (exposure to the film), it was justifiable to conclude that the observed differences in opinions were attributable to the effects of the film.

Compare this film-opinion relationship with a property-disposition relationship such as "Negroes are more alienated than whites." One senses at once certain similarities and certain differences in these two types of findings. The outstanding similarity lies in the *externality* of the independent variable. Some outside force—"The Battle of Britain" or race—has "produced" the effect—attitudes toward the RAF or feelings of alienation. Both results are thus descriptive of social processes. But there are also important differences between these two kinds of findings. These may be focused around four issues: *contiguity, specificity, comparison* (or control), and *unidirectionality.*

In the relationship between the film and the opinion, the two variables are much more *contiguous* than a relationship between race and alienation. The opinion will usually be measured shortly after the film exposure, whereas there is an extended temporal and conceptual gap between being a Negro, starting at birth, and alienation, an attitude evolving over the course of years.

Similarly, if we find that urban youth have higher educational aspirations than rural youth,[19] the place of residence appears as a rather remote influence. What is meant is that rural and urban youth are exposed to a wide variety of different social influences which in the long run eventuate in differential patterns of educational aspiration. The influence of the property on the disposition or behavior is thus rarely that of an immediate, direct agent which creates a specific effect but is rather a remote, abstract, characteristic set of social experiences which eventuates in a given attitude or behavior.

The second difference appears in the quality of *specificity* or *isolability.* If people who have seen the specific film ("The Battle of Britain") differ with regard to an opinion, we know fairly concretely what the effective influence is.[20] But to say that being a Negro is responsible for alienation is much more ambiguous because being a Negro implies such a wide range of experiences, and one does not know which are relevant for the dependent variable. Such a statement is almost like saying that "human communication" is responsible for holding a certain attitude. Both statements are true but unspecific. To know that "communications" produced the attitude is much less enlightening than to know that a specific type of communication (say, a fear-arousing communication) is responsible for the attitude. It is true that the movement of a rocket is due to physico-chemical forces, but no nation will assign its spies to learn this secret from another; they would require much more specific information about the nature of the independent variable.

A third difference between a stimulus-response relationship and a property-disposition relationship lies in the nature of the *comparison groups.* When we say that a film has influenced an attitude, we do so on the basis of two kinds of findings: (1) if two comparable groups are selected, one of which is exposed to the film and the other not, and if differences in opinions emerge, then we attribute this effect to the film: (2) if a group's opinions are measured before exposure to the film and after it, then we attribute the change to the film. In the former case an experimental group is compared with a comparable control group, whereas in the latter case the group is compared with itself.

When one compares groups in terms of properties, we cannot say that the groups are matched in all respects but one. Presumably the soldiers who saw "The Battle of Britain" movie are reasonably like those who did not (within a certain margin of error) in all respects except that of seeing the film. But we cannot say that Negroes are like whites in all respects except their race. Many other qualities are "block-booked" with race. Urban people are not identical with rural people in all regards except residence, nor are men exactly the same as women in all respects except sex. A whole host of experiential and psychological differences are encompassed by these categories. A comparison of groups with different properties must take account of the fact that they are not matched.

A similar problem arises with regard to the "before-after" experimental design. Here we study a group's opinions, expose it to a film, and then study the opinions of this same group again to see what changes have occurred. But this procedure is difficult with relatively fixed properties and impossible with absolutely unalterable properties. One cannot, for example, study a man's alienation before he became a Negro, then make him a Negro, then study his degree of alienation afterward to see what change has occurred. The same is obviously true of sex, national origin, birth order, etc.

Finally, as we have noted, the relationship between a stimulus and response is *unidirectional,* whereas this is not always the case with a property-disposition relationship. In a proper experimental design, it is plain that the film influenced the opinion and that the opinion did not influence the film. With fixed dispositions, of course, the issue is equally clear: being a Negro is responsible for alienation, since alienation cannot be responsible for being a Negro. But suppose we find a relationship between social class and mental illness. Is membership in the lower class responsible for a high rate of schizophrenia or do schizophrenics tend to end up in the lower class? The issue of unidirectionality is usually more ambiguous in a property-disposition relationship than in an experimental design.

There are thus at least four ways in which a relationship based upon an experimental design differs from the usual property-disposition relationship: in the contiguity or remoteness of the two variables; in the specificity of the independent variable; in the matching of the groups compared; and in the unidirectionality of the relationship between the two variables.

Because of these problems, one might be disposed to argue that sociology should confine itself to studies employing the experimental design. But the experimental design simply cannot be applied to many sociological problems. If one wants to study the effect of race on alienation, one cannot take a sample of new babies, assign one group at random to the Negro group and the other to the white group, and then observe the difference in alienation. Even if this were possible, one could not solve the problem of contiguity by studying alienation two weeks after the racial assignment if attitudes of alienation take years to develop. Nor could one, as noted earlier, study the alienation of a sample, make them all Negro, and then study their alienation again to see what change has occurred. Many sociological problems thus are not amenable to experimental manipulation.

The point we wish to make is that consideration of extraneous, component, and intervening variables helps to deal with these problems—not perfectly perhaps, but to some degree.

The issue of *group comparability* is met by the introduction of *extraneous* variables; these help to "control" or eliminate the associated differences between the compared groups. Assume we begin with a relationship between age and religiosity. If, after controlling on a number of relevant variables, one finds that this relationship is still maintained, then one has greater confidence that it is really the factor of age, rather than some associated variable, which exercises the effective influence. The larger the number of extraneous variables controlled, the more do the groups become alike in all ways but one (for example, age). The systematic investigation of extraneous variables, then, enables a survey correlation to approximate to some degree the experimental-control group matching of the after-only experimental design.

The problem of lack of *specificity* in a property-disposition relationship is partly solved through the investigation of *component* variables. The experimental stimulus (a film or a lecture) has a much more precise signification than a property (class or race). We may know that middle-class people are more likely to emphasize self-control as a child-rearing value, but we cannot say what aspect of "middle-classness" (education, income, social prestige, family intactness, etc.) is primarily effective. Analysis of component variables may show that it is the nature of the work people do—the assumption of responsibility and independence—that is the decisive factor in class which accounts for the child-rearing value. The use of component variables thus provides a more precise and specific understanding of the nature of the effective influence, and thereby enables the survey analyst to approach more closely the specificity and concreteness of the experimental stimulus.

The third problem—that of the *remoteness* or *contiguity* of the variables—can in some measure be handled through the use of intervening variables. It is true that there is a much broader temporal and conceptual gap between being a Negro and feelings of alienation than there is between a specific lecture and a particular opinion. The intervening variable helps to fill in that gap. It indicates the more proximate consequences of the independent variable which ultimately issue in the dependent effect. The gap between rural-urban residence and emphasis on obedience as a child-rearing value is partially filled by the traditionalistic orientation. Compared to the original relationship, the independent variable is more contiguous to the intervening variable, and the intervening variable is more contiguous to the dependent variable.

Finally, there is the problem of *unidirectionality*. In the experimental design, the direction of influence is unequivocally from the stimulus to the response, whereas this is not always the case in a survey relationship between a property and a disposition. In large measure, this problem can be met on the basis of general considerations of asymmetrical relationships discussed earlier, particularly the issue of susceptibility to influence. Where the direction of influence is more ambiguous, the panel[21] (re-interview) technique is extremely effective in resolving the issue.

In various ways, then, the introduction of test factors into survey analyses enables one to exploit some of the virtues of the experimental design while avoiding the inappropriateness of experimentation for many sociological problems. The introduction of extraneous, component, and intervening variables into data analysis does not, to be sure, overcome all the problems of correlational analysis. To the extent that they enable the survey analyst to approach the characteristics of the "after-only" experimental design, however, they partake of the strengths of that scientific instrument.

NOTES

1. Hans Zeisel, *Say It With Figures* (New York: Harper & Row Publishers, 1947), p. 191.
2. Paul F. Lazarsfeld, Bernard R. Berelson, and Hazel Gaudet, *The People's Choice* (New York: Columbia University Press, 1948).

3. Morris Rosenberg, *Society and the Adolescent Self-Image* (Princeton, N.J.: Princeton University Press, 1965), chap. 3.

4. *Ibid.*, p. 45.

5. The discrepancy between Tables 3–5 and 3–6 stems from the fact that it was necessary to use one-third of the sample to compute Table 3–6.

6. Erich Fromm, *Man For Himself* (New York: Rinehart, 1947), p. 60.

7. Charles R. Wright and Herbert H. Hyman, "Voluntary Association Memberships of American Adults: Evidence from National Sample Surveys," *American Sociological Review*, XXIII (June 1958), 284–294.

8. David Krech and Richard Crutchfield, *Theory and Problems of Social Psychology* (New York: McGraw-Hill Book Company, 1948), p. 34. [Copyright 1948 by the McGraw-Hill Book Company. Used by permission of McGraw-Hill Book Company. Quoted in Herbert Hyman, *Survey Design and Analysis* (Glencoe, Ill.: The Free Press, 1955), p. 255.]

9. Patricia L. Kendall and Paul F. Lazarsfeld, "Problems of Survey Analysis," in R. K. Merton and P. F. Lazarsfeld, eds., *Continuities in Social Research: Studies in the Scope and Method of "The American Soldier"* (Glencoe, Ill.: The Free Press, 1950), pp. 148–154.

10. A clear exposition of this reasoning appears in Reinhard Bendix and Seymour Martin Lipset, "Karl Marx' Theory of Social Classes," in R. Bendix and S. M. Lipset, eds., *Class, Status and Power* (Glencoe, Ill.: The Free Press, 1953), pp. 26–35.

11. Robert Michels, *Political Parties* (Glencoe, Ill.: The Free Press, 1949).

12. David Weissman, *Dispositional Properties* (Carbondale: Southern Illinois University Press, 1965).

13. Robert K. Merton, *Social Theory and Social Structure* (revised and enlarged ed., Glencoe, Ill.: The Free Press, 1957), p. 299.

14. In the following discussion, we will use the expression "property-disposition relationship" to include also relationships between properties and behavior.

15. John Stuart Mill, *A System of Logic* (8th ed., London: Longmans, Green and Company, 1925), p. 256. [Quoted in Ernest Greenwood, *Experimental Sociology* (New York: King's Crown Press, 1945), p. 23.]

16. The "after-only" design is, of course, only one, and not the best, type of experimental model. Other types of experimental design [Marie Jahoda, Morton Deutsch, and Stuart W. Cook, *Research Methods in Social Relations* (New York: Dryden Press, 1951), Vol. I, 58–74] are the "before-after" design, the "simulated before-after" design, the "before-after with control group" design, the "before-after with two control groups" design, and the "before-after with three control groups" design. Some of the distinctive characteristics of a property-disposition relationship are brought to the fore by comparing it with the "after-only" design, and we shall generally confine our discussion to this model.

17. Carl I. Hovland, Arthur A. Lumsdaine, and Fred D. Sheffield, *Experiments on Mass Communication* (Princeton, N.J.: Princeton University Press, 1949), p. 24.

18. *Ibid.*, p. 36.

19. William H. Sewell, "Community of Residence and College Plans," *American Sociological Review*, XXIX (February 1964), 24–38.

20. The student of communications would, of course, also want to know precisely *what* in the film produced the effect. See Robert K. Merton, Marjorie Fiske, and Patricia Kendall, *The Focused Interview* (Glencoe, Ill.: The Free Press, 1956).

21. Paul F. Lazarsfeld and Morris Rosenberg, eds., *The Language of Social Research* (Glencoe, Ill.: The Free Press, 1955), pp. 231–259.

CHAPTER 4

Suppressor
and
Distorter
Variables

Although sociologists have generally been alert to the danger of extraneous variables producing misleading interpretations, they have been much less aware of the possibility that suppressor and distorter variables may also produce deceptive conclusions. Yet the theoretical consequences of overlooking these test factors may be equally serious. It will soon be apparent why suppressor and distorter variables have generally escaped the attention of survey analysts.

Suppressor Variables

We noted earlier that one may be misled in assuming that a relationship between two variables is real (that is, that there is an inherent link between the variables), whereas in fact the relationship may be due to the intrusion of an extraneous variable. Here we suggest that one may equally be misled in assuming that an *absence* of relationship (sometimes called a zero correlation or noncorrelation) between two variables is real (that is, that there is *not* an inherent link between the variables), whereas in fact the absence of the relationship may be due to the intrusion of a third variable. One may find that certain test factors, which we shall call *suppressor variables,* may intercede to cancel out, reduce, or conceal a true relationship between two variables. Negative findings may thus be just as misleading as positive findings.

A word about the sense in which we will use the term "suppressor variable." A suppressor variable is one which weakens a relationship, which conceals its true strength. In some cases, it may weaken the relationship to the point of causing its complete disappearance, but this situation will not always obtain. So long as it damps down or attenuates the full extent of the relationship, it poses the danger of misleading interpretations.

The theoretical significance of suppressor variables is evident. If one tests an hypothesis based upon a theoretical scheme but finds that the relationship is weak or absent, one may conclude that the theory is defective or erroneous. The theory may, however, be sound, and the data, if properly analyzed, may support it.

For example, a study by Middleton[1] sought to examine the relationship between race and alienation. The theoretical assumption underpinning the hypothesis was that subordinate social status was a disabling social condition which would produce alienation.

Building upon the work of Seeman and others, Middleton recognized that the term "alienation" embraced a variety of different concepts. His conceptual analysis led him to distinguish the following meanings of alienation: powerlessness; meaninglessness; normlessness; cultural estrangement; social estrangement; and estrangement from work. Middleton found that, with regard to five out of six of these measures of alienation, Negroes expressed significantly greater alienation than whites.

Let us focus, however, on the question of cultural estrangement. As Table 4–I shows, 35 per cent of the Negroes and 34 per cent of the whites express such cultural estrangement, suggesting that racial status bears no relationship to this form of alienation. Yet there is reason to believe that as far as cultural estrangement is concerned,

Table 4–1

*Alienation, by Race**

Type of Alienation	PER CENT WHO FEEL ALIENATED Negroes	Whites
Powerlessness	70	40
Meaninglessness	71	48
Normlessness	55	16
Cultural estrangement	35	34
Social estrangement	60	27
Estrangement from work	66	18
Number	(99)	(207)

* Russell Middleton, "Alienation, Race, and Education," *American Sociological Review,* XXVIII (December 1963), 975, Table 2 (abridged). (Reprinted with permission of the American Sociological Association.)

whites, not Negroes, are more alienated, a conclusion which is concealed by the suppressor variable of education. When we control on education (Table 4–2), we find that at each educational level whites are somewhat (though not substantially) more culturally estranged than Negroes. The reason virtually no difference between Negroes and whites appeared originally was that poorly educated people are more culturally estranged and that Negroes are more poorly educated. If education is not considered, however, there is no difference in the cultural estrangement of Negroes and whites. The factor of education accounts for the original *absence* of difference between the races.

A study of the relationship of social class to authoritarianism[2] affords another illustration of this point. Three of the items in this report (a far larger number were considered by the author, but, for the sake of the present illustration, will be ignored) are the following: (1) "All things considered, would you say you think favorably of

Table 4–2

*Alienation, by Race and Years of Education**

	PER CENT WHO FEEL ALIENATED			
	Less than 12 Years of Education		12 Years or More of Education	
	Negroes	Whites	Negroes	Whites
Cultural estrangement	39	42	24	31

* Russell Middleton, "Alienation, Race, and Education," *American Sociological Review,* XXVIII (December 1963), 976, Table 3 (abridged and adapted). (Reprinted with permission of the American Sociological Association.)

Table 4–3

*Social Class, Education and Responses to Authoritarianism
Questions in Three Surveys (Men Only)* *

	PER CENT GIVING AUTHORITARIAN RESPONSE		
		Total Middle Class	Total Working Class
Think favorably of Senator McCarthy		57.2	57.9
". . . will always be war and conflict"		59.7	58.7
". . . women should have less freedom . . ."		19.4	17.3

* Lewis Lipsitz, "Working-Class Authoritarianism: A Re-Evaluation," *American Sociological Review*, XXX (February 1965), 106–108, Table 1 (abridged and adapted). (Reprinted with permission of the American Sociological Association.)

Senator [Joseph] McCarthy, or unfavorably?" (2) "Human nature being what it is, there will always be war and conflict." (3) "It is only natural and right that women should have less freedom than men." Table 4–3 shows that there is virtually no difference between middle- and working-class people in response to these items.

These results would suggest that location in the social and occupational structure has no influence on these particular authoritarian attitudes. In fact, however, class *is* associated with authoritarianism in these cases, but the association has been concealed by the factor of education. In Table 4–4, the relationship between class and the three authoritarian attitudes is examined, controlling on education. Within each educational category, for each of the three items, middle-class people are *more* likely than working-class people to give the authori-

Table 4–4

*Social Class, Education and Response to Authoritarianism
Questions in Three Surveys (Men Only)* *

	PER CENT GIVING AUTHORITARIAN RESPONSE					
	0–8 Years Education		9–12 Years Education		12 or More Years Education	
	Middle Class	Working Class	Middle Class	Working Class	Middle Class	Working Class
Favor McCarthy	68.9	64.5	61.9	54.6	45.4	33.3
War, conflict	71.4	59.7	68.8	62.2	48.2	38.4
Women, freedom	42.8	20.0	20.0	17.3	10.3	0.0

* Lewis Lipsitz, "Working-Class Authoritarianism: A Re-Evaluation," *American Sociological Review*, XXX (February 1965), 106–108, Table 1 (abridged and adapted). (Reprinted with permission of the American Sociological Association.)

tarian response. In other words, were it not for the higher educational levels in the middle class, they would be more authoritarian (in terms of these three items). Contrary to the original finding, occupational level *does* appear to have an effect on authoritarian attitudes, but this effect is concealed, and cancelled out, by the associated factor of education.

In a study of ethnic attitudes of union members,[3] the sample was asked: "What do you think of having Jews on the union staff?" Some union members thought it was a good idea, others considered it a bad idea, and a large proportion said, "Don't care either way." This last response reflects the attitude that a man should neither be favored nor disfavored by virtue of his religious group affiliation.

A question that might be raised is whether length of time in the union might have an effect on this attitude. An examination of the data from Rose's study would appear to indicate that longevity of union membership has no bearing on this attitude. Table 4–5 shows that 50 per cent of those in the union four years or more and 49 per cent of those in the union less than four years said they did not care.

Table 4–5

*Ethnic Attitudes of Union Members and
Longevity in the Union**

"Jews on Union Staff"	In Union Less Than 4 Years	In Union 4 Years or Longer
"Don't care either way"	49.2%	50.4%
Number	(126)	(256)

* Arnold M. Rose, *Union Solidarity* (Minneapolis: University of Minnesota Press, 1952), p. 128, Table 42 (abridged and adapted). (Reprinted with permission of the University of Minnesota Press.)

Despite this virtually zero correlation, union membership *does* appear to make a difference with regard to this attitude, but the effect is concealed by the suppressor variable of age. If one controls on age (Table 4–6), one finds that within each age category, those who have been in the union longer say that being a member of the Jewish faith should neither be an advantage nor a disadvantage in becoming a union staff member.

What accounts for this unexpected result? The reason is that

Table 4–6

*Ethnic Attitudes of Union Members and Longevity in the Union, with Age Held Constant**

	Distribution of Answers by Percentage, According to Age and Longevity					
	29 Years and Under		30–49 Years		50 Years and Older	
	YEARS IN UNION					
Jews on Union Staff	Less than 4	4 or More	Less than 4	4 or More	Less than 4	4 or More
Don't care either way	56.4	62.7	37.1	48.3	38.4	46.1
Number	(78)	(51)	(35)	(116)	(13)	(89)

° Arnold M. Rose, *Union Solidarity* (Minneapolis: University of Minnesota Press, 1952), p. 128, Table 42 (abridged and adapted). (Reprinted with permission of the University of Minnesota Press.)

younger union members are *more* likely to be tolerant but are *less* likely to have been in the union a long time. The test factor is *positively* related to the independent variable but *negatively* related to the dependent variable. Had one not taken account of age, one might have reached the misleading conclusion that longevity in the union had no bearing on this attitude.

In the foregoing examples, we began with a zero correlation (or noncorrelation) and showed, by introducing the suppressor variable, that a definite correlation did in fact exist. As a simple extension of this principle, one may begin with a *weak* correlation and show, by introducing a suppressor variable, that a *stronger* correlation in fact exists.

An illustration of this line of reasoning is presented by Durkheim in his analysis of suicide.[4] On the basis of his theory of social integration, Durkheim reasoned that Jews, who were assumed to be a more integrated group, would have lower suicide rates than Gentiles. And this, in fact, turns out to be the case. But, Durkheim notes, the difference should be ever larger. Jews are more likely to live in cities and to pursue intellectual occupations, and these two conditions are conducive to *higher* suicide rates. "Therefore, Durkheim reasons, if the reported rate of suicide among Jews is lower, despite these conditions, the 'true' Jewish rate must be even lower than the figures reveal it to be."[5]

An empirical example in which a suppressor variable was hypothesized in advance and then confirmed appears in a study dealing with the effects of disaster upon feelings of stress.[6] Some years ago a commercial airliner crashed on a hill near Elkton, Maryland, and all of the crew and passengers perished. Members of a nearby naval station were rushed to the scene of the disaster to help. The first shift arrived in the middle of the night but was prevented by the darkness from searching for bodies and wreckage. The second shift arrived at dawn, and the third arrived four hours later. On a measure of subjective stress administered later, it was found that the second and third shifts experienced greater stress than the first. It was believed that the reason for this differential result was based on the fact that many of the men on the second and third shifts were called upon to handle bodies, whereas this was not true in the first shift.

Obviously, the more direct test of the hypothesis that the handling of bodies had been stress-inducing was to compare the stress scores of the sailors who had handled bodies with those who had done other jobs, for example, guard duty. It turned out that those who had handled bodies did have higher stress scores, but the differences were not statistically significant (0.20 level).

A clue to the possible reason why the differences were not greater came from the finding that those who had handled the bodies had higher scores on the Lykken scale—a scale of sociopathy or "emotional callousness." There was reason to believe that people with sociopathic tendencies would be less likely to find the handling of bodies stressful. What this suggested was that although the sailors were theoretically assigned at random to their various jobs, a principle of self-selection was operative, namely, that those with sociopathic tendencies were more likely to volunteer to handle bodies and those without sociopathic tendencies to avoid it. The principle of self-selection would, in fact, operate to suppress the real relationship between body-handling and the experience of stress.

The procedure, then, was to examine the relationship between body-handling and stress, *controlling on sociopathy* (Lykken scale). If sociopathy was suppressing the relationship, then the size of the relationship should increase when sociopathy was held constant. And such turned out to be the case. When sociopathy was held constant by standardization, the difference in the stress scores between body-handlers and others *increased* by 5 per cent, and the difference was now statistically significant at the 0.05 level.[7]

One might thus say that the "pure," "uncontaminated" effect of body-handling—stripped of the confounding and concealing effect of self-selection by those with sociopathic tendencies—is to produce a subjective experience of stress. This was not evident in the original relationship, where the difference was not statistically significant.

The theoretical relevance of ferreting out such suppressor variables is as obvious as it is important. One begins, let us say, with a certain theoretical basis for assuming that there is a relationship between two variables. One then examines this hypothesis and finds it apparently disconfirmed; no such relationship appears. The empirical data thus cast doubt on the theory and may lead one to consider what is wrong with the theory, how the theory requires modification, what alternative theory accounts for the absence of the relationship, etc.

But all this may do a serious disservice to understanding the phenomenon under consideration. Despite the absence of correlation, a relationship may exist and the theory may in fact be supported. A good deal of theoretical confusion may thus be avoided if one takes account of suppressor variables—variables which produce an absence of relationship, or a weak relationship—when actually a presence of relationship, or a strong relationship, exists.

Negative findings

The discussion of suppressor variables has focused on the theme that negative findings (noncorrelations or weak correlations) may be misleading. But there is another theoretical aspect of the matter to be considered, namely, those cases in which the hypothesis is that a relationship will *not* exist between two variables.

While negative hypotheses in social science are difficult to prove, they may have considerable theoretical relevance. An outstanding case is Sewell's empirical test of the Freudian hypotheses concerning early childhood practices and subsequent psychological states. Sewell's careful study showed that virtually none of the hypotheses deriving from Freudian theory which he tested were supported by the data.[8] The theoretical significance of such negative results is apparent.

Similarly, the finding that there is little relationship between group prestige and self-esteem challenges our theoretical assumptions and forces us to refine our understanding of the thought of Mead and Cooley. Again, when Berelson et al.[9] show that Republicans and Democrats are widely divergent on a great many social and political issues but are in fundamental agreement on the procedures of the political process, their conclusions regarding patterns of consensus and cleavage in American political life are highly enlightening. Hence, negative findings, that is, those showing little or no relationship between two variables, may be of substantial theoretical importance.

Sometimes it is important to establish a negative finding in order to strengthen a positive finding. In his effort to show that social factors were responsible for suicide, Durkheim felt impelled to show that extra-social factors were not. He thus engaged in a detailed examination of the relationship between suicide and psychopathic states, alcoholism, race, heredity, geography, and climate.[10] Through a careful demonstration that these factors were *not* related to suicide, he provided inferential evidence that social factors were essentially responsible for the phenomenon.

If it is theoretically relevant to establish a negative finding, however, then one must guard against the danger that the *absence* of relationship is not spurious. The possibility exists that a positive relationship between the two variables does in fact exist but that it is concealed by the presence of a suppressor variable. How does one deal with this problem? Exactly as one deals with extraneous variables, that is, by controlling on all relevant suppressor variables. If, after controlling on these variables, a relationship still does not emerge, then one's confidence that the negative relationship is real is enhanced.

A suppressor variable is in a sense the obverse of an extraneous variable. In the spurious correlation, it will be recalled, one begins with a positive relationship between two factors. One then introduces a third factor—the test factor—which is extraneous to the original two variables; if the relationship *disappears* within each of the contingent associations, we call the original relationship spurious.

In the present case, we start with a noncorrelation (or low correlation) between two variables. We then introduce a third variable—the test factor—which is extraneous to the original two variables. If the relationship *appears* within each of the partial associations, we call the original *non*correlation spurious.

There is a second parallel between these two procedures which may be noted. If we find a correlation between two variables, we will characteristically check on whether or not it is misleading. If we control on a number of suspect variables and find that the relationship still remains, our confidence increases that the relationship is real. The greater the number of relevant variables controlled, the greater the level of confidence that the relationship is real, although one can never be absolutely certain.

The identical principle applies to noncorrelations. In order to determine whether the noncorrelation is real, it is necessary to control on relevant suspect variables. If the noncorrelation *persists* even after all the suspect variables are controlled, one's confidence in the noncorrelation is enhanced, although, once again, one can never be certain. Such misleading noncorrelations, however, afford a more positive increment to knowledge, for they indicate that a positive relationship between the variables exists and thus provide affirmative evidence in support of a certain theory.

In sum, examination of suppressor variables is important if one wishes to show that the noncorrelation is real or if one wishes to show that it is spurious. If one wishes to show that it is real, one would have to demonstrate that the noncorrelation exists even when one controls on all the relevant variables. If one wishes to show that the noncorrelation is spurious (that is, that a real relationship exists), then one would have to show that a positive relationship *emerges* when the suppressor variable is controlled. Both of these operations may enable one to draw more confident and more correct conclusions about noncorrelations or unduly low correlations.

It may be noted that it is difficult to find suppressor variables in the literature, except as these are unintentionally introduced. One reason is that, while analysts are aware that positive findings may be misleading, they are much less sensitive to the fact that negative findings may also be misleading. The second reason is that, while positive findings are seen to have theoretical relevance, this is much less true of negative findings. Finally, of course, any survey will yield far more negative findings (noncorrelations or low correlations) than positive findings. It may be that a greater awareness of suppressor variables will enable survey research to exploit more fully the theoretical fruitfulness of noncorrelations.

"Distorter" Variables

Perhaps the most striking example of how test factors may avert the danger of misleading conclusions appears when we examine what, for want of a better term, might be called "distorter" variables. A distorter variable reveals that the correct interpretation is *precisely the reverse* of that suggested by the original data.

Since it may be difficult to conceive of such a case, consider the following hypothetical example. In examining the relationship between social class and attitudes toward civil rights, it is found that lower-class people are somewhat more likely to hold favorable attitudes toward civil rights: 45 per cent of them are "high" on a civil rights score, compared with 37 per cent of those from a higher class (Table 4–7). We might interpret this result as indicating, perhaps, that lower-class people have a generally more "liberal" or "progressive" ideology —a political orientation which finds expression in attitudes toward civil rights. One might further proceed to speculate on the bearing of an underprivileged social position on an ideology favoring equal rights.

Table 4–7

*Social Class and Attitudes Toward Civil Rights**

Civil Rights Score	Middle Class	Working Class
High	37%	45%
Low	73	55
Total per cent	100	100
Number	(120)	(120)

* Hypothetical.

Now assume that this study has been conducted in the Washington, D.C., area, an area containing a high proportion of Negroes. When we examine the relationship of class to civil rights attitudes among whites and Negroes separately, we encounter a truly startling result: *the relationship is exactly the opposite of that originally shown.* Among Negroes, as Table 4–8 shows, upper-class people are more likely than lower-class people to favor civil rights and the same is true among whites. We thus see how grossly erroneous is the meaning attached to the original relationship.

Table 4–8

Social Class and Approval of Civil Rights, by Race*

| | Negroes | | Whites | |
| | | SOCIAL CLASS | | |
Civil Rights Score	Middle Class	Working Class	Middle Class	Working Class
High	70%	50%	30%	20%
Low	30	50	70	80%
Total per cent	100	100	100	100
Number	(20)	(100)	(100)	(20)

* Hypothetical.

In this case, we refer to race as a "distorter" variable—a variable which converts a positive relationship into a negative relationship. In the present example, the reversal of the relationship occurs for the following reason: in the Washington, D.C., area, we assume an equal number of whites and Negroes. In this area, Negroes are mostly engaged in manual or service work, whereas the whites, who are largely civil servants, are concentrated in the white-collar group. Now the reason manual workers are more favorable to civil rights is the following: Negroes are much more likely to be manual workers, and Negroes are also much more likely to favor civil rights. The general civil rights score of manual workers is thus artificially elevated by the presence of such a large proportion of (pro-civil rights) Negroes in the group. But it is not being a manual worker which produces such a high civil rights score; it is being a Negro. Hence, when we control on race, cancelling out the effect of the racial distribution of classes, the true relationship appears: within each racial group, the upper class is more strongly in favor of civil rights than the lower class. The *negative* correlation between race and attitudes toward civil rights is actually a *positive* correlation.

That the presence of distorter variables is more than a hypothetical possibility is shown in an empirical study by Schnore.[11] In this study the interest lay in comparing the incomes of city residents and suburban dwellers. After showing the general pattern, however, he notes:

In some cases, a comparison of total income in cities and suburbs is grossly misleading. In the Chattanooga, Tenn. SMA [Standard Metropolitan Area], for example, the median income of all ring [suburban] inhabitants ($1,691) is clearly higher than that of all city dwellers ($1,609). An examination of the city-suburban differentials by color, however, reveals that city incomes are higher—on the average—for both whites and Negroes.

Table 4–9

*Median Income of City and Ring in Chattanooga SMA, by Race**

	Median Income, SMA	Median Income, City	Median Income, Ring
White	1840	1918	1768
Negro	985	1015	819
Total	1642	1609	1691

* Leo F. Schnore, "City-Suburban Income Differentials in Metropolitan Areas," *American Sociological Review*, XXVII (April 1962), 254. (Reprinted with permission of the American Sociological Association.)

The explanation lies in the overwhelming "whiteness" of Chattanooga's suburbs (where Negroes constitute only 4.8 per cent of the total ring population) and the heavier concentration of Negroes in the city (where they make up 30.0 per cent of the Chattanooga population). The higher average income of the more numerous suburban whites raises the overall suburban average above that of the city, despite the fact that city incomes are *higher* for each of the two constituent color groups taken separately.[12]

Schnore cites four other cities in which the same kind of reversal appears.

It is easy to see how one might be misled in this case. Knowing that suburban residents have a higher average income than city residents, one would have reason to assume that the income of suburban whites is higher than that of urban whites and that the income of suburban Negroes is higher than that of urban Negroes. Exactly the reverse, however, is the case—a striking example of the peril of drawing misleading conclusions from data.

How the failure to take account of distorter variables may lead to flatly erroneous conclusions is strikingly illustrated in a case cited by Durkheim. Students of suicide, prior to Durkheim, had reported that married people had higher suicide rates than unmarried ones. As Durkheim noted:

. . . certain authors had once taught that marriage and family life multiply the chances of suicide. Certainly, if in accordance with current opinion one regards suicide primarily as an act of despair caused by the difficulties of existence, this opinion has all the appearance of probability. An unmarried person has in fact an easier life than a married one. Does not marriage entail all sorts of burdens and responsibilities? To assure the present and future of a family, are not more privations and sufferings required than to meet the needs of a single person?[13]

This conclusion is based on the view that suicide is a consequence of life stress induced by social circumstances. But Durkheim has argued repeatedly that suicide does not arise from life stress. People commit suicide *less* in wartime than in peacetime; suicide rates tend to be lower in *poor* than in rich countries; Jews, who suffer severe discrimination, have *lower* rates; enlisted men in the army have *lower* suicide rates than officers; etc.

Married people are assumed to be more highly integrated than unmarried people. Hence, if married people showed higher suicide rates (which they do), this would support the position that life stress was responsible for suicide, contradicting Durkheim's fundamental argument. If, on the other hand, married people had lower suicide rates, this would support the view that social integration was an insulator against suicide, a view which is at the heart of Durkheim's theoretical position. The fact that married people had higher suicide rates is clearly in opposition to Durkheim's view.

But is it? Despite the evidence, Durkheim asserts that marriage actually *reduces* suicide rates. The reason some other writers were misled, he argues, is that they failed to take account of age. Very young people obviously have low marriage rates and also have low suicide rates. When one controls on age, married people have decidedly lower suicide rates than unmarried ones—a result precisely opposite to that of the original relationship. This is revealed clearly in Table 4–10. When one compares the suicide rates of married and unmarried people within age groups, in 16 out of 18 cases the married people have lower rates. The only conspicuous deviation from the pattern is among the youngest men (a finding that Durkheim considers elsewhere).

The finding thus actually supports rather than refutes Durkheim's theory. The original misleading finding was due to the "distorting" factor of age. Once the effect of age was eliminated, the true relationship between marital status and suicide appeared, producing a theoretical interpretation profoundly different from that originally suggested by the data.

Comparison of Test Factors

Having discussed six types of test factors, it may be useful at this point to summarize some of their similarities and differences. We wish first to consider some of the different theoretical contributions which they can make and then compare the statistical properties of the test factors.

A theoretically based social science is a cumulative affair. If the theory underpinning a particular study has power, and if the research is well designed and executed, then there enters into the body of social-scientific knowledge certain generalizations which give rise to new research and stimulate further theoretical advance. It is thus just as important to avoid the acceptance of false conclusions as to attain the acceptance of true ones.

Speaking formally, two dangers lurk in drawing conclusions from

Table 4–10

France (1889–1891): Suicides Committed per 1,000,000 Inhabitants of Each Age and Marital Status Group, Average Year[*]

| | MEN | | WOMEN | |
Ages	Unmarried	Married	Unmarried	Married
15–20	113	500	79.4	33
20–25	237	97	106	53
25–30	394	122	151	68
30–40	627	226	126	82
40–50	975	340	171	106
50–60	1434	520	204	151
60–70	1768	635	189	158
70–80	1983	704	206	209
Above 80	1571	770	176	110

[*] Emile Durkheim, *Suicide* (Glencoe, Ill.: The Free Press, 1951), p. 178, Table XXI (abridged). (Reprinted with permission of The Macmillan Company. Copyright 1951 by The Free Press, A Corporation.)

two-variable relationships: that one will accept a false hypothesis as true, and that one will reject a true hypothesis as false. Extraneous, suppressor, and distorter variables are designed to deal with both problems.

Consideration of *extraneous* variables averts the danger that one will accept a false hypothesis as true, that is, that one will assume that there is an inherent link between the associated variables when the link is in fact accidental. As a simple example, one might find that the death rate in Florida is higher than that in New York State and interpret this as a reflection of the poorer conditions of health in Florida. The reason may simply be, however, that a larger proportion of old people live in Florida—people who have migrated to Florida from elsewhere precisely for reasons of health—and who naturally have higher mortality rates.

Suppressor variables, on the other hand, enable one to avoid the rejection of an hypothesis that is true. A union leader who believes that union life fosters tolerance may be dismayed to learn that men who have been in the union longer are no more tolerant than recent recruits. He may, however, be rejecting a true hypothesis. Union longevity may actually increase tolerance, a conclusion concealed by the fact that older members, who have been in the union longer, are less tolerant by virtue of other factors associated with age.

Finally, consideration of *distorter* variables may enable one to avoid *both* the rejection of a true hypothesis *and* the acceptance of a false one. One might, for example, begin with the hypothesis that well-educated people would be more likely to favor medical care for the aged, on the basis of some theory regarding how *high* education would have this effect. The data, however, might show that the poorly educated hold more favorable attitudes, thus leading to a consideration of how *low* education might have this effect. This latter result, however, might be due to the fact that the poorly educated tend to be older, and older people favor medicare. Controlling on age, we might find that the well-educated are, in fact, more favorable. Without consideration of the distorter variable of age, one would be rejecting a true conclusion (that *high* education leads to more favorable attitudes) and at the same time accepting a false conclusion (that *low* education leads to more favorable attitudes).

If the first contribution of test factors is to avoid being misled in one's conclusions (accepting a false, or rejecting a true, conclusion), the second is to provide more *precise* and *specific* understanding of a two-variable relationship. Employing *component* variables, one is able to find out more exactly what it is about some global indepent variable which is at the heart of the observed relationship. A broad factor may be an effective predictor but may not contribute substantially to scientific understanding. Again, the use of *intervening* variables provides more precise understanding of the temporal and logical process involved in the movement from the independent to the dependent variable. *Antecedent* variables may enable one to extend the causal sequence.

Properly conducted survey research tells us *whether* independent variable A is related to dependent variable B. The introduction of test factors helps to tell us *why* (or why not) the two variables are related. Test factors thus afford important new knowledge and help in filtering out erroneous conclusions, thus contributing importantly to social-scientific understanding and the body of certified knowledge.

In employing test factors in one's analysis, it is important to be aware not only of their divergent theoretical implications, but also of their statistical properties. Extraneous, component, and intervening variables are identical in their statistical properties, while antecedent,

Chart 4-1
Properties of Test Factors

	Extraneous Component Intervening	Antecedent	Suppressor	Distorter
1. Original association between independent and dependent variables is	Positive	Positive	Zero	Positive
2. Relationships in contingent associations are	Zero	Positive	Positive	Negative
3. Compared to the original relationship, the relationships in the contingent associations	Vanish (reduce)	Remain unchanged	Emerge	Reverse
4. Test factor related to independent and dependent variables with	Same signs	Same signs	Opposite signs	Opposite signs
5. Independent, test factor, and dependent all related	Yes	Yes	No	Yes
6. Steps involved in procedure	1	2	1	1

suppressor, and distorter variables differ from these and from one another. Chart 4–1 presents a summary of some of the statistical properties of these test factors, and the following discussion will be rooted in this chart.

Six bases for comparison of these test factors are suggested:

Line 1: Is the original relationship between the independent and dependent variables positive or zero? The term "positive" is arbitrary; it simply means that a relationship is present. Line 1 indicates that with regard to all test factors save one, a positive association exists between the independent and dependent variables. The one exception appears in the case of the suppressor variable, in which the original relationship is zero.

Line 2: Are the relationships in the contingent associations zero, positive, or negative? The term "negative" here is equally arbitrary. It means that the sign of the relationship in the contingent associations is the opposite of that in the original association. The term zero does not literally mean a perfect zero; it means that the contingent associations are closer to zero than the original association. Line 2 indicates that when extraneous, component, or intervening variables are introduced, the contingent associations become zero. With antecedent and suppressor variables, the contingent associations are positive. With distorter variables, the contingent associations are negative.

Line 3: Compared to the original relationship, do the relationships in the contingent associations vanish (or reduce), remain unchanged, emerge, or reverse? This is the crucial question. Line 3 is derived from a comparison of Lines 1 and 2. We see that for extraneous, component, and intervening variables, the original relationship *vanishes* (or is reduced) in the contingent associations. For antecedent variables, the original relationship is *unchanged* in the contingent associations. For suppressor variables, a relationship *emerges* in the contingent associations, even though none existed in the original relationship. And for distorter variables, the original relationship is *reversed* in the contingent associations.

Line 4: Is the factor related to the independent and dependent variables with the same signs (whether positive or negative) or opposite signs? If the test factor is an extraneous, component, intervening, or antecedent variable, then it is related to the independent and dependent variables in the same direction. Among suppressor and distorter variables, on the other hand, the test factor is related positively to one of the variables and negatively to the other.

Line 5: Does a statistical association exist between the independent and dependent variables, the independent variable and test factor, and the test factor and dependent variable? These associations appear in all cases except suppressor variables: in the latter case, one finds a zero relationship between the independent and dependent variables.

Line 6: How many steps are involved in the analytic procedure—one or two? With the exception of antecedent variables, one step is involved, namely, stratifying the original variable by the test factor. This step is also taken with antecedent variables; one must first show that the original relationship remains virtually unchanged in the contingent associations. The second step is to treat the test factor as the independent variable and the original independent variable as the intervening variable. One then treats the table in terms of a typical intervening variable analysis.

Chart 4–1 is designed to serve as a checklist of factors to be considered in employing a particular kind of test factor. The decision to introduce a type of test factor is made on logical and theoretical grounds. Once made, however, there are certain statistical criteria which must be satisfied if the argument is to be sustained. Chart 4–1 suggests what some of these criteria are.

Some of the foregoing discussion of test factors may have offered the appearance of a magician drawing rabbits from a hat. Relationships between two variables, when controlled on an extraneous, component, or intervening test factor, were found to disappear or to be reduced. Conversely, the introduction of a suppressor variable enabled a two-variable relationship to emerge where none existed previously. It was even found that, with the introduction of distorter variables, a relationship in one direction was converted into a relationship of an opposite sort. What manner of fraud or legerdemain is involved in this conversion of relationships into nonrelationships, nonrelationships into relationships, etc.?

As every experienced researcher knows, of course, the answer is to be found in the *marginals*. To the neophyte researcher, on the other hand, the "arithmetic of controls" may be obscure. Readers who are interested in the reason why strange things may happen to two-variable relationships when stratified by a test factor are referred to Appendix B, "The Arithmetic of Controls" for a discussion.

In considering what happens to a relationship when a test factor is introduced, it may be observed that one statistical possibility has not been considered, namely, what if the size or direction of association in the contingent associations are different? This is by no means a rare phenomenon in empirical research. When this occurs, we are in the realm of conditional relationships; the next two chapters consider some of the theoretical contributions which such relationships may potentially make.

NOTES

1. Russell Middleton, "Alienation, Race, and Education," *American Sociological Review,* XXVIII (December 1963), 973–976.
2. Lewis Lipsitz, "Working-Class Authoritarianism: A Re-Evaluation," *American Sociological Review,* XXX (February 1965), 103–109.
3. Arnold M. Rose, *Union Solidarity* (Minneapolis.: University of Minnesota Press, 1952), chap. 5.
4. Emile Durkheim, *Suicide* (Glencoe, Ill.: The Free Press, 1951).
5. Hanan C. Selvin, "Durkheim's *Suicide* and Problems of Empirical Research," *American Journal of Sociology,* LXIII (May 1958), 608.
6. Johanna Stein, Ladd Wheeler, and Bibb Latane, "Environmental Stress, Personality and Variability of Response to Stress" (Unpublished manuscript; June 1965), 29 pp.
7. *Ibid.,* pp. 14 and 26.
8. William H. Sewell, "Infant Training and the Personality of the Child," *American Journal of Sociology,* LVIII (1952), 150–159.
9. Bernard Berelson, Paul F. Lazarsfeld, and William McPhee, *Voting* (Chicago: University of Chicago Press, 1954), chap. 9.
10. Durkheim, *op. cit.,* chaps. 1–3.
11. Leo F. Schnore, "City-Suburban Income Differentials in Metropolitan Areas," *American Sociological Review,* XXVII (April 1962), 252–255.
12. *Ibid.,* p. 254.
13. Durkheim, *op. cit.,* p. 171.

CHAPTER 5

Conditional Relationships: Aids to Interpretation

The process of elaboration, we have seen, involves the introduction of a third variable into a two-variable relationship. By stratifying on the test factor, one can compare the relationships in the contingent associations with the original relationship. Sometimes, we have observed, the relationships in each of the contingent associations vanish (or are reduced); in other cases, they remain unchanged; in still others, relationships emerge (or increase in size); and in some cases, their direction is reversed.

In all such instances, it is assumed that the size and direction of the relationships in the contingent associations are similar. Naturally, one cannot expect a perfect correspondence in all the contingent associations, but one expects to find a general similarity. In many cases, however, dissimilarity appears. Frequently, the relationship in one of the contingent associations may be strong, whereas in another it may be weak; in one, the relationship may be positive, in another, negative; etc.

Assume that we find that city-dwellers are more likely than small-town residents to have high scores on a scale of anomia. We might

Table 5–1

*Distribution of Anomia Scores by Rural-Urban and Race**

| | NEGROES | | WHITES | |
	Rural	Urban	Rural	Urban
High anomia	46%	43%	21%	37%
Low anomia	54	57	79	63
Total per cent	100	100	100	100
Number	(211)	(436)	(89)	(190)

* Lewis M. Killian and Charles M. Grigg, "Urbanism, Race, and Anomia," *American Journal of Sociology*, LXVII (May 1962), 662, Table 1 (adapted). (Reprinted with permission of the University of Chicago Press.)

decide to introduce race as a test factor since there is reason to believe that race is associated both with rural-urban residence and with degree of anomia. We would then emerge with two contingent associations: an association between rural-urban residence and anomia among Negroes, and an association between rural-urban residence and anomia among whites.[1]

Among whites, Table 5–1 shows, urban dwellers are more likely to experience anomia than rural dwellers (37 per cent to 21 per cent). The same is not true among the Negroes, however, where indeed the trend is slightly in the opposite direction (43 per cent to 46 per cent). The relationship between rural-urban residence and anomia thus differs for each group.

Where the relative size or direction of the contingent associations differ, that is, where it is found that "the original relationship is more pronounced in one sub-group than in the other, when the total sample is divided by the test factor,"[2] we speak of *conditional relationships*.[3] Technically, the purpose of examining such relationships is called *specification:* one wishes to specify the conditions under which the original relationship is strengthened or weakened.

Such conditional relationships are not invariably greeted with enthusiasm by the survey analyst. For a science avidly in search of invariant social laws or general relationships between social variables, such conditional relationships are often felt to be an embarrassment, a digression, or simply an irritant. Physical scientists would be extremely uneasy if Newton's law stipulating that every action has an equal and opposite reaction held true in Missouri but not in Nebraska. Similarly,

106

if the physical principle of inertia differed in middle- and working-class homes, then the scientific value of the law would be seriously impaired.

In social science, however, there is no escaping the fact that conditional relationships are often an accurate reflection of social reality. While the descriptive value of conditional relationships is generally recognized in social research, less attention seems to have been paid to their analytic, interpretive, or theoretical potentialities. Not that the descriptive classification which comes from the examination of conditional relationships is without value. To know that the relationship between education and interest in serious music differs for older and younger people provides a more exact description of the relationship of social experience to behavior and is an important contribution to one of the major goals of science, namely, prediction. In this chapter, however, we wish to suggest certain contributions to analysis or theory which may emerge from the focus on conditional relationships. In the following chapter, we will indicate how they may help to clarify the original relationship and the variables involved.

1. Conditional Relationships May Call into Question the Interpretation of an Original Relationship

The serious challenge to an existing interpretation of data is often an important first step in the development of advanced theory. For example, in the afore-mentioned study of students in the later stages of adolescence, the original relationship showed that adolescents from higher social classes had higher levels of self-esteem than students from lower classes.[4] A respectable and easily available body of theory was at hand to explain this relationship. George Herbert Mead had shown that the self is a product of reflected appraisals,[5] and Cooley had described how the individual's self-concept was influenced by his imagination of what others think of him.[6] Since social class is fundamentally a reflection of prestige in the society, it would follow that

Table 5–2
Social Class and Self-Esteem, by Sex[*]

	Boys			Girls		
			SOCIAL CLASS			
Self-Esteem	Upper	Middle	Lower	Upper	Middle	Lower
High	55%	47%	36%	47%	46%	41%
Medium	17	25	26	28	25	27
Low	28	28	39	24	29	32
Total per cent	100	100	100	100	100	100
Number	(89)	(1383)	(168)	(106)	(1311)	(172)

[*] Morris Rosenberg, *Society and the Adolescent Self-Image* (Princeton: Princeton University Press, 1965), p. 41, Table 2. (Reprinted by permission of Princeton University Press.)

those experiencing favorable social regard would tend to develop favorable self-attitudes, and vice versa.

When conditional relationships were examined, however, it was found that the relationship of class to self-esteem was strong among boys but weak among girls[7] (Table 5–2). This finding called into question the interpretation offered above since there is no obvious reason why the principle of reflected appraisals (as determined by social prestige) should not operate in the same way for both sexes. Subsequent analysis revealed that the major reason upper-class boys had higher self-esteem was not their greater social prestige but their closeness to their fathers.

Conditional relationships may thus demand a re-thinking of the interpretation, and this re-thinking may often redound to the advantage of theory. In disturbing the condition of "closure," the conditional relationship is no doubt an irritant, but it is only by breaking such closure that theoretical advance is likely to come.

Durkheim's classical study of suicide[8] affords another illustration of this point. Durkheim noted that in 1882 Bertillon had published a study showing that in areas of high rates of divorce, the suicide rate was high. One of the explanations suggested was that there were many unhappy marriages in such areas and that this marital discord increased the suicide rate.

Durkheim examined the data more carefully, however, and found that the relationship between the divorce rate and the suicide rate existed for men, but not for women. As Durkheim noted: "Actually if it were imputable to the constitution of the family, wives should also be less protected from suicide in countries where divorce is current than in those where it is rare; for they are as much affected by the poor state of domestic relations as husbands. Exactly the reverse is the truth."[9]

Durkheim's conditional relationships thus cast doubt upon Bertillon's originally plausible interpretation of the data, and set in motion an interpretation radically different from that originally advanced, namely, that the divorce rate creates a condition of "domestic anomie" which is suicidogenic.

2. Conditional Relationships May Support or Strengthen the Original Interpretation

This theoretical contribution may appear surprising, since one would assume that if the interpretation were adequate for the original relationship, then it should also explain the relationship in different population subgroups. In fact, however, *different* results in various groups may *strengthen* the interpretation, whereas *similar* results in different groups would *weaken* it.

In the study cited earlier, it was found that adolescents whose parents had been divorced showed somewhat more psychological disturbance than others.[10] It was suggested that this was due to the *social definition* of divorce in the society. Since divorce is disapproved in the society, one could assume that (1) parents who have been divorced have experienced more tension and conflict than others, and (2) the social stigma of divorce would make the child feel different and inadequate.

If this were so, however, then it would follow that in those groups in which the cultural resistance to divorce was strongest, the child's self-esteem would be most affected. The data suggested that the social pressure against divorce was stronger among Catholics and Jews than among Protestants. Further analysis revealed that among Catholics and Jews the association between divorce and emotional disturbance in the child was relatively strong, whereas among Protestants it was weaker (Table 5–3). Rather than calling into question the original interpretation, then, *these conditional relationships made the original interpretation more compelling.* Had the relationships been the same in all religious groups, the adequacy of the interpretation would have been called into question.

Table 5–3

Divorce and Self-Esteem and Psychosomatic Symptoms, by Religion*

Self-Esteem	CATHOLICS		JEWS		PROTESTANTS	
	Divorced	Intact	Divorced	Intact	Divorced	Intact
High	36%	44%	44%	54%	40%	44%
Medium	24	26	17	24	26	25
Low	40	30	39	21	34	32
Total						
per cent	100	100	100	100	100	100
Number	(90)	(1583)	(18)	(514)	(112)	(1391)
Number of Psychosomatic Symptoms						
2 or less	27%	49%	30%	56%	42%	53%
3–5	40	36	50	34	41	35
6 or more	33	15	20	10	16	12
Total						
per cent	100	100	100	100	100	100
Number	(52)	(1097)	(10)	(352)	(73)	(966)

* Morris Rosenberg, *Society and the Adolescent Self-Image* (Princeton: Princeton University Press, 1965), p. 89, Table 2. (Reprinted by permission of Princeton University Press.)

Consider the finding by Sewell and Orenstein that boys from larger cities have higher occupational aspirations.[11] Why should this be? The authors suggest that these differential aspirations are due to differences in direct personal knowledge of people in high status positions. "A youth in immediate contact with persons holding high status positions, or receiving a more or less continuous flow of information concerning their daily activities, will perceive these persons as occupational role models and will feel that their occupational positions are reasonable personal goals. This belief will be reinforced when parents, teachers, and friends encourage high goals. All this is less likely to be the experience of youth from smaller communities."[12]

This is a plausible interpretation. But if it were sound, then one would expect the relationship between size of community and occupational aspirations to be stronger in the upper class than in the lower class. Lower-class boys, one would assume, would have little direct personal knowledge of members of high status occupations, whatever the size of their communities. Members of a higher class, however, might have considerable personal knowledge in large cities but less personal knowledge in farm or village communities. And Table 5–4 shows in fact that the relationship of size of community and occupational aspirations is stronger in the higher than in the lower class. These *differential* results are thus consistent with the original interpretation.

Table 5–4

*Percentage with High Occupational Choices, by Place of Residence and Socio-Economic Status, for Male High-School Seniors**

| Place of Residence | SOCIO-ECONOMIC STATUS | | | |
	Low	Middle	High	Total
Farm	22.0	37.4	49.6	32.9
Village	19.2	37.5	55.6	35.7
Small city	24.3	42.4	64.0	45.4
Medium city	23.8	40.3	66.9	45.7
Large city	34.2	52.7	73.6	57.2

* William H. Sewell and Alan M. Orenstein, "Community of Residence and Occupational Choice," *American Journal of Sociology*, LXX (March 1965), 557, Table 4 (abridged). (Reprinted with permission of the University of Chicago Press.)

Not only may conditional relationships strengthen an interpretation, but certain hypotheses may be of such a nature that they *logically require* conditional relationships for their confirmation. Take the hypothesis that sustained social interaction influences voting behavior in accord with one's group affiliation. One might test this hypothesis by seeing whether people who have resided longer in a community are more likely to vote like the members of their groups than those who are more recent arrivals. Protestants, it is known, tend to vote Republican, and Catholics, Democratic. One would thus expect that, among Protestants, the longer people have lived in the community, the larger the proportion of Republicans. Among Catholics, on the other hand, the longer people have lived in the community, the smaller should be the proportion of Republicans (that is, the larger the proportion of Democrats). The confirmation of the hypothesis thus *requires* opposite results. And Table 5–5 shows that this is precisely in accord with the data.[13] If length of residence were associated with Republican vote for both Protestants and Catholics, the hypothesis would have been disconfirmed.

Table 5–5

*Years of Residence and Republican Vote, by Religion**

	Protestants			Catholics		
	YEARS OF RESIDENCE IN ELMIRA					
	Over 20 years	5–19 years	Under 5 years	Over 20 years	5–19 years	Under 5 years
Per cent Republican	82	75	74	31	40	48

* Bernard R. Berelson, Paul F. Lazarsfeld, and William N. McPhee, *Voting* (Chicago: University of Chicago Press, 1954), p. 68, Chart XXVI (abridged and adapted). (Reprinted with permission of the University of Chicago Press.)

When a survey analyst interprets a relationship, then, he is obliged to confront the further question: *If* this interpretation is correct, then what consequences should follow? In some cases, the logical consequences require differential patterns of association in different groups. Conditional relationships may thus represent a vital basis for confirmation in social science.

3. Conditional Relationships May Modify the Interpretation by Making It More Exact

It is often the case that the interpretation of a relationship may be correct but at the same time incomplete, oversimplified, or inexact. An interesting example is drawn from research on British secondary school students, conducted by Donald Harper. British publicly supported secondary education is primarily divided into "grammar" (superior) schools and "secondary modern" (ordinary) schools.

Assignment to these schools is on a competitive basis. Harper found that those respondents who had siblings in grammar (superior) schools were somewhat more likely to manifest anxiety than those who did not. The interpretation suggested was that the academic success of the sibling placed the respondent under greater pressure to succeed, or generated invidious comparisons, and thus ultimately created anxiety in the individual.

The examination of conditional relationships did not revise the interpretation but modified it to some extent. The sample was divided into four groups: working-class grammar school boys; middle-class grammar school boys; working-class secondary modern school boys; middle-class secondary modern school boys. It turned out that, for the first three groups, there was little or no association between having a grammar school sibling and level of anxiety, but for the last group the relationship was strong. In other words, if the boy was middle class (with a strong pressure to succeed) but was *relatively* inferior to his sibling (he was in an ordinary school, whereas the sibling was in a superior school), then his anxiety level was high. Now consider the other groups. Those boys who were themselves in the superior school were not *relatively* inferior to their siblings in the superior school. At the same time the working-class boy with a successful sibling was less bothered because academic success was less important in the working class. For the middle-class secondary modern school boy, however, *relative* inferiority in an important area of life was a source of anxiety.

The original interpretation suggested by the data was: anxiety is generated when one is confronted with a successful point of reference. The modified, or qualified, interpretation would be: anxiety is generated if one has a *relatively* successful point of reference *in a life area of importance*. Only this qualified statement will cover all four partial associations. In this case, the study of conditional relationships does not actually change the interpretation, nor does it necessarily reduce its level of abstraction, but it modifies the interpretation and makes it more exact.

Another example appears in a detailed study of child-rearing practices conducted by Sears, Maccoby, and Levin. The investigators were interested in learning whether severe toilet training produced emotional upset in the child. The data showed that this was in fact the case: "over half of the most severely trained children showed some disturbance, while not more than a sixth of the least severely trained showed it ($p < .01; r = .47$)."[14]

The authors, however, went on to inquire what the *meaning* of severe pressure is to the mother and child.

> We reasoned that if the mother's punishment was an expression of an underlying hostility or rejection, we might expect it to be more upsetting to the child than punishment which occurred in a context of emotional security. In a sense, the child punished by a hostile mother was in double jeopardy; there was the physical pain of the punishment, plus the anxiety produced by the loss of love implied in the mother's manner while punishing. To the child of the cold and hostile mother, punishment may have meant, "I don't like *you*," while to the child of the warm mother, it may have meant "I don't like *what you did*."

This reasoning led us to expect that severe toilet training would be more anxiety-provoking, and hence more upsetting, for the children of cold mothers than for the children of warm mothers. This proved to be true, as Table 5–6 shows. Severe training produced far more upset in the children of relatively cold mothers, but it had no differential effect whatsoever on the children of warm mothers. This finding requires us to qualify the generalization, made before, that severity of training produced emotional upset. The statement can now be amended and made more precise: *severe toilet training increased the amount of upset in children whose mothers were relatively cold and undemonstrative.*[15]

Table 5–6

*Percentage of Children Who Showed Emotional Upset over Toilet Training, in Relation to Severity of Toilet Training and Warmth of the Mother**

Severity of Toilet Training	Mother Warm	Mother Relatively Cold	Horizontal Differences
Mild toilet training	21%	11%	N.S.
	(112)	(101)	
Severe toilet training	23%	48%	$p = .01$
	(48)	(98)	
Vertical differences	N.S.	$p = .01$	

* Robert R. Sears, Eleanor E. Maccoby, and Harry Levin, *Patterns of Child Rearing* (Evanston, Ill.: Row, Peterson, 1957), p. 125, Table IV: 7. (Reprinted with permission of Harper and Row, Publishers, Inc.)

4. Conditional Relationships May Lead to a Radical Revision of the Original Interpretation

The usefulness of conditional relationships is most dramatically illustrated when this occurs. Donald McKinley had noted that working-class Italian parents tend to use physical violence with their children, insisting on strict obedience to parental prescriptions.[16] He interpreted this result within the framework of the frustration-aggression hypothesis. Working-class Italian fathers, he pointed out, have little opportunity for freedom of decision in their jobs; this is a frustrating condition which finds an outlet in aggression, and insistence on strict obedience, toward their children.

Leonard Pearlin's study of Italian workers also showed that they had little freedom, that they employed physical punishment, and that they stressed obedience in their children.[17] But, Pearlin noted, this was true for boys but not for girls. This finding called into question the appropriateness of the frustration-aggression hypothesis to account for the results. Further analysis suggested that the emphasis on obedience was essentially a teaching phenomenon: the worker knows that he must obey, and he trains his son, who will probably be doing similar work, in the value of obedience. The girl's role will be different, and the father is thus likely to emphasize other kinds of values for her. Conditional relationships have thus produced a change from a frustration-aggression interpretation to a social learning interpretation.

It may generally be suggested that where conditional relationships produce a radical and fundamental revision of the interpretation, they stimulate new types of insight and understanding which are assets in the development of theory.

Durkheim's observation that the relationship between the divorce rate and the suicide rate in an area was strong among men but weak among women is a case in point. In contrast to Bertillon's interpretation that the original relationship in part reflected domestic discord, Durkheim introduced the concept of *domestic anomie*[18] to account for the conditional relationships.

Essentially, Durkheim argues that woman is basically monogamous, whereas man is not. In areas where divorce is prohibited, man knows that there are no other possibilities open to him and adjusts himself to his lot. Where the possibility of divorce exists, however, his hopes and aspirations know no limits. "The result of it all is a state of disturbance, agitation and discontent which inevitably increases the possibilities of suicide."[19] Women, being essentially monogamous, are more restricted in their focus, whether or not divorce is current.

The conditional relationship thus completely transforms the level and type of explanation. Whether or not one is completely persuaded by Durkheim's explanation (and we cannot do full justice to its richness and complexity in this brief space), the point is that the conditional relationships undermine Bertillon's original interpretation and compel the analyst to introduce a radically new and richer theory to account for these observed facts.

5. Conditional Relationships May Enable the Analyst to Choose Between Alternative Interpretations of a Relationship

Everyone engaged in survey research knows that while his data may be clear, the *meaning* of the data often is not. It is commonplace to find two equally plausible or compelling interpretations which neatly fit the results. Conditional relationships sometimes enable one to resolve the issue. If one of the possible interpretations is sound, then it follows that the relationship should be strong under one condition, whereas if the other interpretation is sound, then the relationship should be strong under a different condition.

In a study of adolescents whose parents had been divorced or widowed, it was found, surprisingly, that children whose parents remarried had *lower* self-esteem than children whose parents had not remarried.[20] (In almost all cases of divorce, and in most cases of death, the child was with the mother, and it was therefore the mother who did or did not remarry.) Two interpretations were considered: (1) Freudian theory might suggest that the individual's basic personality is formed in early childhood and that the reinstitution of the Oedipus complex might produce low self-esteem, for example, through the development of a strong and punishing superego (which comes from the father) or through fear of the father which would sap the child's self-confidence. (2) An alternative theoretical interpretation would be phrased in terms of role theory and social integration. Here the argument might run that the absence of the father requires the mother and children to take over the father's roles. In addition, the extra burdens tend to bind mother and children more closely together, since they must face the problems of doing without the aid of the man in the house. When the mother remarries, life becomes easier for mother and child, but the mother may now turn part of her attention to her new husband and possibly stepchildren. As a result, the child is deprived of the self-confidence he had gained from successfully assuming paternal responsibility and at the same time loses his position as the object of central, if not exclusive, interest of his mother.

One way to deal with this problem is to consider the child's *age* at the time of the family rupture. The data show that the relationship of maternal remarriage to the child's self-esteem is stronger among children who were *older* at the time of the family breakup than among children who were *younger* (Table 5–7). In other words, if the child was young at the time (3 years or less), then his mother's remarriage

Table 5–7

*Divorce or Widowhood, Remarriage and Child's Self-Esteem by Child's Age at Time of Family Break-up**

| | Child's Age at Time of Divorce or Death | | | | | |
| | 3 YEARS OR LESS | | 4–9 YEARS | | 10 YEARS OR MORE | |
Self-Esteem	Remarried	Not Remarried	Remarried	Not Remarried	Remarried	Not Remarried
High	32%	37%	33%	46%	32%	49%
Medium	32	27	19	21	27	26
Low	35	37	48	32	41	26
Total per cent	100	100	100	100	100	100
Number	(71)	(41)	(64)	(56)	(37)	(78)

* Morris Rosenberg, *Society and the Adolescent Self-Image* (Princeton: Princeton University Press, 1965), p. 104, Table 14. (Reprinted by permission of Princeton University Press.)

has no deleterious effect upon his self-esteem. If, on the other hand, the child was 10 years or older, then maternal remarriage is strongly associated with lower self-esteem.

The second interpretation thus seems more consistent with these data. By the age of 10 or more, the child has undoubtedly assumed some of the paternal responsibility and has for a long time been united with his mother in dealing with the problems of life. To be thrust out of the center of his mother's stage could thus have consequences for his self-esteem. On the other hand, self-esteem is not lowered among younger children. Hence, the notion of newly developed fear of the father and internalization of a strong superego as a result of this fear—a consequence to be expected in early years—is not supported by the data. We thus see that the examination of conditional relationships at times affords a basis for selection between reasonable alternative interpretations of the original relationship.

6. Conditional Relationships May Reveal Meaningful Results Which Are Concealed in the Original Relationship

There is one particular type of conditional relationship which deserves extended discussion because of its unique nature and its special theoretical fruitfulness. The term "spurious noncorrelation" is sometimes applied to this type of relationship.[21] A spurious noncorrelation is one in which the contingent associations have opposite signs (some of the contingent associations are positive and others negative). As a result, the contingent associations cancel one another, producing a total relationship between the original two variables which is low or completely absent.

The danger of misleading interpretations is particularly acute when the analyst is confronted with no relationship—a zero correlation—between his variables. One is disposed to conclude that one's hypothesis has been in error and to move toward more fruitful lines of inquiry.

But this approach, as we have seen in the discussion of suppressor variables and as we shall again find in spurious noncorrelations, may lead to serious theoretical impoverishment.

Assuming that the analyst does pursue the noncorrelation further and discovers that it derives from a positive association in one of the contingent relationships and a negative association in the other, two types of explanation are possible: (1) He may offer an explanation of why the relationship is positive under one condition and a different explanation of why it is negative under another condition; we will call these *separate interpretations*. (2) He may offer a single explanation which, at a higher level of abstraction, accommodates the two contradictory findings; these are *integrated interpretations*. In the latter case, the contribution of conditional relationships to explanation and theory is particularly striking.

Let us consider an example of separate interpretations—one in which different explanations are presented for the contradictory findings in each of the partial associations. In Merton's study of Craftown, it was found that there was virtually no relationship between job satisfaction and participation in community activities.[22] When one considered this relationship among two social classes, however, opposite results appeared. Among the people who identified with the white-collar group it was the dissatisfied who belonged more to organizations, whereas among working-class identifiers the satisfied belonged more (Table 5–8).

Table 5–8
*Relationship Between Job Satisfaction and Participation in Community Activities According to Class Identification**

Belonging to Some Organiza- tions	Class Identification			
	WHITE COLLAR		WORKING CLASS	
	Satisfied	Dissatisfied	Satisfied	Dissatisfied
Belong	33%	44%	44%	36%
Do not belong	67	56	56	64
Total per cent	100	100	100	100
Number	(42)	(18)	(118)	(99)

* Herbert Hyman, *Survey Design and Analysis* (Glencoe, Ill.: The Free Press, 1955), p. 308, Table XLI (adapted). (Reprinted with permission of The Macmillan Company. Copyright 1955 by The Free Press, A Corporation.)

Although no theoretical integration of these contrary findings is attempted, one might speculate on the reason for these opposite results. It might be suggested that white-collar people who are dissatisfied with their jobs might join organizations, for example, the country club, in order to make contacts for the purpose of improving their occupational opportunities. Working-class people who joined organizations, on the other hand, might be labor union members, and the added security and superior working conditions provided by union shops might make them more satisfied with their jobs. In this case, a separate explanation is provided to account for each of the contingent associations.

Of greater theoretical significance than these separate interpretations is an *integrated* interpretation—one in which the identical principle accounts for the contrary results. Ideally one seeks a single conceptual scheme which satisfactorily accommodates or, even better, *requires* that the conditional relationships be the reverse of one another. In this case, one achieves a theoretical integration of great elegance.

For example, assume one begins with the hypothesis that younger people are more likely to be liberal, whereas older people are more conservative. Democratic affiliation is assumed to represent a liberal persuasion and Republican affiliation, a conservative persuasion. The data show that age bears only a small relationship to political affiliation: 50 per cent of those under 45 and 44 per cent of those over 45 vote Democratic.

When the relationship of age to political affiliation is examined for Protestants and Catholics separately, however, opposite results appear. Among Protestants the younger people are more Democratic, whereas among Catholics the older people are more Democratic.[23] (Table 5–9.) These opposite relationships, when combined, produce a small correlation between the two variables.

These findings can, however, be integrated by an explanation which accommodates both contradictory results, namely, *that the younger generation is less strongly attached to the political affiliation of its religious group* than the older people. Since the Protestants are predominantly Republicans and the Catholics predominantly Democrats, the authors' conclusion is that "within each religious group the

Table 5–9

Religion, Age, and Political Affiliation[*]

	PROTESTANTS		CATHOLICS	
	Below 45 Years	45 Years and Over	Below 45 Years	45 Years and Over
Democrats	43%	34%	72%	84%
Republicans	57	66	28	16
Total per cent	100	100	100	100
Number	(694)	(601)	(214)	(150)

[*] Paul F. Lazarsfeld, Bernard Berelson, and Hazel Gaudet, *The People's Choice* (New York: Columbia University Press, 1948), p. 24, Chart 7 (adapted). (Reprinted with permission of the Columbia University Press.)

younger voters show tendencies of opposition."[24] These apparently inconsistent findings are thus reconciled. The generalization that the new generation tends to deviate from the traditional political orientations of their religious groups is a more abstract conclusion than the simple descriptive statement that there is a small relationship between age and political affiliation. Inconsistent contingent associations, though often puzzling, may well advance the process of theoretical understanding.

Another example of an integrated interpretation is drawn from an investigation of the relationship of social class to certain aspects of authoritarianism.[25] A large-scale study revealed that 61 per cent of the working class and 59 per cent of the middle-class—virtually no difference—agreed, "Any good leader should be strict with people under him in order to gain their respect." When the sample was stratified by education, however, it was found that, among the poorly educated, middle-class people were 16 per cent *more* likely to agree with the statement, whereas among the well-educated, middle-class people were 18 per cent *less* likely to agree (Table 5–10). The results, in opposite directions, tended to cancel one another to produce the spurious noncorrelation.

The concepts of *status crystallization* and *social mobility* would appear to accommodate these contradictory results. Jackson has shown, for example, that people with status discrepancies (for example, inconsistency between their educational and occupational levels) tend to manifest more signs of psychological stress.[26] In the

Table 5–10

*Social Class and Agreement with "Strict Leader" Statement,
by Educational Level (Men Only)* *

	0–8 EDUCATION		9–12 EDUCATION		12 OR MORE YEARS EDUCATION	
	Middle Class	Working Class	Middle Class	Working Class	Middle Class	Working Class
Proportion agreeing with "Strict Leader" statement	83%	67%	58%	56%	44%	62%
Number	(88)	(121)	(121)	(129)	(126)	(13)

* Lewis Lipsitz, "Working-Class Authoritarianism: A Re-Evaluation," *American Sociological Review*, XXX (February 1965), 106–108, Table 1 (abridged and adapted). (Reprinted with permission of the American Sociological Association.)

present case, they also appear to show greater authoritarianism. People of higher class but lower education (the "strivers" or upwardly mobile) are more likely to agree with the statement than the consistent working class, and people of lower class but higher education (the "skidders" or downwardly mobile) are more likely to agree with it than the consistent middle class. In both cases, then, the status discrepants are more likely than the status crystallizers to manifest this aspect of authoritarianism.

A striking illustration of how contradictory trends in partial associations may be encompassed within a single theoretical framework is provided in a study of rural work patterns by Goldstein and Eichhorn.[27] The authors were interested in the Protestant Ethic value of work as an end in itself in relation to the use of farm machinery. The high work-oriented farmers, they found, were somewhat more likely than the low work-oriented farmers to use a two-row rather than a four-row corn planter on their farms. The interesting point, however, is that when one stratifies by size of farm, the relationship between work-orientation and type of farm machinery goes in opposite directions (Table 5–11).

But a single explanation easily covers these opposite results, namely, *the lesser rationality of the highly work-oriented men.* Two-row corn planters are more appropriate for small farms, and four-row planters are better suited for large farms. On small farms, we see, men with

Table 5–11

*Work-Orientation and Type of Corn Planter Used, by Size of Farm**

	Size of Farm					
	60 Acres or Less			More Than 60 Acres		
	WORK-ORIENTATION					
Type of Corn Planters Used	High Work	Middle Work	Low Work	High Work	Middle Work	Low Work
2-row planter	62%	71%	87%	50%	34%	14%
4-row planter	38	29	13	50	66	86
Number	($\overline{37}$)	($\overline{55}$)	($\overline{24}$)	($\overline{30}$)	($\overline{74}$)	($\overline{29}$)

* Bernice Goldstein and Robert L. Eichhorn, "The Changing Protestant Ethic: Rural Patterns in Health, Work, and Leisure," *American Sociological Review*, XXVI (August 1961), 562, Table 1 (abridged and adapted). (Reprinted with permission of the American Sociological Association.)

high work-orientation are *less* likely than others to use two-row planters, whereas on large farms they are *more* likely to do so. According to Goldstein and Eichhorn, ". . . the high work-oriented men are less likely to have the machine best suited to the size of their enterprise. . . ."[28] This single explanation satisfactorily accommodates these opposite results.

The theoretical significance of spurious noncorrelations is also illustrated in a study of the relationship between rural-urban residence and church attendance.[29] It is somewhat surprising to learn that residents of the Central City are slightly more likely than rural dwellers to be regular church attenders (49 per cent to 44 per cent). More interesting, however, is the finding that this relationship is fairly strong among Catholics but is slightly in the reverse direction among Protestants (Table 5–12).

A single interpretation embraces these opposite findings, namely, *that church attendance is greatest where the religious group is most highly concentrated.* Catholics are more likely to be city dwellers, whereas Protestants are relatively concentrated in rural areas. Hence, city or suburban Catholics attend church more than rural Catholics, but rural Protestants attend church somewhat more than city Protestants.[30]

In sum, the spurious noncorrelation, or spuriously low correlation, represents one of the theoretically most fruitful types of conditional relationships. It shows that the absence of a relationship between two

Table 5–12

*Church Attendance by Residential Belts for Protestants and Catholics**

Attend Church	PROTESTANTS				CATHOLICS			
	Central City	Suburban	Adjacent	Rural	Central City	Suburban	Adjacent	Rural
Regularly	36%	37%	38%	42%	72%	77%	67%	57%
Often	23	20	24	26	16	11	14	16
Seldom	34	32	30	25	9	9	12	21
Never	7	11	8	7	3	3	7	6
Total per cent	100	100	100	100	100	100	100	100
Number	(946)	(976)	(1081)	(1179)	(526)	(411)	(216)	(117)

* Bernard Lazerwitz, "National Data on Participation Rates Among Residential Belts in the United States," *American Sociological Review*, XXVII (October 1962), 692, Table 1 (adapted). (Reprinted with permission of the American Sociological Association.)

variables does not necessarily mean that there is no causal connection between them. The connection may be of a complex sort—positive under one test-factor condition and negative under another. These contradictory results may be subject to separate interpretations, or they may be embraced by a single integrated interpretation which satisfactorily embraces the opposite results. Where such integrated interpretations are found—and they are not so rare as might be assumed—they hold promise of yielding theoretical principles of great elegance and power.

It may be useful to digress momentarily to compare these "spurious noncorrelations" with the suppressor variables discussed in Chapter 4. These types of analysis have one salient feature in common, namely, that they both begin with a zero correlation (or low correlation) between the independent and dependent variables. The difference between them is this: In the spurious noncorrelation, the contingent associations have *opposite* signs (one relationship is positive, the other negative); in suppressor variable analysis, the contingent associations have the *same* signs (all positive or all negative). We have attempted to show that both types of analysis may potentially yield rich and fruitful generalizations.

Characteristically, an absence of relationship between an independent and a dependent variable is greeted with disappointment by the survey analyst. But there may be more there than meets the eye, and spurious noncorrelation analysis or suppressor variable analysis may bring it to the surface.

7. Conditional Relationships May Shed Light on Trends or Processes

Since social life consists of change, development, and movement, the sociologist is interested in describing and understanding such change. The matter is complex, and diverse techniques have been applied to the study of change. The examination of conditional relationships is one useful procedure for studying trends or processes; characteristically, this involves the introduction of some aspect of time as a test factor.

For example, it is a well-documented finding that both religious affiliation and socio-economic status are important determinants of voting behavior. But what is the trend in recent generations? Has secularization reduced the influence of religion on vote, or has the "religious revival" increased it? Does the new generation vote in a more or less class-conscious way than its forebears? Or are people voting more "independently," that is, less in accord with either of these groups? Although these questions deal with social dynamics, the examination of conditional relationships within a single survey enables one to deal with them.

Table 5–13 shows that while religious affiliation still plays an important role in voting behavior, its influence has declined substantially in more recent generations.[31] The difference in proportion of Republicans between Protestants and Catholics in the older age group is 70 per cent, whereas in the younger age group this difference is only 28 per cent. As Berelson et al. note: "The succession of generations seems to be softening the religious differences. . . ."[32] Younger people are deviating more from the political norms of their religious groups; religion is declining in importance as a basis for political behavior.

Table 5–13

*Religion and Vote, by Age**

| | AGE | | | | | |
| | 55 and Over | | 35–54 | | Under 35 | |
	Protestant	Catholic	Protestant	Catholic	Protestant	Catholic
Per cent Republican	88	18	82	41	66	38
Difference		70		41		28

* Bernard R. Berelson, Paul F. Lazarsfeld, and William N. McPhee, *Voting* (Chicago: University of Chicago Press, 1954), p. 70, Chart XXVIII (adapted). (Reprinted with permission of the University of Chicago Press.)

Quite the reverse is true of class. Table 5–14 suggests that class is *increasing* as a determinant of political decisions. In the oldest age group the difference between the extreme classes is 18 per cent, whereas in the youngest group it is 37 per cent. Indeed, one can even specify when this class crystallization began; there is a sharp rise in class-based voting in the 35–44 age group, that is, the generation growing up in the New Deal era. The authors note: "Presumably an age generation can be transformed by political events and social conditions into a political generation based on class considerations— a generation that retains its allegiances and norms while succeeding generations are moving in another direction."[33]

If one were simply to compare the influence of religion and socio-economic status on vote, the data would indicate that religion is a more powerful influence. What conditional relationships reveal, however, is that these two influences are moving in opposite directions— religion declining in influence in the younger generation while social class is increasing in influence.

In a study of adolescent society, McDill and Coleman provide an illustration of contradictory contingent associations which shed light on trends or processes.[34] These authors found that boys and girls differed in the value they attached to "brilliance" as a desirable characteristic. What was particularly interesting was the fact that (with the exception of freshmen) in each succeeding year in high school, boys were *increasingly* likely to want to be remembered for brilliance, whereas girls were *decreasingly* likely to value this reputa-

Table 5-14

Socio-Economic Status and Political Affiliation, by Age*

AGE

SOCIO-ECONOMIC STATUS

	55 and Over			45–54			35–44			21–34		
	Higher	Middle	Lower	Higher	Middle	Lower	Higher	Middle	Lower	Higher	Middle	Lower
Per cent Republican	83	71	65	80	75	63	83	74	52	81	56	44
Difference between high and low	18			17			31			37		

* Bernard R. Berelson, Paul F. Lazarsfeld, and William N. McPhee, *Voting* (Chicago: University of Chicago Press, 1954), p. 60, Chart XXII (adapted). (Reprinted with permission of the University of Chicago Press.)

tion. The more sexually mature the girl becomes, the more she seems to fear that a reputation for brilliance reflects negatively on her desirability. Among boys the reverse is true. As they grow older, the values of boys and girls move in opposite directions.[35]

In the clarification of trends or processes, we have noted, the test factor or independent variable in some way reflects the concept of *time*. Since most surveys are conducted at one point in time, the ability of such studies to deal with social change, movement, or development are regrettably limited. To the extent that conditional relationships, using some aspect of time as a test factor, do shed light on such dynamic processes, their contribution is especially to be valued.

Discussion

It is thus apparent that conditional relationships may have an important bearing upon the interpretation of two-variable relationships. They may call into question the original interpretation, confirm the interpretation, modify the interpretation, lead to a radical revision of the interpretation, enable one to select between alternative interpretations, produce meaningful interpretations of noncorrelations, and shed light on trends or processes. Through the confirmation of interpretations, they may importantly contribute to validity. Through the modification of interpretations, they reduce the danger of excessively global and inexact generalizations. Through the radical revision of interpretations, they press theory in new directions. Through the revelation of spurious noncorrelations, they avoid the misleading conclusion that no intrinsic link exists between two variables. And, in revealing trends and processes, they make a contribution to one of the most difficult and important sociological problems, namely, social change. To dismiss conditional relationships as a mere annoyance or source of confusion may at times do a serious disservice to the improvement of theory.

But conditional relationships also serve the functions of specification, clarification, and description. It is these contributions to which we now turn.

NOTES

1. Lewis M. Killian and Charles M. Grigg, "Urbanism, Race, and Anomia," *American Journal of Sociology*, LXVII (May 1962), 661–665.
2. Patricia L. Kendall and Paul F. Lazarsfeld, "Problems of Survey Analysis," in R. K. Merton and P. F. Lazarsfeld (eds.), *Continuities in Social Research: Studies in the Scope and Method of "The American Soldier"* (Glencoe, Ill.: The Free Press, 1950), p. 163.
3. There is still no standard terminology to describe this type of relationship. Hanan C. Selvin, "Durkheim's *Suicide* and Problems of Empirical Research," *American Journal of Sociology*, LXIII (May 1958), 610, notes: "The phenomenon of statistical interaction has been given many different names (e.g., specification, conditional relationship, differential impact, differential sensitivity, and non-additivity of effects.") The test factor is sometimes referred to as the qualifier variable. Lazarsfeld has distinguished two types of qualifier variables: he describes a test factor as a "condition" if it is antecedent to the independent variable and as a "contingency" if it intervenes between the independent and dependent variables [Paul F. Lazarsfeld, "Evidence and Inference in Social Research," *Daedalus*, LXXXVII (1958), 120–121]. In the present discussion, we will use the term *specification* to refer to the process of establishing different degrees of association, *conditional relationships* to the contingent associations which emerge, and *test factor* to the variable upon which the relationship is stratified.
4. Morris Rosenberg, *Society and the Adolescent Self-Image* (Princeton: Princeton University Press, 1965), p. 40.
5. George Herbert Mead, *Mind, Self and Society* (Chicago: University of Chicago Press, 1934).
6. Charles Horton Cooley, *Human Nature and the Social Order* (New York: Charles Scribner's Sons, 1912), p. 152.
7. Rosenberg, *op. cit.*, p. 41.
8. Emile Durkheim, *Suicide* (Glencoe, Ill.: The Free Press, 1951).
9. *Ibid.*, p. 266.
10. Rosenberg, *op. cit.*, p. 86.
11. William H. Sewell and Alan M. Orenstein, "Community of Residence and Occupational Choice," *American Journal of Sociology*, LXX (March 1965), 551–563.
12. *Ibid.*, p. 562.

13. Bernard Berelson, Paul F. Lazarsfeld, and William McPhee, *Voting* (Chicago: University of Chicago Press, 1954).
14. Robert R. Sears, Eleanor E. Maccoby, and Harry Levin, *Patterns of Child Rearing* (Evanston, Ill.: Row, Peterson, 1957), pp. 122–123.
15. *Ibid.*, pp. 124–125. (Reprinted by permission of Harper and Row, Publishers, Inc.)
16. Donald G. McKinley, *Social Class and Family Life* (Glencoe, Ill.: The Free Press, 1964).
17. Leonard I. Pearlin (unpublished manuscript).
18. Durkheim, *op. cit.*, Book II, chap 5.
19. *Ibid.*, p. 271.
20. Rosenberg, *op. cit.*, p. 99.
21. Hans Zeisel, *Say It With Figures* (New York: Harper & Row, Publishers, Inc., 1947), pp. 198–199.
22. Discussed in Herbert Hyman, *Survey Design and Analysis* (Glencoe, Ill.: The Free Press, 1955), p. 307.
23. Paul F. Lazarsfeld, Bernard R. Berelson, and Hazel E. Gaudet, *The People's Choice* (New York: Columbia University Press, 1948), p. 24.
24. *Ibid.*, p. 24.
25. Lewis Lipsitz, "Working-Class Authoritarianism: A Re-Evaluation," *American Sociological Review*, XXX (February 1965), 103–109.
26. Elton F. Jackson, "Status Consistency and Symptoms of Stress," *American Sociological Review*, XXVII (August 1962), 469–480.
27. Bernice Goldstein and Robert L. Eichhorn, "The Changing Protestant Ethic: Rural Patterns in Health, Work, and Leisure," *American Sociological Review*, XXVI (August 1961), 557–565.
28. *Ibid.*, p. 563.
29. Bernard Lazerwitz, "National Data on Participation Rates Among Residential Belts in the United States," *American Sociological Review*, XXVII (October 1962), 691–696.
30. For a more extended discussion and interpretation, see *ibid.*, p. 696.
31. Berelson et al., *op. cit.*, p. 70.
32. *Loc. cit.*
33. *Ibid.*, p. 61.
34. Edward L. McDill and James Coleman, "High School Social Status, College Plans, and Academic Achievement," *American Sociological Review*, XXVIII (December 1963), 905–918.
35. *Ibid.*, p. 915.

CHAPTER 6

Conditional Relationships: Specification, Clarification, Description

From the foregoing illustrations it is plain that the nature of the "conditions" investigated in conditional relationships may vary enormously. They may be environments or "contexts," groups, collectivities, social categories, personality types, or psychological states of any kind—in fact, any type of classificatory basis. Any test factor, when stratified, reveals the relationship under different conditions.

We have used the term *specification* to characterize the process of examining a relationship between two variables under different conditions. A major purpose of specifying a relationship is to "point to" one or another of the contingent associations, singling it out for special attention and stipulating its distinctive significance. The object of this procedure is clarification—clarification of the true value of the relationship, stripped of contaminating factors, clarification of the behavior of the relationship in diverse circumstances, and clarification of the independent variables and test factors themselves. Let us consider some of the different forms this clarification may assume.

1. Conditional Relationships May "Purify," or Reduce Contamination in, the Original Relationship

The size of a relationship between two variables reflects the degree to which an inherent link exists between two variables plus the influence of factors irrelevant to that inherent link. To the extent that one is able to filter out irrelevant conditions, one is able to see the purer and clearer impact of the independent upon the dependent variable.

Assume, for example, that one wished to investigate the relationship of personality to behavior. One might hypothesize that people with "authoritarian" personalities would be more likely than those with "democratic" personalities to discriminate against minority groups. But one would not expect the effect of the personality factor to be the same under all conditions. In the South, for example, one would expect the impact of personality to be less significant because discrimination is a more accepted cultural practice. In this region of the country, a white would probably not invite a Negro to his home, irrespective of whether he had an authoritarian or a democratic personality. In the North, on the other hand, the authoritarian would be less likely than the democratic personality to issue such an invitation. Hence, if one examined the relationship of authoritarianism to discrimination in regions outside the South, the relationship would be "purer" and stronger.

Consider the finding that the lower the adolescent's level of self-esteem, the less likely is he to engage in discussions of political affairs with his high school companions.[1] Here we see the bearing of a particular personality quality on a certain type of social interaction. Adolescents with low self-esteem tend to be self-conscious about expressing their views, are afraid that they will say something stupid, tend to be awkward in their relationships with others, etc. It is thus understandable that they tend to be shy and retiring in expressing their political views.

But the relationship between self-esteem and political discussion is purified if one takes account of the factor of *political interest*. One would not, after all, expect such a relationship among those who are *not* politically interested.[2] If a youth with high self-esteem is not interested in politics, why should he talk about it? The analyst studying the influence of personality factors is thus really concerned with knowing why, among people who *are* politically interested, low self-esteem should lead to low participation in political discussion.

Table 6–1 indicates that among those who are not interested there is little relationship between self-esteem and "intensity of political discussion." (Indeed, those with high self-esteem are somewhat *less* likely to talk politics, which is a rational response in light of their low interest.) This enables one to focus more sharply on the relevant relationship, that is, the relationship between self-esteem and political discussion among those who are politically interested. This relationship is purer, stronger, and less contaminated than the original relationship. The inclusion of low-interest people in the original relationship was simply blurring the clarity of the influence of the personality variable upon the behavior.

The failure to purify the relationship may result in seriously misleading theoretical conclusions. Hamilton illustrates this point strikingly:

When it comes to detailing the meaning of "lower middle class," the tendency in the United States is to turn to the two Census categories, clerical and sales workers. Routine published data show that this "lower middle class" earns less than the best-off manual labor group, the "craftsmen, foremen, and kindred" workers. On the basis of this finding, together with the assumption that things were different in the past, it has been argued on the one hand that the middle class is losing status and is likely to undergo a "status panic," while the working class, on the other hand, is gaining status. From the latter conclusion it has been predicted that we will have less utopian politics (i.e., an end of ideology), more moderation and compromise, and an increasing identity of outlook on the part of voters and parties.[3]

And the income superiority of the skilled manual worker is indeed substantial: his median income of $5,282 is far above the $3,389 median income of the sales and clerical worker—a differential of

Table 6-1

Self-Esteem and Intensity of Political Discussion, Among Those Equally Interested in Public Affairs*

Intensity of Discussion	Interested						Not Interested					
	SELF-ESTEEM						SELF-ESTEEM					
	High 0	1	2	3	4	Low 5-6	High 0	1	2	3	4	Low 5-6
High	63%	56%	46%	53%	44%	43%	5%	5%	11%	8%	12%	4%
Medium	26	32	37	32	30	30	34	38	37	34	42	48
Low	11	12	17	15	25	27	60	57	52	58	46	48
Total per cent	100	100	100	100	100	100	100	100	100	100	100	100
Number	(182)	(254)	(226)	(123)	(63)	(44)	(38)	(58)	(65)	(50)	(26)	(25)

* Morris Rosenberg, "Self-Esteem and Concern With Public Affairs," *Public Opinion Quarterly*, XXVI (Summer 1962), 205, Table 4. (Reprinted by permission of Princeton University Press.)

$1,893. But one would not expect the "status panic" to characterize all of the clerical and sales workers equally. It would not characterize women, for example, since their status is fundamentally dependent upon that of their husbands or fathers. If we just consider men, then (Table 6–2, Line 2) the income differential between the skilled and clerical-sales is only $539—a reduction of over two-thirds of the income differential. Furthermore, one would not properly include foremen in the skilled group because they are as likely to identify with management as with workers. Omitting this group reduces the income differential to $378 (Table 6–2, Line 3).

Many of the clerical and sales workers, it turns out, are students. They will experience no status anxiety since they will anticipate much greater earnings in the future. Omitting this group reduces the income differential to $133 (Table 6–2, Line 4). Finally, status anxiety is likely to appear among those comparing themselves with others during their prime earning years. If one further considers only those between the ages of 21 and 59, one finds that the median income of the clerical-sales group is now $88 *higher* than that of the skilled manual group (Table 6–2, Line 5).

The attribution of "status anxiety" to the white-collar worker is based on the assumption that he compares his income with that of a skilled manual worker more or less *like himself*. In this regard, however, he does not fare poorly at all (as Table 6–2 shows). This conclusion is precisely the reverse of that with which one began, and the

Table 6–2
*Occupation and Income**

	Skilled (Dollars)	MEDIAN INCOME Number	Clerical, sales (Dollars)	Number	Difference (Dollars)
All members of the civilian labor force ages 14 and over	5282	(916)	3389	(1443)	1893
Males only	5334	(891)	4795	(645)	539
Foremen omitted	5173	(786)	4795	(645)	378
Students also omitted	5185	(775)	5052	(579)	133
Age 21 to 59 only	5272	(694)	5360	(480)	— 88

* Richard F. Hamilton, "Income, Class, and Reference Groups," *American Sociological Review*, XXIX (August 1964), 576, Table 1. (Reprinted with permission of the American Sociological Society.)

theoretical implications are radically different. There are, to be sure, at least 16 contingent associations possible, whereas Hamilton has shown but one. Nevertheless, if one can examine the relationship under those conditions most appropriate to the hypothesis (that is, to the *theoretically relevant* group), one is in a better position to see the nature of the relationship clearly.

The principle of purification is implicit in most studies. If one is interested in the relationship of social class to alienation, one does not ordinarily include young children in one's sample. Such inclusion would just produce "don't know" or random responses and tend to muddy up the relationship. Elimination (or separate handling) of this group tends to sharpen, clarify, and purify the relationship.

In this respect social science laws are similar to those in the physical sciences. The law of falling bodies, for example, is assumed to hold true only in a vacuum. Other physical principles may be dependent on temperature. The empirical operation of physical laws is usually meant to apply in the absence of interfering factors. In social science, any generalization is implicitly assumed to obtain, or to obtain most clearly, under specified conditions. Usually this specification remains implicit. We suggest that it may be of value to the analyst to be explicit in stating those conditions under which the interpretation is assumed to be true, and to examine this assumption empirically.

2. Conditional Relationships May Specify Conditions Facilitating the Relationship

It is by now apparent that any relationship between two variables is the result of many currents and cross-currents, often operating differentially—sometimes with differential strength, sometimes in contrary directions—to produce the final result. Some conditions "facilitate" the relationship, whereas others "inhibit" it. Let us first consider the issue of facilitating conditions—what might be called, from the viewpoint of the relationship, "propitious circumstances."

Arnold and Gold's "The Facilitation Effect of the Social Environment"[4] is a good case in point. This study dealt with the campaign and voting for a constitutional convention in Iowa to reapportion state legislative districts. Since the large counties would benefit from such reapportionment and the small counties would lose, it was anticipated that favorableness of response would vary with county size; this hypothesis was strikingly supported by a 0.87 correlation between population size and vote.

One would, of course, interpret this finding as a simple reflection of self-interest. On the basis of other theory and research, however, the authors interpreted this relationship to reflect "social facilitation" as well. It was not simply that each individual privately pursued his self-interest, but that this self-interest was stimulated by impersonal and interpersonal communications which made the issue salient to him, and which activated his latent self-interest. The behavior was not merely a private rational decision but a consequence of interpersonal forces.

If this interpretation were correct, however, then one would expect the relationship between population size and vote to be strongest in those countries in which the issue was most socially salient, that is, where there was heightened general awareness of the issue.

Two forces making for heightened awareness were considered. One was the activity of a citizens' committee (the CCCC) in support of the convention. This group was active in 41 counties and inactive in the remaining 58. In the counties in which the CCCC was active, the correlation between county size and vote was 0.92, whereas in the other counties it was only 0.59.

The other factor presumably increasing awareness of the issue was the presence of a daily newspaper in the county; the assumption was that the newspaper would stimulate interest in the issue. In the 38 counties with a local daily paper, the association between population size and vote was 0.92, whereas in the 61 counties without a paper, the correlation was only 0.56.[5]

Indeed, if the two indices of facilitation are combined, the results are still sharper. In the 28 counties with both a local paper and CCCC activity, the relationship of population size to vote was 0.92; when one of these was present, the correlation was 0.40; and when neither was present, the correlation was only 0.21.

We thus see that the simple explanation of self-interest is insufficient to account for the relationship. The influence of self-interest is strong where the issue has been made salient through press and organizational activity; under other circumstances, self-interest turns out to be a relatively weak determinant of vote.

An interesting example of how a general facilitating condition may integrate *several* diverse results appears in an investigation of the relationship of environmental deviance to arrests or court referrals. In general, the authors find that youngsters from deviant family backgrounds are more likely to encounter difficulty with the law. But Table 6–3 reveals several interesting contingent associations:

(1) A deviant family background increases Negro, but not white, delinquency. (2) A deviant neighborhood increases male, but not female, delinquency. (3) Either kind of deviant influence increases delinquency more among those failing in school than among those succeeding.[6]

These findings suggest, according to the authors, that family and neighborhood deviance tend to lead to delinquency *where there is restricted access to legitimate opportunity*. In other words, this effect appears strongly among those with little chance to succeed in culturally prescribed goals but weakly among those with some chance. Thus, the effect of family and neighborhood deviance is strong among Negroes, but not among whites; among boys, but not among girls (who can achieve the goal of marriage); and among school failures, but not among school successes. These conditional relationships suggest that it is only in the absence of alternative outlets toward achievement of goals that the deviant environment creates delinquency.

Whether there are any general conditions facilitating relationships is unclear at present. What is certain, however, is that the same conditions may facilitate certain types of relationships and inhibit others. A condition frequently considered important by survey analysts is *interest*. Hyman has shown, for example, that low interest very often facilitates the influence of a specific stimulus.[7] In other words, among people who have little interest in politics, some minor factor may

Table 6–3

Family and Neighborhood Deviance and Delinquency,
*by Race, Sex, and School Success**

| | Percentage with One or More Arrests or Court Referrals | | | |
| | Negroes | | Whites | |
	Family Deviant	Family Nondeviant	Family Deviant	Family Nondeviant
	55	39	27	29
Difference		16		− 2

| | Boys | | Girls | |
| | Neighborhood | | Neighborhood | |
	Deviant	Nondeviant	Deviant	Nondeviant
	71	47	14	16
Difference		24		− 2

| | School Failure | | School Success | |
| | Family | | Family | |
	Deviant	Nondeviant	Deviant	Nondeviant
	71	45	33	27
Difference		26		6

| | School Failure | | School Success | |
| | Neighborhood | | Neighborhood | |
	Deviant	Nondeviant	Deviant	Nondeviant
	82	53	44	37
Difference		29		7

* Erdman B. Palmore and Phillip E. Hammond, "Interacting Factors in Juvenile Delinquency," *American Sociological Review,* 29 (December 1964), 850–851, Tables 2–5 (adapted). (Reprinted with permission of the American Sociological Association.)

change their minds. On the other hand, there is some evidence to suggest that the influence of properties are often facilitated by a *high* level of interest and involvement. Berelson et al., show that the greater the political interest, the sharper the party differences on major issues[8] (Table 6–4). The same condition, we see, may have a facilitating or an inhibiting effect, depending upon the type of relationship under consideration.

There is thus patent value in specifying—in "pointing to"— those conditions, such as environmental influences, group affiliations, or subjective states, under which the relationship appears with special sharpness. Social science has been justly criticized for its neglect of

Table 6–4

Political Affiliation and Stand on Issues, by Level of Interest[*]

| | Level of Political Interest | | | | | |
| | GREAT DEAL | | QUITE A LOT | | NOT MUCH OR NONE | |
	Republican	Democrat	Republican	Democrat	Republican	Democrat
Percentage for						
Taft-Hartley	81	33	68	46	57	41
Difference		48		22		16
Percentage for						
price control	44	83	58	79	60	67
Difference		39		21		7

[*] Bernard R. Berelson, Paul F. Lazarsfeld, and William N. McPhee, *Voting* (Chicago: University of Chicago Press, 1954), p. 196, Chart XCI (adapted). (Reprinted with permission of the University of Chicago Press.)

situational factors. One may know that general principles obtain, but one does not know whether these principles have predictive value in specific circumstances. The specification of facilitating conditions affords some aid in dealing with this problem.

3. Conditional Relationships May Specify Conditions Inhibiting or Blurring the Relationship

In many cases it is of value to the survey analyst to specify those conditions under which a relationship is particularly *weak*. One purpose of separating the weak relationship, as noted, is to "purify" or reduce contamination in the relationship. The purpose we wish to stress here, however, is the inherent interest in the inhibiting condition itself. Otherwise expressed, the fact that a relationship is weak under a particular condition may tell us a great deal about that condition.

An investigation of the relationship between faith in people and success-orientation affords an illustration of this point. College students with low faith in people, it was found, were more likely to stress the importance of getting ahead in life.[9] The interpretation offered was that those with low faith in people tended to view the world as a jungle in which only the fittest could survive. Hence, the striving for success was to them a means of gaining power (money, prestige, etc.), which was the prime objective in the struggle for survival.

The investigator suggested, however, that the general cultural pressure to succeed would tend to "mute" or "inhibit" the relationship between faith in people and success-orientation.

We would thus expect that the impact of faith in people upon one's desire to get ahead would tend to be strongest upon those who are not under strong cultural pressure to be successful. One simple fact which is overlooked surprisingly often in discussions of success is that the value is considered much more appropriate for men than for women. Women are much more likely to attain higher status through the success of their husbands than through their own achievements. This certainly tends to be the case among the members of our sample; only 29 per cent of the women, compared with 51 per cent of the men, considered it "very important" to get ahead in life. We would thus expect the influence of the individual's degree of faith in people on his success-orientation to be greater among the women than among the men since, in the former case, this relationship is less likely to be adulterated by a general social pressure to succeed. The results in Table 6–5 confirms this expecations.

Among the men, 59 per cent of those with low faith in people considered it "very important" for them to get ahead, compared with 52 per cent of those with medium faith and 48 per cent of those with high faith. The male's basic interpersonal attitude thus has *some* influence on his desire for success, but it is not a very strong one; the difference between men with the lowest and highest degrees of faith in people is only 11 per

Table 6–5

*Faith in People and Desire to Get Ahead, by Sex**

Important to Get Ahead	Men			Women		
	FAITH IN PEOPLE					
	High	Medium	Low	High	Medium	Low
Very important	48%	52%	59%	19%	34%	51%
Not very important	52	48	41	81	66	49
Total per cent	100	100	100	100	100	100
Number	(444)	(491)	(200)	(229)	(137)	(51)

* Morris Rosenberg, "Faith in People and Success-Orientation," in P. F. Lazarsfeld and M. Rosenberg, eds., *The Language of Social Research* (Glencoe, Ill.: The Free Press, 1955), p. 161, Table 3. (Reprinted with permission of The Macmillan Company. Copyright 1955 by The Free Press, A Corporation.)

cent. Even men with high faith in people often accept the cultural value of success quite completely. Among the women, however, fully 51 per cent of those with low faith in people were particularly anxious to be successful compared with only 19 per cent of those with high faith, a difference of 32 per cent, or nearly three times as great as that obtaining among the men. . . . Many men in American society, irrespective of their attitudes toward humanity, accept the idea that they should do their best to get ahead. Consequently, the relationship between these two variables in this population subgroup, though significant, is considerably smaller than that among women, who are not exposed to the same amount of cultural pressure to get ahead.[10]

How a broad community environment may mute or inhibit the influence of family tradition is shown in a study of voting behavior in Elmira.[11] While sons of Republicans, as expected, were more likely to vote Republican than sons of Democrats, nearly half of the sons of Democrats supported the Republican Party. This latter finding suggested to the authors that the predominantly Republican atmosphere of Elmira strongly influenced those whose family heritage was Democratic. But if the community environment operated to change one's party affiliation in the majority direction, then it would follow that the longer one had been exposed to this community environment, the greater would be the change in the Republican direction.

In order to examine this question, the sample was divided into those who were long-established members of the Elmira community and those who were relatively recent arrivals. Table 6–6 shows that the

Table 6–6

*Relationship Between Father's Vote and Own Vote According to Length of Residence in Elmira**

| | OLD-TIMER | | NEWCOMER | |
	Republican father	Democratic father	Republican father	Democratic father
Republican	87%	53%	85%	37%
Democratic	13	47	15	63
Total per cent	100	100	100	100
Number	(284)	(189)	(47)	(27)

* Herbert Hyman, *Survey Design and Analysis* (Glencoe, Ill.: The Free Press, 1955), p. 307, Table XXXIX (adapted). (Reprinted with permission of The Macmillan Company. Copyright 1955 by The Free Press, A Corporation.)

relationship of father's vote to own vote is weaker among the long-term residents of Elmira than among the newcomers. The general Republican atmosphere of Elmira has operated to mute, tone down, or adulterate the significance of family tradition for one's own political affiliation. These data reveal the positive power of the community atmosphere in overcoming the influence of political tradition.

4. Conditional Relationships May Stipulate Necessary Conditions

The survey analyst examining an asymmetrical relationship does so on the basis of some theoretical assumption concerning the impact of the independent upon the dependent variable. But implicit in virtually every such relationship is the assumption that certain necessary conditions obtain which render the observed effect possible. In a sense, virtually every relationship is a conditional one, that is, is assumed to hold under certain conditions but not others. Ordinarily, these necessary conditions are implicit, but they are usually so obvious that their specification is unnecessary.

Assume that a survey analyst, on the basis of the examination of his data, concludes that working-class family members are more alienated than middle-class family members. But he does not seriously mean this generalization to apply under all conditions, that is, all social environments, groups, categories, psychological states, etc. It is not meant to apply, for example, to two-year olds, to members of the Kwakiutl or Trobriand tribes, nor in all probability to the seriously mentally defective. But there is no point in saying these things, since they are implicit in the conclusion. The relationship is assumed to hold only in the presence of certain necessary conditions.

Let us consider an obvious necessary condition. Some people like the appearance of a Rolls-Royce, while others find its styling unattractive. We would naturally expect that people who like the appearance of Rolls-Royces would be more likely to buy them. Table

6–7 (hypothetical) shows that this in fact is the case, but that the difference is small: 8 per cent of those who are attracted by the styling and 4 per cent of those who dislike the styling purchase the car. This would suggest that response to the styling is of some, but not great, importance in the decision to make the purchase.

Table 6–7

*Response to Appearance of Rolls-Royce and Purchase**

	Like Appearance	Dislike Appearance
Purchase Rolls-Royce	8%	4%
Do not purchase	92	96
Total per cent	100	100
Number	(330)	(110)

* Hypothetical.

Table 6–8, however, examines this relationship among those who are or are not wealthy. Among respondents who are not wealthy, there is almost no relationship: a relatively poor person who likes the Rolls-Royce styling is hardly more likely than an equal-income person who does not like the appearance to purchase one. Among wealthy people, on the other hand, preference has a very strong influence on purchase. The reason, of course, is that a necessary condition for the purchase of a Rolls-Royce is a lot of money. Only when this necessary condition is satisfied can the determinant factor— attitude toward the appearance of the automobile—influence the purchase.

Table 6–8

*Response to Appearance of Rolls-Royce and Purchase,
by Income Level**

	NOT WEALTHY		WEALTHY	
	Like Appearance	Dislike Appearance	Like Appearance	Dislike Appearance
Purchase Rolls-Royce	3%	2%	60%	20%
Do not purchase	97	98	40	80
Total per cent	100	100	100	100
Number	(300)	(100)	(30)	(10)

* Hypothetical.

Now consider an actual empirical example. Sewell finds that among high school graduates, boys are more likely to plan to go to college than girls.[12] But the stronger male emphasis upon college attendance is not basically assumed to operate under all conditions; it is assumed to operate *chiefly among those who are college material*. This is evident when we examine the relationship of sex to college plans, stratifying by intelligence (Table 6–9). Among those low in intelligence, there is little difference (2 per cent) in plans to attend college, whereas in the high-intelligence group the difference is substantial (14 per cent). It is only when the necessary condition of a superior level of intelligence is satisfied that the male norm of college attendance makes its influence felt.

Table 6–9

*Percentage with College Plans by Intelligence,
for Male and Female High School Seniors**

| | Intelligence | | | | | |
| | LOW | | MIDDLE | | HIGH | |
	Male	Female	Male	Female	Male	Female
Percentage planning to go to college	14	12	34	27	62	48

* William H. Sewell, "Community of Residence and College Plans," *American Sociological Review*, XXIX (February 1964), 28, Table 2 (abridged and adapted). (Reprinted with permission of the American Sociological Association.)

Conditional relationships may thus provide a more complete causal analysis by stipulating the necessary conditions under which the determinative factors make their effects felt. Unlike the cases cited above, these necessary conditions are not in all cases so obvious.

Since a two-variable relationship is typically the outcome of complex processes, *time* is frequently a necessary condition for a relationship to emerge. Consider the following example drawn from a study of attitudes toward military service. In this study, soldiers were asked about their willingness for further service in the Army.[13] As Table 6–10 shows, soldiers who had served overseas objected more to further military service than those who had not yet left the States. However, when one stratifies the sample according to length of service, one finds that this effect is strong among those who have been in the Army a

Table 6–10

Relationship Between Theater of Service and Willingness for Further Service[*]

	Overseas	Not Yet Overseas
Willing to serve further	51%	68%
Not willing	49	32
Total per cent	100	100
Number	(1462)	(253)

[*] Herbert Hyman, *Survey Design and Analysis* (Glencoe, Ill.: The Free Press, 1955), p. 302, Table XXXIV (adapted). (Reprinted with permission of The Macmillan Company. Copyright 1955 by The Free Press, A Corporation.)

long time but not among those who have been in less time. In other words, if one has served less than three years, there is no conspicuous feeling that one should be discharged even if one has served overseas. Among these people, this issue is not really problematical (Table 6–11). Among those who have been in longer than three years, however, the question of discharge becomes problematical. This is the necessary precondition for giving serious consideration to the idea of discharge. Once this necessary condition is satisfied, then the determinant factor—overseas service—operates strongly to influence attitudes toward further service.

One cannot always assume, however, that the introduction of time as a test factor means that the relationship is the end product of a long process. Sometimes time has another meaning: it is a reflection of an historical condition. In *The American Soldier,* for example, it was found that better educated soldiers were more likely to gain

Table 6–11

Relationship Between Theater and Willingness for Further Service According to Length of Service[*]

	3 PLUS YEARS		2–3 YEARS	
	Overseas	Not Yet Overseas	Overseas	Not Yet Overseas
Willing to serve further	33%	66%	60%	68%
Not willing	67	34	40	32
Total per cent	100	100	100	100
Number	(465)	(57)	(997)	(196)

[*] Herbert Hyman, *Survey Design and Analysis* (Glencoe, Ill.: The Free Press, 1955), p. 303, Table XXXV (adapted). (Reprinted with permission of The Macmillan Company. Copyright 1955 by The Free Press, A Corporation.)

promotions[14] (Table 6–12). This finding would lend support to the functionalist interpretation that those with superior training are more likely to achieve upward social mobility.

But one would have to modify this conclusion to specify the conditions under which it is more or less free to operate. The findings suggest that this principle operates more powerfully when the oppor-

Table 6–12

*Relationship Between Rank Among Enlisted Men and Educational Level**

Rank	High School Graduate or Better	Less than High School Graduate
Noncommissioned officer	61%	43%
Private or private-first-class	39	57
Total per cent	100	100
Number	(3222)	(3152)

* Herbert Hyman, *Survey Design and Analysis* (Glencoe, Ill.: The Free Press, 1955), p. 300, Table XXX. (Reprinted with permission of The Macmillan Company. Copyright 1955 by The Free Press, A Corporation.)

tunities for mobility are ample than when they are restricted. This is suggested by the findings of Table 6–13. There it will be seen that among those who have been in the Army two years or more, education is more clearly associated with rank than among those who have been in less time. This is probably due to the fact that early in the war many opportunities for promotion existed, but that later

Table 6–13

*Relationship Between Rank and Educational Level According to Length of Service**

	Length of Service			
	LESS THAN 2 YEARS		2 YEARS OR MORE	
	High School Graduate	Less than High School Graduate	High School Graduate	Less than High School Graduate
Noncommissioned	23%	17%	74%	53%
Private or Pfc.	77	83	26	47
Total per cent	100	100	100	100
Number	(842)	(823)	(2380)	(2329)

* Herbert Hyman, *Survey Design and Analysis* (Glencoe, Ill.: The Free Press, 1955), p. 300, Table XXXI (adapted). (Reprinted with permission of The Macmillan Company. Copyright 1955 by The Free Press, A Corporation.)

the Tables of Organization tended to be filled up. It was under conditions of ample opportunity for promotion that the impact of superior training on upward mobility was more likely to make itself felt.

5. *Conditional Relationships May Clarify the Nature of the Independent or Dependent Variables*

Social science is obliged to convert its concepts into concrete empirical indicators or indices, but these indices are inevitably inexact reflections of the concepts. The danger thus arises that the analyst's interpretation of the meaning of an index may be more or less wide of the mark, which must inevitably introduce some error into the interpretation. Conditional relationships may at times clarify the meaning of an index, either for the total sample or for one of the sample subgroups.

Pearlin's work provides an illustration of this point. Pearlin sought to examine the relationship between remoteness from the locus of authority in the mental hospital and feelings of alienation of the staff.[15] The particular dimension of alienation upon which he focused was "feelings of powerlessness"—the feeling that one was deprived of control over the direction of affairs within one's immediate province. He then asked the hospital personnel to specify the person who, in their opinion, was the most important figure (excluding themselves) on how the ward was run—doctors, nursing supervisors, head nurses, and charge attendants. It turned out that the greater the hierarchical distance between the respondent and the assumed source of power, the more alienated was the respondent, that is, the less he felt that he had an influence on how things were run[16] (Table 6–14).

But Pearlin then examined this relationship under different conditions. He classified his respondents as high or low in "status obeisance"—whether they accepted or rejected the principle of unquestioning authority. Among those who were low in obeisance, the

Table 6–14

*Positional Disparity in Authority Relations and Alienation**

Score of Alienation	Four-Step Disparity	Three-Step Disparity	Two-Step Disparity	Adjacency
Low 0	2%	12%	15%	19%
1	25	31	25	29
2	34	23	34	23
3	29	18	14	18
High 4	11	16	12	11
Number	(56)	(238)	(358)	(314)

* Leonard I. Pearlin, "Alienation From Work: A Study in Nursing Personnel," *American Sociological Review*, XXVII (June 1962), 317, Table 1. (Reprinted with permission of the American Sociological Association.)

relationship between positional disparity and alienation was particularly strong; among those high in obeisance, the relationship was weaker (Table 6–15).

In other words, the individual feels powerless when he is remote from the locus of authority *only if he desires independent power or influence*. If he feels that the authorities are omnipotent and omniscient and feels they *should* make the decisions, then there is no frustrating feeling of powerlessness. Alienation, then, is not just a feeling of powerlessness; it is a *frustration* at the feeling of powerlessness stemming from an inability to exercise influence. When there is no *desire*

Table 6–15

*Status Obeisance, the Positional Disparity Between Superordinate and Subordinate and Alienation**

Aliena-tion Score	LOW AND MODERATE OBEISANCE				HIGH OBEISANCE			
	Four-Step Disparity	Three-Step Disparity	Two-Step Disparity	Adjacency	Four-Step Disparity	Three-Step Disparity	Two-Step Disparity	Adjacency
Low 0	..%	12%	16%	22%	5%	13%	12%	12%
1	22	30	21	25	32	32	32	36
2	28	18	33	20	41	27	35	31
3	34	22	16	20	18	18	12	13
High 4	16	18	14	13	5	11	9	8
Number	(32)	(148)	(248)	(220)	(22)	(85)	(98)	(86)

* Leonard I. Pearlin, "Alienation From Work: A Study of Nursing Personnel," *American Sociological Review*, XXVII (June 1962), 317, Table 2. (Reprinted with permission of the American Sociological Association.)

to exercise influence, the individual does not feel alienated. As Pearlin expresses the point:

> Given such status values [high obeisance], situations of great positional disparity do not result in feelings of deprivation, for one does not experi-ence loss in not having something he does not feel is rightfully his. . . . Evidently those who regard authority with deference and awe do not seek a voice in their own affairs; they are willing to have their superordinates speak for them.[17]

In this case, we see, the meaning of the dependent variable of aliena-tion is clarified by the introduction of conditional relationships.

6. Conditional Relationships May Shed New Light on the Test Factor Categories

Not only may conditional relationships add to our understanding of the nature of the independent or dependent variables, but they may also enable one to learn more about the test factor itself. In the foregoing discussion, we have indicated how the stipulation of con-ditions enables one to increase one's understanding of the relationship between the independent and dependent variables. Here we suggest that the reverse is also true—that the examination of differential relationships can tell us something about the different conditions under which they hold.

For example, in a five-nation study of citizenship, the investigators examined the relationship between social class position and the belief that one would receive equal treatment before the law. The questions posed were the following: "Suppose there were some question that you had to take to a government office—for example, a tax question or housing regulation. Do you think you would be given equal treatment—I mean, would you be treated as well as anyone else?" "If you had some trouble with the police—a traffic violation maybe, or being accused of a minor offense—do you think that you would be given equal treatment? That is, would you be treated as well as anyone else?"[18]

As one would expect, there is a definite relationship between the individual's social position and his expectation of equal treatment. Lower-status people are less likely to expect equal treatment before the laws. But this is not *equally* true in all countries. In the English-speaking countries (as Tables 6–16 and 6–17 show), lower-class people are slightly less likely than higher-class people to expect equal treatment; in Germany, the difference is greater; and in Italy and Mexico, the differences are very great. In the two English-speaking countries, then, location in the stratification system has little effect on one's view of the impartiality of the law, whereas in the two Latin-speaking lands the effect is considerable. These findings shed light on the nature of the stratification systems in these countries and the degree to which their legal systems are seen to operate "without fear or favor." We do not learn more about the relationship between the independent and dependent variables (status and equal treatment), but we do learn more about the test factor (for example, how the United States differs from Italy).

Similarly, in a study of staff attitudes toward patients in a mental hospital,[19] it was found that staff members who worked on predominantly Negro wards in the hospital were somewhat more likely to maintain attitudes of "status distance" toward patients (the feeling that one should avoid intimate, equalitarian relations with patients) than staff members on predominantly white wards. Further analysis showed, however, that this relationship was quite striking among charge attendants in the wards but was nonexistent among nursing assistants (Table 6–18). (In total there was no difference in the status distance of both groups.) These results suggest that charge attendants were more sensitive or responsive to the race of the ward patients (and were probably more prejudiced) than nursing assistants.

Again, we do not learn a great deal more about the relationship between the racial composition of the ward and the status distance of the nursing staff, but we do learn more about the differences in attitudes of nursing assistants and charge attendants; the data suggest that the latter are more prejudiced against Negroes. The findings teach us something about the test factor categories.

Table 6-16

*Expectation of Treatment by Governmental Authorities and Police,
by Education in the United States, United Kingdom, and Germany
(in Per Cent)* *

Per Cent who Expect Equal Treatment	UNITED STATES			UNITED KINGDOM			GERMANY		
	Primary or Less	Some Secondary	Some University	Primary or Less	Some Secondary	Some University	Primary or Less	Some Secondary	Some University
. . . in government office	80	84	88	81	87	88	64	73	77
. . by police	81	87	89	88	90	96	70	81	88
Number	(338)	(443)	(188)	(593)	(321)	(24)	(788)	(123)	(26)

* Gabriel A. Almond and Sidney Verba, *The Civic Culture* (Princeton: Princeton University Press, 1963), p. 110, Table 4 (abridged). (Reprinted by permission of Princeton University Press.)

Table 6-17

*Expectation of Treatment by Governmental Authorities and Police,
by Education in Italy and Mexico (in Per Cent)* *

Percentage who Expect Equal Treatment	ITALY Education				MEXICO Education			
	None	Some Primary	Some Secondary	Some University	None	Some Primary	Some Secondary	Some University
. . . in government office	30	51	65	59	19	45	58	68
. . . by police	27	53	68	74	14	33	54	51
Number	(88)	(604)	(245)	(54)	(221)	(656)	(103)	(24)

* Gabriel A. Almond and Sidney Verba, *The Civic Culture* (Princeton: Princeton University Press, 1963), p. 112, Table 5 (abridged). (Reprinted by permission of Princeton University Press.)

Table 6–18

*Position of Nurses, the Racial Composition of Their Wards,
and Status Distance from Patients*[*]

| | ASSISTANTS | | | CHARGE ATTENDANTS | | |
Status Distance	P. N.[†] Wards	Mixed Wards	P. W.[‡] Wards	P. N.[†] Wards	Mixed Wards	P. W.[‡] Wards
High	49%	47%	48%	65%	53%	31%
Moderate	26	31	32	15	12	24
Low	25	22	20	20	35	45
Number	(97)	(133)	(209)	(34)	(34)	(58)

[*] Leonard I. Pearlin and Morris Rosenberg, "Nurse-Patient Social Distance and the Structural Context of a Mental Hospital," *American Sociological Review*, XXVII (February 1962), 59, Table 3. (Reprinted with permission of the American Sociological Association.)
[†] Predominantly Negro.
[‡] Predominantly White.

7. Conditional Relationships Make Descriptive Statements More Exact

Although it is not always possible to provide a single integrated interpretation which satisfactorily embraces the diverse partial associations, the simple descriptive fact of such conditional relationships may have important practical consequences. For example, a team of psychiatrists was interested in studying the effects of various medications on mental patients.[20] They thus brought together the data from all American, British, and Canadian studies on six antidepressant drugs published during the previous five years, pooling the results in a single summary report. The results appear in Table 6–19.

Attention is called to the fact that of the six antidepressants considered, Nialamide appears to be the least effective, showing the lowest mean rate of improvement. The psychiatric practitioner might thus be disposed to discard this drug as a candidate for use. But Table 6–20, revealing conditional relationships, would lead to a radically different conclusion (assuming an adequate number of cases were available). Among psychiatric depressions of recent onset, Nialamide is indeed strikingly lower in effectiveness than the other five

Table 6–19

Reported Improvement by Treatment Modality[*]

Treatment	No. of Studies	No. of Patients	Mean Per Cent Improvement
Imipramine	44	2178	64.7
Iproniazid	25	786	44.4
Phenelzine	21	919	49.0
Isocarboxazid	17	756	63.5
Nialamide	13	624	39.4
Amitriptyline	11	601	65.1
Total drugs	131	5864	56.7
Placebo	25	638	23.2
EST	9	211	72.0

[*] Henry Wechsler, George H. Grosser, and Milton Greenblatt, "Research Evaluating Antidepressant Medication on Hospitalized Mental Patients: A Survey of Published Reports During a Five-year Period," *Journal of Nervous and Mental Disease,* CXLI (August 1965), 232, Table 1 (abridged). (Reprinted with permission of The Williams and Wilkins Company.)

drugs; but among the chronic depressive, schizophrenic, and geriatric patients, it is the *most* effective of the six drugs.

One cannot, of course, "interpret" this relationship, since one does not know precisely how the medications exercise their psychic effects. But (assuming a more adequate sample) the practitioner is provided with a basis for avoiding the use of Nialamide with one type of diagnostic category but employing it with another.

Now let us consider the relevance of such descriptive results for

Table 6–20

Treatment Results by Type of Patient Sample[*]

	PRIMARILY DEPRESSIONS OF RECENT ONSET			PRIMARILY CHRONIC DEPRESSION, SCHIZOPHRENIA, AND GERIATRIC PATIENTS		
	No. of Studies	No. of Patients	Mean % Improvement	No. of Studies	No. of Patients	Mean % Improvement
Imipramine	35	1771	69.3	9	407	45.0
Iproniazid	16	479	59.7	9	307	20.5
Phenelzine	18	788	55.8	3	131	7.6
Isocarboxazid	16	676	66.0	1	80	42.5
Nialamide	12	595	39.0	1	29	48.3
Amitriptyline	10	582	66.2	1	19	31.6

[*] Henry Wechsler, George H. Grosser, and Milton Greenblatt, "Research Evaluating Antidepressant Medications on Hospitalized Mental Patients: A Survey of Published Reports During a Five-Year Period," *Journal of Nervous and Mental Disease,* CXLI (August 1965), 223, Table 2 (abridged). (Reprinted with permission of The Williams and Wilkins Company.)

sociological investigations. A major concern of sociology is the investigation of group norms—customs, folkways, mores, etc. In a complex society, subcultures are customarily the units of investigation, and the research aim is to discover such cultural differences. While the norms of a group may be viewed as culturally arbitrary, the student of comparative social systems is interested in learning how the norms of various subcultures differ. The specification of conditional relationships enables one to avoid misleading generalizations about the total culture when these generalizations hold differentially in various subcultures.

An illustration of differential generalizations applicable to different subcultures appears in a study of the relationship of mothers' work experience and students' post-high-school plans.[21] It turns out that if the mother worked before marriage, the student is more likely to plan to attend college. But, as Table 6–21 shows, this is true in the working-class subculture but not in the middle-class subculture. Such conditional relationships help to describe the differences between the two classes.

The same is true if one's test factor is a total society or culture. For example, Marie Osmond examined the hypothesis that the amount of female contribution to the economy would be associated with monogamy or polygyny in a society.[22] The relationship turned out to be conditional. "Type of marriage is significantly associated with female economic contribution only in the more rudimentary agricultural

Table 6–21

*Students' Post-High School Plans and Mother's Occupational Status Prior to Marriage, by Social Class**

| Student's Post-High School Plans | WORKING CLASS | | MIDDLE CLASS | |
	Mother Worked	Mother Did Not Work	Mother Worked	Mother Did Not Work
College	48%	35%	64%	65%
Technical school	28	33	19	22
No further education	24	32	17	14
Total per cent	100	100	100	100
Number	(191)	(196)	(179)	(88)

* Irving Krauss, "Sources of Educational Aspirations Among Working-Class Youth," *American Sociological Review*, XXIX (December 1964), 870, Table 3 (abridged). (Reprinted with permission of the American Sociological Association.)

economies (such as hoe agriculture or horticulture). Among these societies, monogamy is associated with minimal and polygyny with maximal female economic contribution."[23] The relationship does not appear in the more advanced societies.

In producing results more specific than those revealed in the original relationship, conditional relationships advance the scientific goal of prediction. If we know that a relationship is strong in Group A but weak in Group B, we can usually make a better prediction than if we simply know that the relationship is moderate for the combined sample. By combining both groups (that is, just treating the original relationship), we weaken the predictive power of the data.

Discussion

In a sense, all relationships may be considered conditional since it is always possible to stratify a relationship by a test factor and to examine the relationship in the different test factor categories. If one begins with a relationship between social class and anomia, for example, one may further examine this relationship among men and women; whites and Negroes; socially integrated and socially isolated people; authoritarian and democratic personality types; and so on. The total relationship is, in fact, a complex "sum" of all these contingent relationships.

Usually the relationships will be fairly similar in the various test factor categories. Then one will ordinarily interpret the test factor as an extraneous variable, component variable, intervening variable, etc. Often enough, however, the size, and even the direction, of the relationship will differ under varying circumstances. Such differential relationships are not "simple," but it is evident that they may have substantial theoretical relevance.

Where an interpretation succeeds in encompassing, or satisfactorily accommodating, divergent contingent associations simultaneously, we speak of *integrated* interpretations. At their best, these integrated interpretations not only have great elegance but also raise the original interpretation to a higher level of abstraction, thus generating broader, more comprehensive, or even new theories. In other cases, of course, one is obliged to apply *separate* interpretations to the several contingent associations. But whether one uses integrated or separate interpretations, one is able to make more exact or more refined statements about the nature of social life. To the extent that conditional relationships are fruitful in generating new insights, either with regard to the meaning of a relationship, the meaning of a variable, or the existence of unconsidered variables, they deserve the attention of the social investigator.

It is true that we often find something discomforting about conditional relationships, for they seem to violate our sense of order and parsimony. Admittedly, with the glittering model of physical science, with its universal laws, dangling invitingly before our eyes, it is much more tempting to search for universals. But, as noted, conditional relationships may show "inconsistent" findings in various groups which produce a consistent interpretation; indeed, they may strengthen rather than weaken the interpretation. In other cases, they may modify the interpretation or lead to a completely new theoretical formulation. Furthermore, in making interpretations more exact, affording a basis for selecting between alternative interpretations, showing noncorrelations to be theoretically meaningful, revealing trends and processes, purifying relationships, and clarifying the influence of test factors, conditional relationships deepen, enrich, and strengthen survey data analysis.

NOTES

1. Morris Rosenberg, "Self-Esteem and Concern with Public Affairs," *Public Opinion Quarterly*, XXVI (Summer 1962), 201–211.
2. To be sure, personality factors may influence level of political interest, but that is an issue for separate examination.

3. Richard F. Hamilton, "Income, Class, and Reference Groups," *American Sociological Review*, XXIX (August 1964), 576.
4. David O. Arnold and David Gold, "The Facilitation Effect of Social Environment," *Public Opinion Quarterly*, XXVIII (Fall 1964), 513–516.
5. *Ibid.*, p. 515.
6. Erdman B. Palmore and Phillip E. Hammond, "Interacting Factors in Juvenile Delinquency," *American Sociological Review*, XXIX (December 1964), 851.
7. Herbert H. Hyman, *Survey Design and Analysis* (Glencoe, Ill.: The Free Press, 1955), p. 298.
8. Bernard R. Berelson, Paul F. Lazarsfeld, and William N. McPhee, *Voting* (Chicago: University of Chicago Press, 1954), p. 196.
9. Morris Rosenberg, "Faith in People and Success-Orientation," in P. F. Lazarsfeld and M. Rosenberg, eds., *The Language of Social Research* (Glencoe, Ill.: The Free Press, 1955), pp. 158–161.
10. *Ibid.*, pp. 160–161. (Reprinted by permission of The Free Press.)
11. Cited in Hyman, *op. cit.*, pp. 306–307.
12. William H. Sewell, "Community of Residence and College Plans," *American Sociological Review*, XXIX (February 1964), 28.
13. Samuel A. Stouffer et al., *The American Soldier: Adjustment During Army Life* (Princeton, N.J.: Princeton University Press, 1949). (Cited in Hyman, *op. cit.*, p. 302.)
14. *Ibid.*, p. 249.
15. Leonard I. Pearlin, "Alienation from Work: A Study of Nursing Personnel," *American Sociological Review*, XXVII (June 1962), 314–326.
16. *Ibid.*, p. 317.
17. *Ibid.*, p. 318.
18. Gabriel A. Almond and Sidney Verba, *The Civic Culture* (Princeton, N.J.: Princeton University Press, 1963), p. 108.
19. Leonard I. Pearlin and Morris Rosenberg, "Nurse-Patient Social Distance and the Structural Context of a Mental Hospital," *American Sociological Review*, XXVII (February 1962), 56–65.
20. Henry Wechsler, George H. Grosser, and Milton Greenblatt, "Research Evaluating Antidepressant Medications on Hospitalized Mental Patients: A Survey of Published Reports During a Five-Year Period," *Journal of Nervous and Mental Diseases*, CXLI (August 1965), 231–239.
21. Irving Krauss, "Sources of Educational Aspirations Among Working-Class Youth," *American Sociological Review*, XXIX (December 1964), 867–879.
22. Marie W. Osmond, "Toward Monogamy: A Cross-Cultural Study of Correlates of Type of Marriage," *Social Forces*, XLIV (September 1965), 8–16.
23. *Ibid.*, p. 11.

CHAPTER 7

Conjoint
Influence

The basic procedure of survey analysis, we have seen, is to begin with a relationship between two variables. One then introduces a third variable into the analysis by stratifying on the test factor categories. This procedure helps to clarify the meaning of the two-variable relationship by showing how it is affected by test factors, and it specifies how this relationship varies under different conditions, that is, conditional relationships.

The survey analyst, however, may also wish to learn something else about the third variable. He may be interested in seeing how it and the independent variable separately or jointly determine the dependent variable. In this case the third variable is not a test factor in the usual sense but is rather seen as another independent variable.

An example may clarify the distinction. Assume that we find a relationship between race and liberalism, and we stratify this relationship by social class. Three general purposes might be served by introducing the third variable: (1) One purpose is to see if the relationship between race and liberalism is spurious, that is, whether the reason Negroes are more liberal is actually due to the fact that they are more likely to belong to the working class. If this were so, then class would be an extraneous variable. (2) A second purpose is to examine the relationship of race to liberalism under different conditions. Is this relationship stronger in the middle than in the working

class? Are the relationships in the same direction? (3) The third purpose is to ask: Do race and class each influence liberalism independently of one another? Which is the stronger determinant of liberalism—race or class? Do both factors jointly account for liberalism
better than either alone? Do certain special "types" of people—say,
middle-class Negroes—show an unusually high level of conservatism
or liberalism?

Certain distinctive statistical properties characterize the third variable under these circumstances. In the determination type of analysis,
we noted, the test factor is related both to the independent and dependent variables. In the present type of analysis—what we will call
the *conjoint influence* type of analysis—the third variable may or may
not be related to *either* the independent or the dependent variables.
Different statistical properties will characterize the different purposes
served by test factors.

Four types of conjoint influences may be distinguished: the independent effect; the relative effect; the cumulative effect; and the "typological" or "emergent" effect. Since each of these serves distinctive
purposes and has different interpretive or theoretical consequences,
they will be considered separately.

Independent Effects

When the third variable introduced into an analysis serves as an
independent variable, one is faced with two independent variables.
Assume that both of these variables are related to the dependent
variable. The first question one would ask is: is each of the variables
related to the dependent variable independently of the other? As a
consequence of the interaction of the independent variables, each may
separately be related to the dependent variable, but one may not be so
related when the other is held constant.

A study of voting behavior affords a pertinent illustration.[1] One
begins with a relationship between religion and voting behavior, and
one then introduces a test factor, socio-economic status. In the Erie

Table 7–1

*Religion and Political Affiliation, by Socio-Economic Status**

	SOCIO-ECONOMIC STATUS							
	A + B		C+		C−		D	
	Protes-tant	Catho-lic	Protes-tant	Catho-lic	Protes-tant	Catho-lic	Protes-tant	Catho-lic
Democrats	24%	71%	34%	75%	46%	77%	57%	86%
Republicans	76	29	66	25	54	23	43	14
Total per cent	100	100	100	100	100	100	100	100
Number	(269)	(42)	(413)	(134)	(386)	(113)	(217)	(76)

* Paul F. Lazarsfeld, Bernard Berelson, and Hazel Gaudet, *The People's Choice* (New York: Columbia University Press, 1948), p. 22, Chart 6 (adapted). (Reprinted with permission of the Columbia University Press.)

County study, it is found that both social class and religion are strongly related to voting behavior. But is each related when the other is held constant? Table 7–1 shows that they are. Within socio-economic status groups, it will be noted, Catholics are more likely to be Democrats than Protestants (71 to 24 per cent, 75 to 34 per cent, 77 to 46 per cent, and 86 to 57 per cent). Conversely, within each *religious* group, *class* is associated with vote. Among Protestants, the proportion voting Democratic, as one descends the SES scale, is 24, 34, 46, and 57 per cent; among Catholics, the corresponding figures are 71, 75, 77, and 86 per cent. We thus see that each variable exercises an influence independent of the other.

That the demonstration of independent effects may have important theoretical implications is shown in Blau's ingenious analysis of "structural effects."[2] The question posed was: Does the attitude of a group exercise an influence on behavior, independent of the individual attitudes that constitute it? Let us see how he deals with this intriguing question.

Blau's study dealt with the attitudes of caseworkers in a social agency toward their clients. Caseworkers were organized into units of five or six under a supervisor. Caseworkers who felt that public assistance to their clients should be increased were characterized as "positive" in their client orientation. If most of the *group* members favored such an increase, then the group was characterized as "positive." One can thus characterize a group as positive (the structural effect) and an individual as positive (the individual effect).

The dependent variable to be explained was "casework service" orientation. Some caseworkers were chiefly concerned with the formal tasks of their jobs, such as checking eligibility, whereas others were more involved in their social work tasks, that is, providing casework service. The latter were considered to have a "casework service" orientation. The question is: Are caseworkers who are "positive" in their attitudes toward clients more likely to have a "casework service" orientation? More important, are positive *groups* more likely to have this orientation *independent* of the caseworkers' attitudes?

Table 7–2 shows that each independent variable is associated with the dependent variable, independently of the other. Within similar groups, caseworkers who feel clients should receive additional assistance are more likely to have a casework service orientation. More interesting, however, is that *even among individuals holding the same views,* those in *groups* dominated by the attitude that clients should receive additional assistance are more likely to stress casework service than those in other *groups.* This is shown by the fact that among *equally positive (or not positive) individuals,* those in positive *groups* are more likely to have a "casework service" orientation (60 to 44 per cent and 44 to 27 per cent). This is especially interesting in view of the fact that the characterization of the *group* as positive is based exclusively on the responses of the *individuals.* Blau thus shows that the structural variable has an *impact separate from the individual variable, even when they are based upon responses to the same questions.*

We deal here with a crucial theoretical problem, for it bears upon

Table 7–2

*Effects of Value Orientation Toward Clients**

| | Group's Prevailing Value Orientation Toward Clients | | | |
| | POSITIVE Individual's Orientation | | NOT POSITIVE Individual's Orientation | |
	Positive	Not positive	Positive	Not positive
"Casework service" orientation	60	44	44	37

* Peter M. Blau, "Structural Effects," *American Sociological Review,* XXV (April 1960), 181, Table 1 (abridged). (Reprinted with permission of the American Sociological Association.)

a fundamental dictum propounded by Durkheim in his *Rules of the Sociological Method,* namely, that social facts are external to the individual. Referring to Durkheim's *Suicide,* Blau notes: "After admitting, notwithstanding his social realism, that 'social consciousness' exists only in individual minds, he states that the social force it exerts, nevertheless is *'external to each average individual taken singly.'* "[3] Blau's data provide striking confirmation of this seminal insight.

The issue of whether the determinant variables exercise an influence independent of one another is of conspicuous importance when the independent variables are strongly related. In many cases these variables may appear to reflect much the same thing. In ordinary social research, one encounters many pairs of overlapping variables: education and intellectual sophistication, social class and social class identification, age and feeling old, etc. Since each independent variable also reflects the other to some extent, the task is to disentangle their influence.

Consider the following two findings from a study of occupational choices of college students:[4] (1) Students whose fathers had high incomes were more likely than those of low income families to choose business and the free professions. (2) Students who identified with the upper social class were more likely than those identifying with lower classes to choose business and the free professions.

Father's income stands for the student's class *membership group,* and his class identification reflects his *reference group.* These are obviously closely related variables and the effect of one clearly implicates the other. Two questions are directly generated: Is the effect of father's income due to class identification? If so, then a reference group explanation is supported. Second, is the effect of class identification due to father's income? If so, then the membership group factor would appear to be decisive. The obvious procedure is to examine the effect of each, controlling on the other.

Table 7–3 shows the relationship of income to occupational choice, controlling on class identification, and Table 7–4 shows the relationship of class identification to occupational choice, controlling on income.

Table 7–3 shows that, with the exception of working-class students

Table 7-3

Father's Income and Occupational Choice, by Class Identification*

	Class identification																	
	UPPER CLASS						MIDDLE CLASS						WORKING CLASS					
	Father's Income (in Thousands of Dollars)																	
Occupational Choice	5	5-7.5	7.5-10	10-20	20-30	30+	5	5-7.5	7.5-10	10-20	20-30	30+	5	5-7.5	7.5-10	10-20	20-30	30+
Business, free pro-fessions	—	38	53	63	69	71	42	41	53	56	67	71	32	38	37	—	—	—
Number	(9)	(21)	(30)	(81)	(67)	(87)	(419)	(421)	(273)	(252)	(68)	(47)	(412)	(69)	(16)	(—)	(—)	(—)

*Morris Rosenberg, *Occupations and Values* (Glencoe, Ill.: The Free Press, 1957), p. 56, Table 32 (abridged and adapted). (Reprinted with permission of The Macmillan Company. Copyright 1957 by The Free Press, A Corporation.)

Table 7-4

Class Identification and Occupational Choice, by Father's Income*

	FATHER'S INCOME (DOLLARS)																	
	Under 5,000			5,000-7,500			7,500-10,000			10,000-20,000			20,000-30,000			Over 30,000		
	CLASS IDENTIFICATION																	
Occupational Choice	Upper	Middle	Low	Upper	Middle	Low	Upper	Middle	Low	Upper	Middle	Low	Upper	Middle	Low	Upper	Middle	Low
Business, free pro-fessions	—	42	32	38	41	38	53	53	37	63	56	—	69	67	—	71	71	—
Number	(9)	(419)	(412)	(21)	(421)	(69)	(30)	(273)	(16)	(81)	(252)	(—)	(67)	(68)	(—)	(87)	(47)	(—)

*Morris Rosenberg, *Occupations and Values* (Glencoe, Ill.: The Free Press, 1957), p. 56, Table 32 (abridged). (Reprinted with permission of The Macmillan Company. Copyright 1957 by The Free Press, A Corporation.)

(where the number of cases in the well-to-do categories is too small for analysis), there is a strong relationship between father's income and occupational choice; almost without exception, the higher the income, the greater the choice of business and the free professions. At the extremes, the difference in the upper class is 33 per cent and in the middle class, 29 per cent.

Table 7–4, on the other hand, shows that the relationship between class identification and occupational choice is weak when father's income is controlled. In only one of the six partial associations is there a substantial difference at the extremes (16 per cent). (For the total sample, on the other hand, upper-class people are 32 per cent more likely than working-class people to choose business and the free professions.)

The point is, then, that if one has two independent variables which are intertwined and mutually contaminating, one may be interested in unraveling their effects. Among people with the same class identification, income importantly influences occupational choice; but among people with similar incomes, class identification seems to have only a minor bearing on occupational choice. In light of the recent emphasis in social psychology on the power of reference groups as determinants of attitudes, this result may come as a surprise. It suggests that one must first determine which attitudes are *relevant* for the reference group rather than automatically assuming that reference group identification will have certain attitudinal consequences.

Another case of contaminated variables whose separate influence is to be assessed is the following: In his study of "structural effects," as we noted earlier, Blau[5] had found that if one examined the attitudinal composition of the *group,* one was able to predict the behavior of the individual. In another study, Simpson[6] had found that if one knew the attitudes of the individual's *friends,* one could also make such a prediction. But obviously these two influences—the structural (group) and the interpersonal (friends)—are likely to be closely related. The attitudes of the group and the attitudes of one's friends in the group will often be the same. In apparently demonstrating the influence of one, one may actually be demonstrating the influence of the other.

Campbell and Alexander[7] sought to examine this issue with regard to high school students' college plans. Using the social status of the *school* as an indicator of a "structural effect," they found that this independent variable was positively related to college plans (Table 7–5, Column 1). (This is true at each level of parental education.) Using the social status of one's *two best friends* as an indicator of interpersonal influence, they also found that this second independent variable was positively related to college plans (Column 2). Both independent variables, then, were related to college plans. These independent variables, furthermore, were strongly related to one another (Column 3). The main question, then, was: What is the relationship of school status to college plans when friends' status is controlled, and what is the relationship of the friends' status to college plans when school status is controlled?

The results appear in Columns 4 and 5. When the relationship between school status and college plans is examined, holding friends' status constant, the relationship virtually disappears (Column 4). On the other hand, when the association between friends' status and college plans is examined, holding school status constant, the relationship remains strong (Column 5). In other words, the reason school

Table 7–5

*Correlations Among School Status, Friends' Status, and College Plans of High School Seniors, by Parental Educational Level**

| Parental Educational Level | ZERO-ORDER CORRELATIONS | | | PARTIAL CORRELATIONS | | |
| | School Status with College Plans | Friends' Status with College Plans | School Status with Friends' Status | | | Number |
	(1)	(2)	(3)	(4)†	(5)‡	(6)
Both parents college	0.10	0.15	0.49	0.03	0.12	172
One parent college	0.16	0.29	0.36	0.06	0.26	183
Both parents high school graduates	0.15	0.28	0.50	0.01	0.24	147
One parent high school graduate	0.07	0.19	0.34	0.01	0.18	178
Neither parent high school graduate	0.14	0.31	0.40	0.02	0.28	295

* Ernest Q. Campbell and C. Norman Alexander, "Structural Effects and Interpersonal Relationships," *American Journal of Sociology*, LXXI (November, 1965), 286, Table 1. (Reprinted with permission of the University of Chicago Press.)
† School status with college plans, holding friends' status constant.
‡ Friends' status with college plans, holding school status constant.

status is associated with college plans is that the individual's immediate friends within the school tend to be of that status. On the other hand, the relationship of friends' status to the individual's occupational plans is not due to the fact that they are found in a school in which their status predominates.

Campbell and Alexander conclude:

Given knowledge of an individual's immediate interpersonal influences, the characteristics of the total collectivity provide no additional contribution to the prediction of his behaviors in these data. Thus we have no indication that an important structural effect exists independently of interpersonal influences. So little additional variation is explained by school status that we could easily regard the remainder as due to our inability to involve in the analysis *all* of the relevant interpersonal influences (e.g., the individual's additional friends of the same sex, his friends of the opposite sex, his "ideal" referents in the system, etc.).[8]

The theoretical relevance of independent effects is thus apparent. It enables one to deal with such questions as: Does a structural variable have an effect independent of the individual responses which constitute it? In occupational decisions, do objective economic factors and reference group factors exercise an influence independent of one another and, if not, which is the effective variable? If structural variables and interpersonal variables have an effect on college plans, is only one of these the truly effective variable, and, if so, which one? In many cases, the decisive answers to important theoretical questions can be derived only from the examination of independent effects.

A digression on format

In this last example, the method of control has been partial correlation. In most cases of survey analysis, however, subgroup classification is the method employed. If each variable has very few categories, there is usually little difficulty in determining by inspection —by simply reading across the table and examining comparable categories—whether each independent variable is related to the dependent variable, independently of the other. When one deals with variables possessing a large number of categories, however, it sometimes becomes difficult to tell by inspection whether each variable is associated independently of the other. There is a certain confusion involved as one must select out comparable categories across the page.

A simplifying format commonly employed enables one to examine one independent variable on the horizontal axis and the other on the vertical axis, with each cell consisting of the "per cent positive" on the dependent variable.

Consider the following illustration from a study of "happiness."[9] On the basis of responses to a series of items, the investigators classified their respondents as high, medium, or low on "positive feelings" and high, medium, or low on "negative feelings." People who were high on positive feelings were more likely to describe themselves as "very happy" and the same was true of those who were low on negative feelings. Since one would assume that positive and negative feelings overlapped—that a strong inverse relationship existed between the two—one might wish to examine the influence of each independently of the other.

Table 7–6 presents the data using the usual format. In order to examine the impact of positive feelings independently of negative feelings, one's eye must move back and forth across the page, picking up the comparable categories (comparing all the lows, all the mediums, all the highs). However, the same data can be presented by setting one of the variables on the vertical axis and the other on the horizontal axis, with the proportions in each cell representing the per cent "very happy." This is shown in Table 7–7.

As one reads across the table, one sees that positive feelings are

Table 7–6

Positive and Negative Feelings and "Happiness"*

	Positive Feelings								
	HIGH			MEDIUM			LOW		
	Negative Feelings								
	Low	Medium	High	Low	Medium	High	Low	Medium	High
Per cent "very happy"	47	33	24	34	24	13	22	24	8

* Norman M. Bradburn and David Caplovitz, *Reports on Happiness* (Chicago: Aldine Press, 1965), p. 20, Table 2–9 (abridged and adapted). (Reprinted with permission of the National Opinion Research Center and the Aldine Publishing Company.)

Table 7–7

Positive and Negative Feelings and "Happiness" [*]

| | (Cell Figures Are Per Cent "Very Happy") | | |
| | POSITIVE FEELINGS | | |
Negative Feelings	High	Medium	Low
Low	47	34	22
Medium	33	24	24
High	24	13	8

[*] Norman M. Bradburn and David Caplovitz, *Reports on Happiness* (Chicago: Aldine Press, 1965), p. 20, Table 2–9 (abridged and adapted). (Reprinted with permission of the National Opinion Research Center and the Aldine Publishing Company.)

related to happiness independently of negative feelings. As one reads down the table, one sees that negative feelings are related to happiness independently of positive feelings. Indeed, it was one of the most fruitful findings of the study to learn that these two types of feelings had effects independent of one another. This format has the merit of enabling one to see the independent effects much more easily.

This format can only be used, of course, when one is able to dichotomize the dependent variable. Where dichotomization leads to the concealment of essential data, then the more cumbersome usual format must be used. This simplified format may also be used for some of the other types of conjoint effects to be described. We shall, however, continue to use the traditional format, since most examples in the literature are presented in this way.

Relative Effects

Assuming that each independent variable has an effect on the dependent variable separate from the other, one is naturally disposed to ask the further question: Which has the greater effect?[10]

For example, the authors of *The American Soldier* found that unmarried soldiers had higher morale (were in "good spirits") than married soldiers, and that men who had been in the service a shorter

Table 7–8

Attitudes Reflecting Adjustment, as Related to Army Experience,
by Marital Condition—May 1945*
(Overseas Noncommissioned Officers)

| Combat Troops— | Years in Army | | | |
| | 3 OR MORE | | 2–3 | |
All but Air Force	Married	Unmarried	Married	Unmarried
Per cent in "good spirits"	22	27	33	38

* Samuel A. Stouffer et al., *The American Soldier: Adjustment During Army Life* (Princeton: Princeton University Press, 1949), p. 111, Chart I (abridged and adapted). (Reprinted by permission of Princeton University Press.)

time had higher morale than the old-timers.[11] Table 7–8 shows that each independent variable is related to morale, independently of the other.

But which experience—marital status or longevity—is *more strongly* related to the dependent variable? This question can be answered by comparing the unmarried men who have been in the Army longer with the married men who have been in service less time. Thirty-three per cent of the latter, but 27 per cent of the former, were in "good spirits," suggesting that longevity is the more important variable. If you are in the Army a shorter time, even though married, your spirits are higher than if you are in the Army longer, even though unmarried.

Many important theoretical issues may be met through the examination of relative effects. In particular cases, one might be able to say whether a psychological or a demographic variable is more important in producing a certain result, whether a structural influence is stronger than an interpersonal influence, which of two psychological variables (or two demographic variables) is the more powerful, etc.

One type of analysis, representing a common concern of sociological research, involves the comparison of the relative effects of two *demographic* variables. For example, Lenski[12] found that both religion and "old family" were associated with voting behavior. Protestants were more likely than Catholics to vote Republican, and third or higher generation Americans were more likely than first or second generation Americans to vote Republican. But which is the more important determinant of vote—religion or generation? The

Table 7–9

Percentage of Working Class Whites Expressing a Party Preference Who Identify as Republicans, by Religious Group, and Immigrant Generation (Non-Southern-Born Only) *

	Working-Class Whites			
	PROTESTANTS		CATHOLICS	
	Third or Higher Generation	First or Second Generation	Third or Higher Generation	First or Second Generation
Per cent Republican	41	32	21	10

* Gerhard Lenski, *The Religious Factor* (Garden City, N.Y.: Doubleday and Company, Inc., 1961), p. 164, Table 27 (abridged and adapted). (Copyright 1961 by Gerhard Lenski. Reprinted by permission of Doubleday and Company, Inc.)

answer is that religion appears to have a greater effect than generation, for first or second generation Protestants are more likely to vote Republican than third or higher generation Catholics (32 per cent compared with 21 per cent).

The comparison of the relative effects of demographic variables will often have great substantive interest. Which is a more important determinant of voting—education or income? Which variable is the more powerful determinant of alienation—class or race? Does religion or class have the greater influence on political orientation? Is race or class the stronger determinant of delinquency? Similar questions may easily be directed to any body of data.

In other cases the survey analyst may be interested in comparing the relative effects of two *psychological* variables. In a population study in Peru,[13] it was found that those people who felt that another child would be a *danger to health* were likely to want no more children, and those who felt that another child would be an *economic burden* also tended to want no additional offspring. But which was the stronger deterrent to family increase among the Peruvians—the health danger or the economic burden? Apparently the economic burden was somewhat more influential. Among those who were *not* worried about a health danger but *were* concerned about an economic burden, 73 per cent wanted no more children; among those worried about health, but not about money, the proportion was 64 per cent (Table 7–10).

Table 7–10

*Per Cent Who Want No More Children, by Opinion About Impact of
an Additional Child on Health and Economic Situation, Lima**

	HEALTH WOULD BE HARMED		HEALTH WOULD NOT BE HARMED	
	Economic Situation Harmed	Economic Situation Not Harmed	Economic Situation Harmed	Economic Situation Not Harmed
Want no more children	90	64	73	48

* J. Mayone Stycos, "Social Class and Preferred Family Size in Peru," *American Journal of Sociology*, LXX (May 1965), 654, Table 4 (adapted). (Reprinted with permission of the University of Chicago Press.)

Questions involving the relative effects of psychological variables spring readily to mind. Which is the more important determinant of occupational choice—one's occupational values or one's self-perceptions? Which is the more important determinant of vote—image of the candidate or political ideology? Which has the greater effect on delinquency—attitudes toward society or attitudes toward oneself? The value of investigating such questions is apparent.

Just as it is interesting to compare the relative effects of demographic variables and of psychological variables, so it is often useful to compare the effects of interpersonal influences. A clear case in point involves an issue of considerable importance today, namely, the relative effects of peer and parental influences. Indeed, one of the problems frequently discussed is that adolescents are more likely to conform to the norms of their peers than the prescriptions of their parents. For example, Rosen[14] asked a small sample of Jewish adolescents about the observance of religious rituals in the home. "When you get married are you going to use kosher meat in your home?" and "Is kosher meat now used in your home?" Information of intended observance of religious practices was also obtained about peers. The results in Table 7–11 show that both peer influences and parental influences play roles independent of one another. But among adolescents with observant parents but nonobservant friends, 38 per cent plan to follow the practice of using kosher meat; among those with nonobservant parents but observant friends, 75 per cent intend to observe the ritual. In this case, the influence of friends seems to be

Table 7-11

*Peer Group Attitude by Adolescent's Attitude When Parental
Attitude Is Controlled**

Adolescent Attitude	Observant Parents		Nonobservant Parents	
	PEER GROUP ATTITUDE			
	Observant	Nonobservant	Observant	Nonobservant
Observant	83%	38%	75%	12%
Nonobservant	17	62	25	88
Total per cent	100	100	100	100
Number	(12)	(13)	(8)	(17)

* Bernard C. Rosen, "Conflicting Group Membership: A Study of Parent-Peer Group Cross-Pressures," *American Sociological Review*, XX (April 1955), 158, Table 2. (Reprinted with permission of the American Sociological Association.)

much greater than that of parents in influencing conformity to religious group norms.

Many similar comparisons are possible. Who is more influential in determining an adolescent's attitudes—his father or his mother, his teacher or his friends, his siblings or his friends, boy friends or girl friends, etc. One might also compare the relative influence of interpersonal and impersonal communications: for example, are the mass media or interpersonal influences stronger in determining political orientation?

It is also possible to compare the effects of two *global* structural variables. By a global variable we refer to a classification which is not based on the cumulation of properties of individuals, but which in a sense defines their environment. For example, Breton[15] was interested in the "institutional completeness" of ethnic communities and the personal relations of immigrants. Some ethnic communities contain a number of formal organizations—"religious, educational, political, recreational, national, and even professional. Some have organized welfare and mutual aid societies . . . it may have its own churches and sometimes its own schools."[16] Two questions arise: (1) is the presence of these formal organizations in the community associated with a greater tendency among the ethnic group members to associate with other ethnic group members; and (2) is the presence of one type of organization more closely associated with intra-ethnic associations than another type of organization?

The two types of organization considered were (1) the number of churches in the community, and (2) the number of welfare organizations in the area. Neither independent variable, it may be noted, is based on characteristics of the individual; they are general properties of the community.

Breton found that if there was a relatively large number of churches in the community, then there was a higher proportion whose interpersonal relations were centered in the ethnic group, and the same was true if welfare organizations appeared in the community (Table 7–12). But which factor bore the stronger relationship to the dependent variable? The answer is that presence of churches was more important than presence of welfare organizations. If there were many churches but no welfare organizations, 75 per cent of the respondents had the majority of their relations within their ethnic groups, whereas if there were few churches and some welfare organizations, the proportion was only 54 per cent.

Many other uses of relative effects could be made. Research may involve variables at the same or different levels of analysis, and a comparison of their relative effects may often give rise to extremely interesting interpretations. Of course, such interpretations are not always as simple as we have implied, but they enable us to get at the question of which factors are more important in accounting for dependent variables and, in the process, to deal with significant theoretical issues.

Computing relative effects

In the examples cited above, we have confined our discussion to dichotomous independent variables. The procedure has been to compare the proportions in the two "counter-directional" groups (groups "high" on one variable and "low" on the other). The larger proportion indicates the more powerful variable.[17]

When one compares two counter-directional categories, one is actually *comparing the average percentage difference of each variable controlled on the other.* Consider the earlier example (Table 7–11) comparing the relative power of parental and peer influence on religious observance. If the parents were nonobservant and the peers

Table 7–12

Churches, Welfare Organizations, and Extent of In-Group Relations[*]

	Number of Churches in Community			
	2 OR LESS		3 OR MORE	
	Welfare Organizations			
	None	Some	None	Some
Percentage of individuals with majority of relations within ethnic group	26	54	75	95

[*] Raymond Breton, "Institutional Completeness of Ethnic Communities and the Personal Relations of Immigrants," *American Journal of Sociology*, LXX (September 1964), 200, Table 5 (abridged). (Reprinted with permission of the University of Chicago Press.)

observant, then 75 per cent of the adolescents were observant, whereas if the parents were observant and the peers were not, then only 38 per cent of the adolescents were observant. The influence of peers is thus greater than that of parents by a margin of 37 per cent.

Now let us make the same comparison, using average percentage differences. The average effect of parental observance, controlling on peer group attitudes, is 17 per cent ($83 - 75 = 8$; $38 - 12 = 26$; average of $8 + 26$ is 17). Conversely, the average effect of peer influence, controlling on parental attitudes, is 54 per cent ($83 - 38 = 45$; $75 - 12 = 63$; average of $45 + 63$ is 54). The effect of peer influence independent of parental influence is thus much greater than the effect of parental influence independent of peer influence, namely, 54 per cent to 17 per cent. In fact, the difference between these average differences is 37 per cent ($54 - 17$) *which is precisely the difference which appeared when we compared the two counter-directional categories.* Counter-directional comparisons, then, actually reflect the average percentage differences of each variable when controlled on the other. The results are identical using either average percentage differences or counter-directional categories, although inspection of the counter-directional categories is obviously simpler;[18] we have therefore used this method exclusively in our discussion of relative effects.

The comparison of counter-directional categories is satisfactory if both independent variables are dichotomized, but becomes difficult if either variable has more than two categories. In such a case, one is obliged to use average percentage differences.

Consider the case in which one compares the relative effect of an individual characteristic and a demographic characteristic. In the aforementioned study of "happiness,"[19] Bradburn finds that people who participate socially have higher "positive feelings," and that higher SES groups also have higher "positive feelings." The participation index has four categories, ranging from a high score of 3 to a low score of 0. The SES variable is dichotomized. The results appear in Table 7–13 (using the format discussed earlier).

The effect of SES, controlling on participation, is 11 per cent (the average of the difference between 49 and 33, 37 and 31, 32 and 24, and 32 and 18). The effect of participation, controlling on SES, is 16 per cent (the average of the difference between 49 and 32, and 33 and 18). Participation thus appears to be somewhat more closely related to positive feelings when SES is controlled than the other way around.

Using percentage differences as a measure of effect, however, gives the variable with the larger number of categories an "unfair advantage." Assuming that the relationship between an independent and a dependent variable is linear, it follows that the larger the number of categories, the greater the percentage differences at the extremes. Thus, the percentage difference between score 3 and score 0 on the participation index is quite large, even though the difference between any two contiguous categories may not be so great. The more one "stretches" a linear variable, the greater is the percentage difference between the highest and lowest groups.

The importance of this factor is shown if we reduce the four participation categories to two (Table 7–14). Since participation and

Table 7–13

Participation, Socio-Economic Status, and Positive Feelings*

SES	PARTICIPATION INDEX			
	High			Low
	3	2	1	0
	(Per cent "Positive Feelings")			
High	49	37	32	32
Low	33	31	24	18

* Norman M. Bradburn and David Caplovitz, *Reports on Happiness* (Chicago: Aldine Press, 1965), p. 44, Table 2–23h (adapted). (Reprinted with permission of the National Opinion Research Center and the Aldine Publishing Company).

Table 7–14

Participation, Socio-Economic Status, and Positive Feelings

	PARTICIPATION INDEX			
	High 2–3		Low 0–1	
	High SES	Low SES	High SES	Low SES
Per cent "positive feelings"	44	32	32	21

* Norman M. Bradburn and David Caplovitz, *Reports on Happiness* (Chicago: Aldine Press, 1965), p. 44, Table 2–23h. (adapted). Reprinted with permission of the National Opinion Research Center and the Aldine Publishing Company.)

SES are both dichotomized, one can assess their relative effects by comparing the counter-directional categories. These are both 32 per cent, suggesting that the effects of participation and SES are equal. One thus obtains different results if a different number of categories is used. If a larger number of SES categories had been used, then *its* effect might have been greater.

This problem is solved if both independent variables have an equal number of categories—both dichotomous, both trichotomous, both with four categories each, etc. This can be accomplished either by collapsing categories, in order to make the number in each variable equal, or by starting with an equal number of categories.

There are two further problems which, while not unique to the study of relative effects, are especially prominent in this connection. These are the issues of the cutting points of the variables and the adequacy of the indicators.

Consider first the issue of cutting points. Assume that we characterized students with A or B averages as good students and those with C or D averages as poor students. We found that good students who were poor athletes were less popular than poor students who were good athletes, suggesting that athletic ability contributed more to popularity than academic success. But let us say that we had decided that only A students were good students. It might be that these people, though poor athletes, were more popular than poor students who were good athletes. One might then be led to conclude that academic performance was more important than athletic ability. In some sense, then, the cutting points of the two variables must be comparable; if the athletic ability cutting point differentiates *outstanding* athletes (varsity members) from all others, then the academic cutting point should differentiate *outstanding* scholars (A students) from all others. These cutting points should, for example, differentiate approximately equal proportions of the population. Since, however, it is often difficult to find comparable cutting points, this method of relative effect must be used with caution.

The second problem revolves about the relationship between the indicator and the concept. In drawing conclusions from data analysis, we are interested in being able to state that one conceptual variable is more effective than another conceptual variable, not that one indicator is more influential than another. Assume we had reason to believe that both social class and religious conviction were associated with criminal behavior and that we wished to know which was the more effective influence. We might use the Hollingshead socio-economic index[20] as a measure of social class and church attendance as a measure of religiosity. If we found that higher-class church abstainers had lower criminality records than lower-class church attenders, we might conclude that class was more important than religiosity as a determinant of criminal behavior. But, in fact, it might not be that religiosity is less important than class but that church attendance is a less satisfactory indicator of religiosity than the Hollingshead scale is of class. If one had a deep probing of the religious area, including views of God, ethical principles, religious rituals and traditions, etc., then this measure of religiosity might be more powerfully related to criminal behavior than social class.

The problems of cutting points and of adequate indicators exist with regard to all the types of analysis cited above, but they are particularly acute when it comes to evaluating the relative influence of two independent variables upon a dependent variable. Assuming that we are interested in evaluating concepts, rather than the indicators which represent them (that is, rejecting "operational definitions"), we are in serious danger of being misled in our conclusions. If, however, the indicators are equally adequate to the concepts, if the cutting points are comparable, and if the independent variables have the same number of categories, then the information to be derived from analyses of relative effects is often highly enlightening.

Cumulative Impact

If one question is to ask which of two independent variables is the stronger, a second question would be: How strong is their combined effect? If X and Y (independent variables) are each related to Z (dependent variable), then X and Y combined may be even more strongly related to Z than either alone. Of course, the combined effect is not simply additive. Several factors are involved, the most important of which is the size of the relationship between X and Y.

Investigation of the cumulative impact is of particular value for purposes of prediction. If one wishes to understand what factors are responsible for the dependent variable—technically, if one wishes to explain more and more of the variance—then one must consider whether several independent variables, considered simultaneously, have a stronger relationship to the dependent variable than any single one considered separately.

While more powerful statistics can be used in the treatment of quantitative variables, we will confine our discussion to percentage differences, which are suitable for both quantitative and qualitative variables. The cumulative impact of variables can then best be seen by comparing the extreme consistent groups.

Consider the example cited earlier dealing with the effects of parental and peer influence on religious observance among adolescents.[21] The findings show that if parents are observant, then 60 per cent of their children are observant; if parents are not observant, only 32 per cent of the children are. Similarly, if peers are observant, then 80 per cent of the adolescents are also observant; if the peers are not observant, then only 23 per cent of the adolescents are.

Thus, both peer and parental influence are strongly associated with the adolescent's religious beliefs. But what if *both* the parents and peers are in agreement on the issue? Does this produce an effect greater than either considered individually? Table 7–15 shows that it does. If both membership groups are observant, then 83 per cent of

Table 7–15

*Relationship Between Adolescents' and Membership Groups' Attitude
When Membership Groups' Attitude Is Homogeneous**

Adolescent Attitude	PARENT AND PEER GROUP ARE OBSERVANT Per Cent	PARENT AND PEER GROUP ARE NONOBSERVANT Per Cent
Observant	83	12
Nonobservant	17	88
Number	($\overline{12}$)	($\overline{17}$)

* Bernard C. Rosen, "Conflicting Group Membership: A Study of Parent-Peer Group Cross-Pressures," *American Sociological Review*, XX (April 1955), 158, Table 3 (abridged). (Reprinted with permission of the American Sociological Association.)

the adolescents are observant; if both groups are nonobservant, then only 12 per cent are observant. Comparison of the unidirectional categories—the extreme "consistent" groups—shows that both variables have a cumulative impact on the adolescent's religious orientation. This cumulative impact is considerably greater than the impact of either independent variable considered alone.

Just as in the case of relative effects, one can examine variables at the same or different levels of analysis. Consider an example of the cumulative impact of three independent variables—two demographic characteristics (sex and race) and a behavior characteristic (church attendance)—upon attitudes of sexual permissiveness. Reiss finds that permissiveness is higher among males than females, among Negroes than whites, and among non-church attenders than church attenders.[22] The cumulative effect is particularly strong. Only 5 per cent of female white church attenders express sexually permissive attitudes, compared

Table 7–16

*Church Attendance and Permissiveness in the Student Sample,
by Race and Sex**

	MALE				FEMALE			
	Negro		White		Negro		White	
	CHURCH ATTENDANCE							
	Low	High	Low	High	Low	High	Low	High
Per cent highly permissive	91	83	77	40	58	44	53	5

* Ira L. Reiss, "Premarital Sexual Permissiveness Among Negroes and Whites," *American Sociological Review*, XXIX (October 1964), 693, Table 4 (abridged and adapted). (Reprinted with permission of the American Sociological Association.)

with fully 91 per cent of male Negro non-church attenders (Table 7–16).

One might also wish to examine the cumulative impact of a structural and a demographic variable. The structural variable is the respondent's friendship environment (the political attitudes held by his three closest friends); the demographic variable is religion. The dependent variable is vote.

Table 7–17 shows that both friendship environment and religion are related to vote independently of one another. Their cumulative impact appears most striking in comparisons of the extreme unidirectional groups—the Protestants with all Republican friends and the Catholics with all Democratic friends. Over 9 out of 10 of the former, but only 1 out of 10 of the latter, vote Republican. When both variables exercise their effect in a consistent direction, their predictive power may be very strong indeed.

Sociologists tend to focus their interest on the effects of objective demographic variables, whereas psychologists tend to center their attention upon the effects of subjective factors. When both factors are considered in conjunction, they may permit predictions superior to either considered individually.

It is known, for example, that people with a conservative political ideology are more likely to vote Republican and that Protestants are more likely to vote Republican. But among conservative Protestants, 98 per cent vote Republican, whereas among liberal Democrats, only 17 per cent do so (Table 7–18). This difference substantially exceeds that of either variable considered alone.

Table 7–17

*Religion and Republican Vote, by Political Affiliation of Three Friends**

| | Political Affiliation of Three Friends | | | | | | | |
| | RRR | | RRD | | RDD | | DDD | |
	Protes-tant	Cath-olic	Protes-tant	Cath-olic	Protes-tant	Cath-olic	Protes-tant	Cath-olic
Per cent Republican of two-party vote	93	62	85	42	57	36	21	10

* Bernard R. Berelson, Paul F. Lazarsfeld, and William N. McPhee, *Voting* (Chicago: University of Chicago Press, 1954), p. 101, Chart XLV (abridged and adapted). (Reprinted with permission of the University of Chicago Press.)

Table 7–18

*Religious Affiliation Is as Strong an Influence upon
Vote as "Liberalism-Conservatism"* *

| | "CONSERVATIVE" | | "MIDDLE OF ROAD" | | "LIBERAL" | |
	Protestant	Catholic	Protestant	Catholic	Protestant	Catholic
Per cent Republican	98	69	76	36	67	17

* Bernard R. Berelson, Paul F. Lazarsfeld, and William N. McPhee, *Voting* (Chicago: University of Chicago Press, 1954), p. 66, Chart XXV (adapted). (Reprinted with permission of the University of Chicago Press.)

It should not be assumed that if two independent variables are related to the dependent variable, then their cumulative impact will reflect the combined power of each independent variable. The joint influence may in fact be strong or weak, depending upon the interaction of X and Y (as well as other factors). For example, if education is related to vote and occupation is related to vote, the cumulative impact of education and occupation on vote may be no greater than the impact of either independent variable alone because the two independent variables are so closely related. It thus becomes an empirical question whether the cumulative impact of two or more independent variables is greater than any smaller number considered individually.

Typological Effects

In the discussion of independent, relative, and cumulative effects, we have dealt with two independent variables, each of which is associated with the dependent variable. There are, however, certain conditions under which an independent variable which is *not* correlated with the dependent variable may affect the original relationship; in fact, two uncorrelated independent variables may, when considered conjointly, bear upon the dependent variable.

The point is that certain combinations of independent variables may have special effects which cannot be inferred from the examination of each independently. This will occur when the two independent variables become "fused" in such a way as to constitute a single independent variable.

When new effects are produced through a fusion or amalgamation of two variables which produces a new emergent possessing a distinctive unity—a unity which is something more than, or different from, the two separate variables which constitute it—we speak of a *typology*. One then no longer thinks of a two-variable interaction but of the effect of a single influence. To be sure, the typology may be substructed into its component variables, but conceptually it is a unity which is over and above the variables that constitute it.

Such a typology is symbolized by the relationship of the whole to the parts. While the whole obviously cannot be greater than the sum of its parts, it is nevertheless different from the sum. One can have all the parts of a watch but not have a watch. On the other hand, one cannot have a watch without the parts. Similarly, Gestalt psychologists have shown how holistic perception is radically different from the perception of the parts.

Take a simple example. Assume one wishes to examine the relationship between parental attitudes and childhood behavior. One independent variable is the father's attitude, and another independent variable is the mother's attitude. Let us say that the father stresses obedience and the mother stresses obedience. Considering these two variables together, one emerges with a new single independent variable —the variable of *parental agreement*. This variable cannot be deduced from the separate examination of each of the independent variables, or through adding the variables, etc. Agreement is a new emergent. Similarly, if the father stresses obedience and the mother does not, one encounters the new emergent of *parental disagreement* or inconsistency. This is now a single variable, and its influence cannot necessarily be inferred from the separate variables which constitute it.

The fact that the emergent is not implied in the individual dimensions themselves has certain implications for analytic procedure. Ordinarily, if one independent variable is related to the dependent variable and the other independent variable is not, we would not be inclined to consider the independent, relative, or cumulative effects of these two independent variables. One would assume that the second variable would add nothing to the predictive power of the first. But this is not necessarily the case. The uncorrelated variable may fuse with the correlated variable to produce a type which has a unique effect. Indeed, one may have both independent variables which are uncorrelated with the dependent variable but which, when fused into a type, may have a distinctive effect. It is even possible for one of the independent variables to be *negatively* associated with the dependent variable but to create a type which accentuates the *positive* effect of the other independent variable.

The independent variables may fuse in different ways. For this reason, we have distinguished four kinds of types: a distinctive type, a modified type, a consistent type, and a relative type.

Distinctive type

Let us say we classify our respondents in terms of two dimensions: opinion leadership and concern with local affairs. Those opinion leaders concerned with local affairs are, in Merton's terms, "locals"; those concerned with affairs of broader scope are "cosmopolitans."[23] (Two other types are also possible: the average non-opinion leader whose interests are confined to his immediate environment—perhaps designated as John Q. Public; and the other man who has little to do with others but reflects on the broader problems of the world—a sort of "detached intellectual.") A "local," however, means more than the two dimensions by which he is characterized; it also means a way of thinking, a way of acting toward others, a certain set of life experiences, a characteristic style of life, a certain place in society, etc. The local, then, is a distinctive type—as is the cosmopolitan—which connotes a good deal more than the additive effect of the two variables.

Consider a case in which we have one independent variable which is not associated with the dependent variable and another which is. The point to note is that when the correlated variable is considered in association with the uncorrelated variable, the relationship is stronger than when it is considered separately.

The study in question dealt with certain social factors associated with level of self-esteem.[24] The *uncorrelated* variable was sex; adolescent boys and girls did not differ in self-esteem levels. The *correlated* variable was possession of siblings; "only" children had somewhat higher levels of self-esteem than children with siblings. In considering these two independent variables in conjunction, however, it was found that "only" boys had particularly high self-esteem, whereas this was not true of "only" girls. Fifty-four per cent of the only boys, but 44 per cent of boys with siblings had high self-esteem; among girls, the corresponding proportions were 47 and 44. The uncorrelated variable—sex—did play a role in self-esteem when considered in association with possession of siblings. To be an "only boy" implies a set of experiences over and above being an only child and being a boy. In other cultures, the "eldest son" has a position and set of experiences above what could be inferred from the knowledge that he is a son or that he is the eldest.

Sibling structure may produce many distinctive types. In this study of self-esteem, two factors in the sibling structure of the family were considered: (1) whether the boy was surrounded mostly by sisters or mostly by brothers, and (2) whether the boy was in the "first half" or "last half" in sibling birth order. The results showed that boys who had mostly sisters had higher self-esteem than those who had mostly brothers (the correlated variable). However, there was no difference in self-esteem emerging from being early or late in birth order (the uncorrelated variable). Nevertheless, being in the first or last half of the family did have an effect when considered in conjunction with sex distribution.

The data are these. Among boys in predominantly male families, 41 per cent have high self-esteem, compared with 50 per cent of the boys in predominantly female families. Overall, there was no difference in the self-esteem of boys in the first or last half of the family. However, if boys who had mostly sisters were in the last half of the family, 56 per cent had high self-esteem, compared with 48 per cent of boys in predominantly female families who were among the older children (Table 7–19). A particular combination of characteristics, then—a younger boy with mostly older sisters—thus produces a particularly strong effect on the dependent variable. Birth order in itself makes no difference, but it has an important modifying effect

Table 7–19

Proportion of Brothers and Sisters, Ordinal Position, and Self-Esteem, Among Males (Families of Three or More Children) [*]

| | NO BROTHERS OR BROTHERS IN THE MINORITY | | BROTHERS IN THE MAJORITY OR EQUAL | |
	Respondent First Half or Middle of Family	Respondent Last Half of Family (Younger Minority)	Respondent First Half or Middle of Family	Respondent Last Half of Family
Per cent high self-esteem	48	56	41	40

[*] Morris Rosenberg, *Society and the Adolescent Self-Image* (Princeton: Princeton University Press, 1965), p. 114, Table 4 (abridged and adapted). (Reprinted by permission of Princeton University Press.)

on the influence of sex distribution. Expressed more technically, one would say that the uncorrelated variable accentuates the effect of the correlated variable.

It is even possible that a *negatively* correlated variable may accentuate the effect of a *positively* correlated variable. Assume that we find that men tend to have greater knowledge of public affairs than women and that professors have greater knowledge than others. But the joint influence of these variables might not reflect the typological influence. A particular type—the woman professor—might have the greatest knowledge of any group.

Similarly, one might find that people of working-class origins are more likely to favor labor unions and that men who are currently rich are more likely to oppose them. But a man from the working class who has become rich might be more strongly opposed to unions than anyone else. Since he has risen from the ranks on his own merits, and perhaps been scorned for his ambitions at an earlier age, he might be particularly hostile to worker organizations. For this type, the negatively related variable accentuates the power of the positively related variable.

The frequent conservatism, if not reactionary bias, of the nouveaux riches is a familiar case in point. Although "old family" and wealth are both conducive to conservatism, the "newly wealthy" may be the most conservative of all. They may be "more royalist than the king."

Modifying type

A second situation in which the two independent variables produce a type which is different from their separate influences is one in which the new independent variable modifies the nature or quality of the original independent variable. This type of conjoint influence is illustrated in a study by Suchman and Menzel.[25]

In this study the dependent variable is party affiliation. Two independent variables are considered: (1) ethnic membership and (2) degree of identification with ethnic group. The first factor is found to be related to vote, the second is not. In other words, if one is Italo-American, Catholic, Negro, or Jewish, one tends to vote Democratic, but if one is a white Protestant, one tends to vote Republican. If one simply asks whether a person identifies strongly with his ethnic group, however, one finds no relationship to vote. The latter variable, however, accentuates the effect of the former. Thus, a Catholic who considers his religious group very important to him is more likely to vote Democratic than a Catholic who does not, and the same is true among Jews, Italo-Americans, and Negroes. The effect of group identification, therefore, is to intensify the influence of group membership. It is not simply the influence of group membership, but the influence of "socially or psychologically real groups"[26] that is revealed by this analysis.

The consistent-inconsistent type

When a type is classified on the basis of the agreement or disagreement with regard to two independent variables, then we have a new emergent which is not even implied in either of the variables considered independently. The concept of consistency implies a *relationship* between two or more variables; a consideration of each independent variable separately or cumulatively gives no hint of this type.

The emergence of a single new variable out of two or more independent variables is, of course, a theoretical, rather than an empirical, task. One concept which has attracted considerable interest in recent years is Lenski's idea of "status crystallization." Jackson describes this concept in the following way: "The accuracy of the traditional view of social stratification, that of individuals placed above or below other individuals in a single status hierarchy, has been questioned by many writers, who proposed instead that individuals are ranked simultaneously on a number of different status hierarchies. This multidimensional theory implied the existence of a new variable, the consistency of the status ranks of an individual. For this research, status consistency is defined as the degree to which an individual's rank positions on important societal status hierarchies are at a comparable level."[27]

The status dimensions employed in this study were occupation, education, and racial-ethnic background. Three ranks were assigned for each pattern. These three dimensions were fused to form a single dimension of status consistency, which differentiated four types: (1) status consistents—status patterns 111, 222, or 333; (2) moderate inconsistents—persons with two like ranks and a deviation of one step in the third—112, 323, etc.; (3) persons with no like ranks—123, 312, etc.; (4) two-rank deviates—persons with two like ranks and a deviation of two steps in the third, for example, 113, 313, etc.

In terms of symptoms of stress, the results show that consistents and moderate inconsistents differ little, but that those of no like rank show somewhat higher symptoms of stress and that those with two-rank deviates show considerably higher symptoms (Table 7–20). In this analysis the three independent variables are not even considered

Table 7–20

*Status Consistency and Symptom Level**

Degree of Status Consistency	PER CENT AT EACH SYMPTOM LEVEL			
	Low	Medium	High	N(100%)
Consistent	27	57	16	392
Moderately inconsistent	27	55	18	931
Sharply inconsistent:				
No like ranks	24	52	24	206
Two-rank deviates	16	48	36	144

* Elton F. Jackson, "Status Consistency and Symptoms of Stress," *American Sociological Review*, XXVII (August 1962), 473, Table I. (Reprinted with permission of the American Sociological Association.)

individually; their sole significance lies in the new dimension emerging from the fusion of the dimensions.

The archetype of the consistency-inconsistency type of conjoint influence is the phenomenon of "cross-pressures." In studies of political campaigns, for example, it is found that people who are under cross-pressures, that is, those showing some kind of psychological, sociological, interpersonal, or behavioral inconsistency, tend to delay their final vote decision more than others.[28]

Table 7–21 shows six types of inconsistency. The first type of inconsistency is between objective social factors—people whose religious affiliation and economic status lead in different political directions (for example, upper-class Catholics or working-class Protestants). A second type of inconsistency is reflected in conflicting interpersonal forces, represented by those whose families are politically divided. A third type of inconsistency is represented by a conflict between an objective and subjective factor (a membership and a reference group), exemplified by the person whose actual and self-defined social statuses differ. Fourth, behavioral inconsistency is represented by people who changed their votes between the two presidential elections. Finally, subjective inconsistency (cognitive dissonance) is shown by those who report a trend toward the other party and, to some extent, by those who adopt a position contrary to that of their party on the relative importance of business versus governmental experience. Table 7–21 shows the relationship beween each type of inconsistency and late final voting decision, controlling on level of political interest. In each case, we see, the inconsistents are more likely to make a late decision than the consistent people.

In this example, even if neither independent variable is related to the dependent variable, the newly emergent type may be strongly related. Consider the example of the family. It may be that people from Democratic families are neither more nor less likely than those from Republican families to make a late vote decision, and that Democratic respondents do not differ from Republican respondents about when the decision is made. But people in conflict—Democrats in Republican families or Republicans in Democratic families—may be considerably more likely than others to delay their decisions. The theoretical fruitfulness of concepts such as "status crystallization" and

Table 7-21

Cross-Pressures and Late Final Voting Decisions, by Interest in the Election
(Percentage Making Relatively Late Final Voting Decisions) *

CROSS-PRESSURES

	Political Influence of Religious Affiliation and Economic Status Differ †		Actual and Self-Defined Social Status Differ		Person's Vote in 1936 was Different		Family Politically Divided		Notices Trend Toward the "Other" Party		Importance of Business vs. Governmental Experience Contradicts Party Affiliation	
	No	Yes	No	Yes	No	Yes	No	Yes	No	Yes	No	Yes
Great Interest in the Election	32	44	36	44	28	55	25	52	33	35	34	48
Less Interest in the Election	52	64	63	67	44	78	44	71	45	62	51	73

* Paul F. Lazarsfeld, Bernard Berelson, and Hazel Gaudet, *The People's Choice* (New York: Columbia University Press, 1948), pp. 58–59, Chart 20 (abridged and adapted). (Reprinted with permission of the Columbia University Press.)
† Poor Protestants or rich Catholics.

"cross-pressures" testifies to the value of employing multidimensional concepts.

The relative type

The final kind of emergent variable is one in which the two independent variables achieve meaning by virtue of comparative positions. The individual is higher or lower on one dimension than on another.

For example, Pearlin was interested in studying feelings of powerlessness among members of the staff of a mental hospital.[29] In order to learn whether staff members felt they had little personal control over their work activities, they were asked: ". . . who has the *most* say or influence in what you do in your daily work?" Two independent variables could be considered: (1) the position of the person in authority, and (2) the position of the individual himself. By fusing these two variables, one can come out with a new emergent variable which Pearlin calls "positional disparity"—the hierarchical distance between the individual and his superior.

Five levels of authority were distinguished in the mental hospital: the doctor, the nursing supervisor, the head nurse, the charge attendant, and the nursing assistant. One could thus compute the disparity between any two levels. For example, the disparity between an assistant and a head nurse would be the same as that between a head nurse and a doctor, namely, two steps. The significance of this positional disparity for feelings of powerlessness at work was shown in Table 6–14. Pearlin noted "that there is a tendency for alienation to be most intense under conditions of great disparity and to decrease with positional distance between superordinate and subordinate parties."[30]

One prominent area of sociological research in which the relative type of conjoint influence predominates is that of *social mobility*. A major concern of sociologists is the effect of movement up and down the status scale, either within or between generations. If one wishes to study intergenerational mobility, the effect of each of the two independent variables—the father's status and the respondent's status —is contained in the relationship between the two. The man who surpasses his father is upwardly mobile; the man who fails to achieve his father's level is downwardly mobile (a "skidder").[31] It is not *what* each level is, but the *relative* standing of each, that defines the type.

The theoretical importance of this variable is illustrated in Greenblum and Pearlin's study of vertical mobility and prejudice.[32] In discussing Table 7–22, they note:

A comparison of the three groups in our total sample shows the stationary group, in contrast to Bettelheim and Janowitz's findings, to be almost consistently less intolerant than either mobile group. . . . This is especially clear in the case of both cognitive anti-Semitic items. Thus, our first hypothesis, derived above from Park and Williams, regarding a greater relative frequency of prejudice among mobile, in contrast to stationary groups, would seem to be substantiated with slight modifications.[33]

Vertical mobility has also been found to be associated with certain child-rearing values. In Lenski's study,[34] four groups were differentiated: Middle-class sons of middle-class fathers (middle: nonmobile); middle-class sons of working-class fathers (middle: upwardly mobile); working-class sons of middle-class fathers (working: downwardly mobile); and working-class sons of working-class fathers

Table 7–22

*Occupational Status Mobility (Upward vs Downward) and Prejudice**

							STEREOTYPE	
		(Per Cent)						
		"KEEP OUT"		"TOO MUCH POWER"			"Jews	
						Foreign	Dis-	"Negroes
	Number	Jews	Negroes	Jews	Negroes	Born	honest"	Lazy"
Total Sample								
Upward								
mobile (UM)	(154)	15	71	29	9	16	36	45
Station-								
ary (S)	(415)	11	59	20	7	16	28	39
Downward								
mobile (DM)	(95)	13	63	27	16	21	42	39
Total	(664)							
Difference:								
UM and DM		2	8	2	−7	−5	−6	6

* Joseph Greenblum and Leonard I. Pearlin, "Vertical Mobility and Prejudice: A Socio-Psychological Analysis," in R. Bendix and S. M. Lipset, eds., *Class, Status and Power* (Glencoe, Ill.: The Free Press, 1953), p. 486, Table I (abridged). (Reprinted with permission of The Macmillan Company. Copyright 1953 by The Free Press, A Corporation.)

Table 7–23

*Percentage of Urban-Born Detroiters Valuing Intellectual Autonomy
Above Obedience, by Class and Mobility Status*

	CLASS AND MOBILITY STATUS			
	Middle:	Working:	
	Middle:	Upwardly	Downwardly	Working:
	Nonmobile	Mobile	Mobile	Nonmobile
Value intellectual autonomy above obedience	74	77	48	55

* Gerhard Lenski, *The Religious Factor* (Garden City, N.Y.: Doubleday and Company, Inc., 1961), p. 202, Table 40 (abridged and adapted). (Copyright 1961 by Gerhard Lenski. Reprinted by permission of Doubleday and Company, Inc.)

(working: nonmobile). The dependent variable dealt with the degree to which the individual valued intellectual autonomy above obedience as an important quality in his child. It turned out that the upwardly mobile people were most likely to do so and the downwardly mobile were least likely to do so (Table 7–23). This conclusion is not implicit in the class difference of the two groups or the class of origin difference. It is a function of the particular types created by the joining of these two variables.

In this discussion, four types of conjoint influences have been differentiated: distinctive, modified, consistent-inconsistent, and relative types. Each is an emergent from the original two independent variables; it is not based on the statistical characteristics of both variables considered separately. It is for this reason that basic statistical techniques, such as partial or multiple correlation, fail to detect their effects. Nevertheless, they represent one of the most valuable contributions afforded by the introduction of a third variable into an original two-variable relationship.

Discussion

In the foregoing chapters, we have been concerned with one basic question: what happens when a third variable is introduced into a two-variable relationship? First of all, we have seen, the third variable may serve as a test factor, enabling one to understand the original two-variable relationship better. Second, the third variable represents a specifying condition, showing how this two-variable relationship differs among various groups. Finally, as the present discussion has suggested, the third variable may serve as another independent variable, interacting in various ways with the original independent variable to produce a certain effect. In the last case, one can investigate whether each independent variable exercises an influence separate from the other, which independent variable is the stronger, what is the cumulative impact of the two independent variables, and what is the effect of new types, emerging from a fusion of the independent variables. Each procedure may potentially contribute to a fuller, deeper, richer understanding of the data.

NOTES

1. Paul F. Lazarsfeld, Bernard R. Berelson, and Hazel E. Gaudet, *The People's Choice* (New York: Columbia University Press, 1948).
2. Peter M. Blau, "Structural Effects," *American Sociological Review,* XXV (April 1960), 178–193.
3. *Ibid.,* p. 180.
4. Morris Rosenberg, *Occupations and Values* (Glencoe, Ill.: The Free Press, 1957).
5. Blau, *op. cit.*
6. Richard L. Simpson, "Parental Influence, Anticipatory Socialization, and Social Mobility," *American Sociological Review,* XXVII (August 1962), 517–522.
7. Ernest Q. Campbell and C. Norman Alexander, "Structural Effects and Interpersonal Relationships," *American Journal of Sociology,* LXXI (November 1965), 284–289.
8. *Ibid.,* p. 288.
9. Norman M. Bradburn and David Caplovitz, *Reports on Happiness* (Chicago: Aldine Press, 1965).
10. Hubert M. Blalock, Jr., "Evaluating the Relative Importance of Variables," *American Sociological Review,* XXVI (December 1961), 866–874, has distinguished between the "quantitative criterion" and the "causal criterion" of relative effects. Our discussion deals only with the quantitative criterion. The causal criterion is dealt with separately in the earlier discussion of test factors.

11. Samuel A. Stouffer et al., *The American Soldier: Adjustment During Army Life* (Princeton, N.J.: Princeton University Press, 1949), p. 110.

12. Gerhard Lenski, *The Religious Factor* (Anchor edition, Garden City: Doubleday & Company, Inc., 1963).

13. J. Mayone Stycos, "Social Class and Preferred Family Size in Peru," *American Journal of Sociology*, LXX (May 1965), 651–658.

14. Bernard C. Rosen, "Conflicting Group Membership: A Study of Parent-Peer Group Cross-Pressures," *American Sociological Review*, XX (April 1955), 155–161.

15. Raymond Breton, "Institutional Completeness of Ethnic Communities and the Personal Relations of Immigrants," *American Journal of Sociology*, LXX (September 1964), 193–205.

16. *Ibid.*, p. 194.

17. It should be emphasized that where the data are in such a form that more powerful statistics may appropriately be used, they will yield more confident conclusions about the relative effects of independent variables. Probably the soundest way of calculating relative effects is through partial correlation. One examines the relationship of each independent variable to the dependent variable, controlling on the other independent variable. (The Campbell and Alexander example cited earlier is a case in point.) One may also use the procedure of standardization [Morris Rosenberg, "Test Factor Standardization as a Method of Interpretation," *Social Forces*, XLI (October 1962), 53–61], by standardizing each independent variable on the other.

18. I am indebted to Melvin Kohn for calling this point to my attention.

19. Bradburn and Caplovitz, *op. cit.*

20. August B. Hollingshead and Frederick C. Redlich, *Social Class and Mental Illness* (New York: John Wiley & Sons, Inc., 1958), pp. 390–397.

21. Bernard Rosen, *op. cit.*

22. Ira L. Reiss, "Premarital Sexual Permissiveness Among Negroes and Whites," *American Sociological Review*, XXIX (October 1964), 688–698.

23. Robert K. Merton, "Patterns of Influence: A Study of Interpersonal Influence and of Communications Behavior in a Local Community," in P. F. Lazarsfeld and F. N. Stanton, eds., *Communications Research, 1948–1949* (New York: Harper & Row, Publishers, Inc., 1949), pp. 180–219.

24. Morris Rosenberg, *Society and the Adolescent Self-Image* (Princeton, N.J.: Princeton University Press, 1965).

25. Edward A. Suchman and Herbert Menzel, "The Interplay of Demographic and Psychological Variàbles in the Analysis of Voting Surveys," in P. F. Lazarsfeld and M. Rosenberg, eds., *The Language of Social Research* (Glencoe, Ill.: The Free Press, 1955), pp. 148–155.

26. *Ibid.*, p. 155.

27. Elton F. Jackson, "Status Consistency and Symptoms of Stress," *American Sociological Review*, XXVII (August 1962), 469.

28. Lazarsfeld, Berelson, and Gaudet, *op. cit.*, pp. 56–64.

29. Leonard I. Pearlin, "Alienation from Work: A Study of Nursing Personnel," *American Sociological Review*, XXVII (June 1962), 314–326.

30. *Ibid.*, p. 316.

31. Harold L. Wilensky and Hugh Edwards, "The Skidder: Ideological Adjustments of Downward Mobile Workers," *American Sociological Review*, XXIV (April 1959), 215–231.

32. Joseph Greenblum and Leonard I. Pearlin, "Vertical Mobility and Prejudice: A Socio-Psychological Analysis," in R. Bendix and S. M. Lipset, eds., *Class, Status and Power* (Glencoe, Ill.: The Free Press, 1953), pp. 480–491.
33. *Ibid.*, p. 483.
34. Lenski, *op. cit.*, p. 224.

CHAPTER 8

The Strategy of Survey Analysis I

It is sometimes assumed, either explicitly or implicitly, that there is a single correct approach to survey analysis and that approaches which deviate from this path are in error. We would suggest, on the contrary, that several approaches are available and that the research worker should be flexible in conducting his analysis in a way which will maximize theoretical fruitfulness and will permit more confident conclusions.

Hypothesis Testing

The model of scientific procedure involves the testing of preformulated hypotheses which have been derived from strict deductive reasoning or more general theoretical considerations. Certain logical operations must thus precede the collection of the data. If the hypothesis derives directly from these logical operations, and if the empirical data turn out to confirm the hypothesis, then the theory which engendered the hypothesis is supported.

As a simple example, one might hypothesize that Negroes in American society would be more alienated than whites. This prediction might be based on the assumption that people who are systematically deprived of the rewards of the society would be little disposed to adopt the dominant value system of that society. If the empirical data agreed with the prediction, one would say that the hypothesis was confirmed and the theory supported.

There is thus a strong mutual dependence of data and theory, the theory determining which of the multitudinous facts of social life are to be selected for investigation, and the data lending support to the theory. Hypothesis testing has long represented the model of research procedure because the hypothesis is presumably drawn from theoretical considerations and because it is potentially nullifiable by empirical data.

While hypothesis testing, in this strict sense, is of great value in survey research, it is by no means the sole, nor even the dominant, procedure employed. There are several reasons why this is the case.

The first point is that even if the hypothesis is drawn from a theory and is supported by the data, the data do not prove the theory; they only support it. While the findings may be consistent with the theory which gave rise to the hypothesis, they may also be consistent with other theories.

Goode and Hatt offer some interesting illustrations of being right for the wrong reasons.[1] It was once popularly believed that one could prevent colds by hanging a bag of asafetida around one's neck. Had this hypothesis been put to a test, it might well have turned out that those who wore the asafetida had fewer colds. The reason for the effect would have been, in fact, that the obnoxious odor of the asafetida kept people at a distance, thereby reducing the danger of contagion. The alleged hygienic properties of the chemical did not exist, despite the correctness of the prediction.

Similarly, suppose one begins with the hypothesis that Negroes are innately inferior intellectually. One tests this hypothesis by comparing

Negro and white IQ scores, and the data apparently support the hypothesis. But they do not prove it. An alternative interpretation—that the differences are environmentally determined—is equally consistent with the results. Hypothesis testing, though a relatively severe criterion of the adequacy of one's theoretical reasoning, is far from foolproof.

Actual research affords a number of illustrations. In a study of self-images among adolescents, the hypothesis was advanced that upper-class adolescents would have higher self-esteem than lower-class adolescents. This hypothesis derived logically from a cogent body of theory. Mead had suggested that the self was a product of reflected appraisals, and Cooley had stressed that self-estimates were fundamentally determined by our assumptions concerning others' attitudes toward us. Since social class reflects societal prestige, it would follow that people who are generally well regarded and respected in society would have greater self-respect than those who are disdained. And the empirical data did, in fact, agree with the hypothesis; the upper-class adolescents did have higher self-esteem than the lower-class respondents. While the results were thus consistent with the theoretical reasoning of Mead and Cooley, they did not prove its correctness. Further analysis, in fact, suggested that this theory had little to do with the results—that the results were actually due to certain normative patterns of closeness of fathers to sons and fathers to daughters in the several social classes.[2]

Another example of the support of an hypothesis but the undermining of the theory behind it appears in a study of social isolation and schizophrenia by Kohn and Clausen.[3] In the early thirties, Faris and Dunham had demonstrated that schizophrenic mental patients were especially likely to come from socially disorganized areas of the city. They interpreted this finding to suggest that the low level of social solidarity in these areas was conducive to social isolation, and that schizophrenia, which entails a breakdown of social communication, was a consequence of this human isolation.

This plausible post-factum interpretation represented the theoretical basis for the testing of the hypothesis some years later. A group of hospitalized mental patients from a Maryland community was individually paired with controls from the community on the basis of age, sex, and occupation (or father's occupation). "By this method, it was possible to accomplish matching as of a period well before the onset of illness—on the average, 16 years before hospitalization. In roughly half of the cases the patient and his control had attended the same class in public school."[4] The results of the interviews showed that the schizophrenics were far more likely than the controls to have been social isolates. Only 42 per cent of the schizophrenics, but 80 per cent of the controls, were nonisolates at the age of 13–14.

The data thus supported the theory that social isolation leads to schizophrenia. But they did not prove the theory on which the hypothesis was based. The theory involved the assumption that certain aspects of the structure of the environment were responsible for the individual's social isolation. But a careful analysis of the data indicated that there were no differences in the structure of the social environments of the isolates and nonisolates; there was nothing about social experience per se that was isolating the isolates. This finding (in addition to certain other data) suggested that the same factors which ultimately produced the schizophrenia were also responsible for the social isolation at an earlier age. We thus see that the hypothesis was confirmed, but that the theory which gave rise to the hypothesis was disproved.

The second reason why hypothesis-testing cannot serve as the sole scientific procedure is this: that even if the hypothesis is confirmed in survey analysis, one's job is still not done. The possibility still remains that the relationship may be spurious, that is, may be due to extraneous variables. It is thus often necessary to control on certain variables to insure that there is an inherent link between the independent and dependent variables. In the experimental method, the "block-booking" problem is overcome by insuring that the experimental and control groups are as alike as possible (either through matching or through random selection). The empirical support of an hypothesis in survey research represents weaker confirmation than hypotheses tested by means of experimentation. Some form of elaboration is thus almost always required in a theoretically based survey.

The third point is that much can be learned in survey analysis which is not based on the explicit testing of clearly stipulated pre-formulated hypotheses. Indeed, the strict and exclusive adherence to hypothesis-testing as the sole scientific model may seriously impoverish research. The wide range of knowledge which can be obtained through the various processes of elaboration, the flow of analysis, the "pursuit of an idea," and the assaying of evidence is largely cut off through strict adherence to the model of hypothesis-testing. Pure hypothesis-testing is a valuable research model and should be employed where appropriate, but research can be severely cramped if it is employed as the *sole* method of analysis.

Elaboration

At least as common in survey analysis is the process of elaborating the relationship between two variables by introducing a third variable into the analysis. The purpose is to "explain" or to "specify" the relationship, thus making it more meaningful or more exact. Elaboration helps to answer the questions of "why" and "under what circumstances."

The basic format suggested in our discussion of analysis involves a relationship between two variables which is stratified according to the categories of a test factor. When this simple step is taken, an enormous amount of information is potentially available. The information which the table can yield, however, *depends entirely upon the perspective one brings to bear on it*. The data are unable to speak for themselves; they are only able to respond to the questions asked of them.

Two errors commonly made in the elaboration of a two-variable table are these: one is to look at only one item of information in the table, the other to look at all the information at once. The first procedure is wasteful, the second confusing. A great deal of information can potentially be derived by introducing a third variable into the analysis, but the full exploitation of this information is possible only if one treats the various questions separately and asks some of the essential questions first. *Elaboration may thus properly be viewed as a sequence of steps*. How does the process of elaboration proceed?

Take the familiar and well-documented finding that working-class people are more likely to vote Democratic than those in the middle class. What questions might one pose of such a finding that could be answered by the introduction of a third variable? In principle, a surprisingly large number are susceptible of systematic investigation.

1. The first question one would always pose is whether the relationship is symmetrical, reciprocal, or asymmetrical. If the relationship is viewed as symmetrical, then one would not undertake to examine how one variable determines the other since neither variable is dependent nor independent. If the relationship is seen as reciprocal, then, in the presence of panel data, one could examine their mutual interaction to determine the dominant direction of influence. In the case of the relationship of social class to vote, the relationship is obviously asymmetrical, and the direction of influence is clear. A man's vote can hardly determine his social class; plainly, the class factor must be responsible for the vote and must therefore serve as the independent variable.

2. Having determined that the relationship is asymmetrical, and that class is independent and vote dependent, one would immediately ask whether the relationship is real or whether it is actually attributable to an *extraneous* variable. The analyst would certainly consider whether the relationship might be due to religion, that is, to the possibility that middle-class people tend to vote Republican because they are more likely to be Protestants. Or perhaps race is the extraneous factor; possibly working people vote Democratic because they are more frequently Negro. Even geographical region might be implicated: perhaps lower-class people vote Democratic because the South has a lower economic level but is Democratic for reasons of history. In rare circumstances, it could turn out that one of these is a "distorter" variable and that the true relationship between class and vote is precisely the reverse of what it appears to be. If, on the other hand, the original relationship is maintained when the relevant extraneous variables are considered, then one would have greater confidence

that the factor of class was, in fact, responsible for the voting behavior.

3. Having established that the original relationship was real, one might be interested in examining *component* variables. Social class is a broad category; most analysts would be interested in specifying more precisely the decisive element which was responsible. Which element of class is crucial: income, economic power (bourgeoisie or proletariat); type of occupation (manual versus white-collar); educational level; etc.? If the relationship vanished when education was controlled, but remained strong when the income and occupational variables were controlled, then one would have a more precise understanding of what it was about class which gave rise to the political behavior.

4. The next step might involve the quest for *intervening* variables. The speculation might proceed as follows: the social category (class) produces an attitude (liberalism) which results in behavior (voting). If liberalism were in fact the intervening variable, then the relationship of class to voting behavior should vanish when liberalism was controlled. The causal connection between the independent and dependent variables would become more complete.

5. Although *suppressor* variables will usually be sought when there is an *absence* of relationship between two variables, one should always be aware of its possible relevance when a relationship does exist. Perhaps the observed relationship would be even stronger if the suppressor variable were controlled. It is known, for example, that Jews, who are a relatively well-educated group, tend strongly to vote Democratic. Controlling on religious affiliation might thus have the effect of *enhancing* the size of the relationship between class and vote.

6. In some cases (though probably not in the present example), one might be interested in extending the causal chain by seeking antecedent variables. Social class may be responsible for a man's vote, but what is responsible for his social class? For one thing, his father's social class. After showing that the relationship between class and vote was *maintained* when

father's class was controlled, one could then examine the relationship between the father's class and the respondent's vote, controlling on the respondent's class. If the relationship *vanished,* one would conclude that the father's class was an antecedent variable. Or one might consider whether time of family immigration was an antecedent variable, reasoning that families who came to America earlier had descendants who were more likely to end up in a higher class, which would in turn lead to a Republican orientation.

7. Having considered these possibilities, one might then turn one's attention to conditional relationships. Much valuable information can be gained from this aspect of elaboration.

Assume, for example, that one interpreted the relationship between class and voting in terms of a theory of economic interest: the higher classes vote Republican because they feel that the government will protect their economic interests, whereas the lower classes vote Democratic for the same reason. But suppose this relationship turns out to be strong in the East but weak in the West. Should economic self-interest play less of a role on the Pacific than on the Atlantic coast? One's interpretation is thereby *challenged* by the data and must either be defended in terms of special circumstances or must exert pressure for an alternative interpretation which will effectively accommodate these divergent results.

One might also examine conditional relationships in an effort to *confirm* the interpretation. Assume that one had interpreted the relationship in reference group terms—that voting derived from an identification with a class group and adherence to its political norms. One could thus expect the relationship of class to voting to be stronger among those who firmly identified with their class groups than among those whose identification was weaker. If such turned out to be the case, it would add strength to the interpretation; if not, it would tend to undermine it.

Conditional relationships might not change the interpretation but might *modify* it to some extent. Interpreting the relationship of class to vote as due to self-interest, one might find that the relationship is great among factory workers and owners but not among other people. One might then conclude that economic self-interest does operate *if the presence of economic power is highly visible,* as in the factory. The interpretation has not been changed, but modified.

Conditional relationships might also reveal *trends.* Assume one examined the relationship of class to vote, controlling on age. If the relationship grew weaker as the age level decreased, this might suggest a decreasing level of class consciousness in the population in recent generations. If the relationship increased, the conclusion would be the reverse.

The analyst might also be interested in conditions that *mute* or *amplify* the relationship. He would probably find, for example, that the relationship between social class and support of the Republican or Democratic Parties was weak in the South, though strong in the North. The factor muting the relationship in the South would be the power of race and tradition on vote which would submerge the class factor.

On the other hand, the investigator might find that the relationship was stronger in cities than in small towns. This finding might suggest that the intensive intra-class interaction characteristic of densely populated areas would foster class polarization and class consciousness, whereas this would be less true of thinly populated areas.

Similarly, one would expect no relationship between class and vote unless certain *necessary conditions* obtained. In some sections of the South, particularly in local elections, victory in the Democratic primary is virtually tantamount to election. If the Republican Party in these regions is virtually defunct, one would expect little association between class and Republican or Democratic vote. A necessary condition for this association is serious two-party competition.

These illustrations perhaps suffice to suggest the abundance of information inherent in conditional relationships. Few analysts would be interested in looking at all these questions, of course, but an awareness of the range may alert the analyst to seek useful information he might otherwise overlook.

8. Finally, there is much to be learned from the study of conjoint influence. Assume one finds that both social class and religious affiliation are related to voting behavior. But does class exercise an influence independent of religion, and religion, an influence independent of class? The study of *independent effects* is often essential to an understanding of the observed relationships.

Having established that both class and religion have effects independent of one another, one might want to know which independent variable has the stronger effect. Is class or religion more powerfully associated with vote when each is controlled on the other? Such *relative effects* enable one to understand the importance of independent variables.

The *cumulative effect* of variables may also be of interest. If working-class people are more likely to vote Democratic than middle-class people, and Catholics more likely than Protestants, then are working-class Catholics *especially* likely to vote Democratic and middle-class Protestants particularly *unlikely* to do so? For predictive purposes, one would be extremely interested in such information.

Finally, the research worker can investigate whether the simultaneous consideration of two independent variables may create a distinctive *type* which cannot be inferred from the variables that constitute it. Low-income people may tend to vote Democratic and people from Tennessee to vote Democratic, but a low-income Tennessean—perhaps the mountaineers who supported the Union in the Civil War—might vote Republican for traditional reasons. Again, one might study the voting behavior of people under "cross-pressures," for example, high-income Catholics and low-income Protestants. A number of interesting types can be generated through a simultaneous examination of two independent variables, and a much greater number through consideration of three or more. The only danger lies in becoming lost in a host of purely formal types which have little substantive meaning.

In the analysis of survey data, then, there are a number of steps, corresponding to a series of questions, which should be considered in penetrating more deeply into the relationship. The vein of research data is almost always richer than it appears to be on the surface, but it can only be of value if mined. The purpose of the foregoing discussion has been to make explicit some of the contributions to understanding which can be gained by introducing a third variable. To the extent that the analyst is more explicitly aware of these varied contributions, his chances of more fully exploiting his data are increased.

The "Flow of Analysis"

It is thus apparent that, in survey analysis, the two-variable relationship represents the start, not the completion, of the analysis. But the formal procedure of elaboration is also not the end of the analysis. As each of the varied types of information is gained in the process of elaboration, it may yield results which suggest further investigation. This is the "flow of analysis." As the research analyst investigates a particular idea, his attention is captured by data which suggest new ideas, which in turn exert pressure to examine new data, and so on. Any of the types of information acquired through elaboration may serve as a springboard for this process.

This type of analysis inevitably involves a close interplay of theory and data. The data suggest, stimulate, and generate the theory and the theory is restrained, controlled, and disciplined by the data. The separation of theory and research becomes impossible when guided by the flow of analysis procedure.

We may begin with a simple illustration suggested by Lazarsfeld.[5] Let us say one finds that married women working in factories have a higher rate of absenteeism than single women. But there is the obvious danger that this relationship is misleading: perhaps it is not the marital status (imposing, for example, additional family responsibilities) that is actually responsible, but the extraneous factor of *age*. Married women tend to be older, and older women are less able to stand the strain of factory work. If the relationship vanishes when age is controlled, we would conclude that the marital status in itself does not determine absenteeism.

Rather than completing one's analysis at this point, however, one might go on to ask: Why do *older women* have higher rates of absenteeism? Is it because they have less physical stamina? Is it because they were raised at an earlier historical epoch, when female factory employment was normatively disapproved, and are therefore in conflict about factory work? Or is it simply because they are more likely to have men who support them? One might, for example, examine this last question by controlling on economic support from men (husbands or fathers). If the relationship of age to absenteeism vanished, then one would know that it was not age, but male support, that was crucial.

And so on. Each result, we see, generates a new question leading to the examination of new data which may generate still another question. These potentialities for analysis are all too often overlooked.

The flow of analysis is particularly likely to be fruitful when one is seeking to trace out a causal sequence by means of intervening variables. As we observed earlier, any true relationship between two variables is actually the product of a lengthy causal sequence; it is, in effect, like a relationship between A and E, with B, C, and D as possible intervening variables. In order to understand the relationship of A to E better, we introduce C as an intervening variable. If the relationship vanishes, then we have reason to believe that A leads to C and that C leads to E. But we might want to go further by attempting to improve our understanding of the relationship of C to E; we would do so by introducing the intervening variable D. If, once again, the relationship of C to E vanishes, then we have spelled out with still greater specificity the causal sequence leading from A to E. To the extent that this can be accomplished—and it is difficult indeed —one is able to deal with one of the most difficult and important problems in sociological research, namely, the tracing of a complex causal sequence.

Consider a hypothetical illustration. Assume one finds a relationship between father's income and son's college ambition. One then introduces as an intervening variable the type of secondary school attended; boys from poor families are much more likely to attend slum schools. If the original relationship vanishes, then we have reason to believe that rich fathers have sons who go to good schools and that these good schools stimulate an interest in college.

But now one might wish to probe still further by examining the relationship between slum schools and lack of college ambition. The intervening variable might be the absence or presence of apathetic hostile teachers. If one were able to control on this variable and found that the relationship again vanished, then one would have reason to believe that boys attending slum schools encounter apathetic or hostile teachers who stimulate little academic interest or college ambition.

The original relationship between father's income and son's college ambition has thus been interpreted, not purely on speculative grounds, but on disciplined speculation guided by data. One can now suggest that fathers with low incomes tend to move into neighborhoods where their sons attend slum schools. Here these boys tend to be exposed to hostile or apathetic teachers who stifle, rather than stimulate, their interest in intellectual matters, and this lack of interest tends to abort their desire to attend college.

It may be noted that even in this analysis, some untested speculation enters into the picture. As we observed earlier, it is never possible to test a complete causal sequence (for example, physico-chemical processes in the brain intervene to explain all action, but we know virtually nothing about these processes). The more intervening variables we can successfully specify in our analysis, the more complete, exact, and sure is our interpretation of the causal sequence leading from the original independent to the final dependent variable. Only thus can one achieve both scientific confidence and richness of meaning.

In other cases, one might find that a conditional relationship analysis may yield results which will lead to an extraneous variable analysis. In a study of adolescents from broken homes, it was found that youngsters whose mothers had remarried had lower self-esteem than those whose mothers had not.[6] But the relationship turned out to be conditional: If the child was young at the time of the marital breakup, remarriage made no difference; whereas, if the child was older, remarriage had a substantial effect.

But one might then ask whether this latter contingent association— the association of maternal remarriage and child's self-esteem among children who were older at the time of the marital breakup—was spurious. Is it the remarriage as such which is responsible for the lower self-esteem, or may it be some accidentally associated personality characteristic. Perhaps mothers who are "flighty" are more likely to remarry and are also more likely to have children with low self-esteem. It would thus not be the factor of remarriage as such, but the associated factor of personality, that was responsible.

If the data indicated that this possible extraneous factor was not responsible, then one might shift from a conditional relationship analysis to an intervening variable analysis. One might suggest that the reason maternal remarriage appears to have this deleterious effect on the child's self-esteem is that the mother's interest in her child decreases as her interest in her new husband, and possibly stepchildren, increases. If one controlled on maternal interest in the child and found that the relationship vanished, one would have a more complete explanation of this contingent association.

In other cases, a conditional relationship may lead to a further conditional relationship, as the process of specification becomes more exact. One might, for example, begin with the finding that Negroes are more alienated than whites. The introduction of a *specifying variable* might show that this was true in the working class, but not in the middle class. But the significant contingent association might be further specified. Within the working class, one might find, the relationship of race to alienation might be strong in the North, but weak in the South. Such additional specifications may have any of the theoretical consequences suggested in the chapter on conditional relationships.

It is apparent that the flow of analysis characteristically derives directly from the earlier steps in elaboration. Its movement is rarely predicted in advance; it is, on the contrary, suggested, directed, or dictated by the results emerging from the earlier steps of the analysis.

The "Pursuit of an Idea"

In actual practice, much survey analysis involves the hot pursuit of an idea down paths and byways which have little to do with one's original hypotheses. In this case, the investigator displays a willingness to be led by his data along unexpected paths although he of course also gives direction to the analytic course. A reluctance to follow the lead of the findings may stultify and abort a good deal of promising research. Since the procedure is more easily illustrated than formalized, we will present one example in detail.

In the study of adolescent self-esteem, the investigator undertook to examine the relationship of sibling structure to self-esteem.[7] It turned out that neither birth order nor size of family (except "only" boys) appeared to show a clear or consistent relationship to self-esteem. However, the investigator was also interested in the *sex distribution* of children in the family. Considering families of three or more children, he found that among boys in predominantly male families, 41 per cent had high self-esteem, whereas 50 per cent of the boys in predominantly female families had high self-esteem. The self-esteem of girls, however, was not enhanced by being surrounded by brothers.

It occurred to the investigator that the boy in a family consisting mostly of girls would be considered something "special" by his father, mother, and sisters, and that this would be especially true if he were a younger boy with older sisters. The respondents were thus divided into those who were in the "first half" or "last half" of their family birth orders. Table 8–1 shows that 56 per cent of the "last half" boys with mostly sisters (the "younger-minority" boys) have high self-esteem, compared with 48 per cent of the older boys with mostly younger sisters and 41 per cent of the boys with mostly brothers.

This finding naturally generated the next question, namely, what accounts for the higher self-esteem of the "younger-minority" boys? The investigator considered the reaction of the father, mother, and sisters separately. He reasoned that the father, having sired several

Table 8–1

Proportion of Brothers and Sisters, Ordinal Position, and Self-Esteem Among Males (Families of Three or More Children) [*]

Self-Esteem	NO BROTHERS OR BROTHERS IN THE MINORITY		BROTHERS IN THE MAJORITY OR EQUAL	
	Respondent First Half or Middle of Family	Respondent Last Half of Family (Younger Minority)	Respondent First Half or Middle of Family	Respondent Last Half of Family
High	48%	56%	41%	40%
Medium	24	20	26	28
Low	29	24	34	31
Total per cent	100	100	100	100
Number	(244)	(127)	(544)	(237)

[*] Morris Rosenborg, *Society and the Adolescent Self-Image* (Princeton: Princeton University Press, 1965), p. 114, Table 4. (Reprinted by permission of Princeton University Press.)

daughters, would be particularly eager to have a boy and that the longer the son's arrival was deferred, the more welcome the child would be. The family's dependence upon the status of the male, the desire to carry on the family name, and the desire to recapture his own childhood would dispose the father very favorably to the boy for whom he had waited so long.

As far as the mother's reaction was concerned, an examination of the literature suggested that her reaction would be the same. A careful study by Sears, Maccoby, and Levin revealed "that when the new child is a boy, and the family already has girls but no boys, 50 per cent of the mothers are classified as very warm toward the child during infancy, whereas if the family already has boys but no girls, only 17 per cent are classified as very warm. . . . Conversely, the latter are twice as likely as the former to be described as 'relatively cold.' "[8] When the new child is a girl, on the other hand, these advantages do not obtain.

Further evidence on this point appeared in a question on parental favoritism. When asked, "Who was your mother's favorite child?" girls were more likely than boys to cite a younger brother, and the same was true on a question dealing with the father's favorite child.

As far as the sisters were concerned, it was assumed that they would welcome the opportunity to rehearse the mother role with a baby brother, and that fewer invidious comparisons would be made of siblings of different sexes than siblings of the same sex.

The investigator, however, was interested in learning more precisely the mechanisms through which family favor became converted into subjectively high self-esteem. One possibility considered was the following: Other analysis had revealed that academically successful students tended to have higher self-esteem than those who did poorly in school. This raised the possibility that the younger-minority boy, upon whom the family hopes were strongly pinned, was given special attention, help, and encouragement in his school work by his father, mother, and sisters, and that his consequent academic success helped to enhance his self-esteem level. It was thus decided to examine the school grades of these several groups.

Table 8–2 indicates that, contrary to expectations, younger-minority boys had significantly *lower* grades than other boys. In other words, they did not have higher self-esteem *because* of their academic success but *despite* their academic mediocrity.[9]

This finding led to the decision to examine the relationship of grades to self-esteem among the several groups separately. The relationships turned out to be conditional. It was found that grades were clearly related to self-esteem among all groups *except the younger-minority boys*. For this group, the self-esteem of those with low grades was at least as high as that of adolescents with high grades.

Table 8–2

Sex Distribution of Siblings, Ordinal Position, and Grades, Among Males (Families of Three or More Children) *

| Grade Average | NO BROTHERS OR BROTHERS IN THE MINORITY | | BROTHERS IN THE MAJORITY OR EQUAL | |
	Respondent in First Half or Middle of Family	Respondent in Last Half of Family (Younger Minority)	Respondent in First Half or Middle of Family	Respondent in Last Half of Family
A–B	34%	24%	32%	36%
C	47	57	48	40
D–F	18	19	20	25
Total per cent	100	100	100	100
Number	(233)	(118)	(536)	(230)

* Morris Rosenberg, *Society and the Adolescent Self-Image* (Princeton: Princeton University Press, 1965), p. 120, Table 7. (Reprinted by permission of Princeton University Press.)

Table 8–3

Sex Distribution of Siblings, Ordinal Position, Grades, and Self-Esteem, Among Boys (Families of Three or More) *

	No Brothers or Brothers in the Minority					
	RESPONDENT IN FIRST HALF OR MIDDLE OF FAMILY			RESPONDENT IN LAST HALF OF FAMILY (YOUNGER MINORITY)		
	Grades			Grades		
Self-Esteem	A–B	C	D–F	A–B	C	D–F
High	56%	45%	41%	46%	60%	64%
Medium	20	27	27	19	18	18
Low	24	28	32	35	22	18
Total Per Cent	100	100	100	100	100	100
Number	(79)	(104)	(41)	(26)	(65)	(22)

	Brothers in the Majority or Equal					
	RESPONDENT IN FIRST HALF OR MIDDLE OF FAMILY			RESPONDENT IN LAST HALF OF FAMILY		
	Grades			Grades		
Self-Esteem	A–B	C	D–F	A–B	C	D–F
High	51%	40%	29%	42%	44%	30%
Medium	26	27	18	32	33	20
Low	23	32	53	26	23	50
Total per cent	100	100	100	100	100	100
Number	(168)	(240)	(102)	(78)	(86)	(56)

* Morris Rosenberg, *Society and the Adolescent Self-Image* (Princeton: Princeton University Press, 1965), p. 121, Table 8. (Reprinted by permission of Princeton University Press.)

This finding suggested to the researcher the possibility that the younger-minority boy might be characterized by a particular *type* of self-esteem, namely, *unconditional self-acceptance*. While the self-esteem of others appeared to be influenced by their level of academic performance, the self-esteem of the younger-minority boy appeared to be relatively impervious to it. It might thus be that the self-esteem of the younger-minority boy was so firmly established in the family by the interest and affection of his father, mother, and older sisters that it was relatively independent of later extra-familial experiences.

In order to see if other evidence supported this supposition, further indicators of objective success were sought. The only available evidence dealt with social success—opinion leadership, participation in extra-curricular activities, election to class offices, etc. In all, six such indicators of social participation and success were available. For the total sample, the socially more active and successful students always had higher self-esteem. For the younger-minority boys, however, in five out of these six cases, social success or failure, activity or passivity, was *unrelated* to self-esteem. As in the case of academic achievement, the self-esteem of the younger-minority boy appeared to be relatively unaffected by social success or failure in the high school. This finding provided additional support for the interpretation that the younger-minority boy was characterized by unconditional self-acceptance.

The purpose of pursuing this example at such length has been to highlight the contrast between typical survey analysis and the pure hypothesis-testing model. As noted earlier, it is generally assumed that one begins with a theory, develops hypotheses on the basis of this theory, collects one's data, and then examines them to see if the hypothesis is supported or nullified. The "pursuit of an idea" clearly does not correspond to this model. Indeed, it is worth considering what would be implied in the hypothesis-testing model in the present example.

1. The researcher would have hypothesized in advance, on the basis of some theory, that boys who are surrounded by sisters would have higher self-esteem than boys surrounded by brothers, but that girls in the minority sex in the sibling structure would enjoy no self-esteem advantage over girls in the majority sex.

2. He would have hypothesized in advance that younger boys with mostly older sisters would have higher self-esteem than older boys with mostly younger sisters.

3. Despite his knowledge that grades were positively associated with self-esteem, he would have hypothesized in advance that these younger-minority boys would be significantly *poorer* students than other boys.

4. The researcher would further have hypothesized in advance that grades would be positively related to self-esteem for the other three groups of boys, but that grades would be unrelated to self-esteem for the younger-minority boys.

5. The researcher would have made the same prediction with regard to social activities and social success.

It may be suggested that it is highly unlikely that researchers will generally (if at all) have the theoretical acumen to establish these specific hypotheses in advance. Indeed, it seems evident that the empirical findings outrun the theory. The "pursuit of an idea" often involves a complex interplay between theory and data—the data exercising pressure on the theorist to account for them, the consequent theory pointing the direction to the appropriate data for testing or elaborating the theory. This research strategy is possible only if one demonstrates a willingness to be led by the data but, at the same time, to direct it in accord with some interpretive or theoretical position.

NOTES

1. William J. Goode and Paul K. Hatt, *Methods in Social Research* (New York: McGraw-Hill Book Company, 1952), p. 60.
2. Morris Rosenberg, *Society and the Adolescent Self-Image* (Princeton, N.J.: Princeton University Press, 1965), chap. 3.
3. Melvin L. Kohn and John A. Clausen, "Social Isolation and Schizophrenia," *American Sociological Review*, XX (June 1955), 265–273.
4. *Ibid.*, p. 266.
5. Paul F. Lazarsfeld, "Evidence and Inference in Social Research," *Daedalus*, LXXXVII (1958), 122–123.
6. Rosenberg, *op cit.*, chap. 5.
7. *Ibid.*, chap. 6.
8. Robert R. Sears, Eleanor E. Maccoby, and Harry Levin, *Patterns of Child Rearing* (Evanston, Ill.: Row, Peterson, 1957), p. 107.
9. Rosenberg, *op. cit.*, chap. 6.

CHAPTER 9

The
Strategy
of
Survey
Analysis
II

We have seen that elaboration, the flow of analysis, and the pursuit of ideas are complex procedures involving a dynamic interplay between theory and data. It is useful to call attention now to three somewhat different aspects of the strategy of analysis, namely, the concern with, and alertness to, unhypothesized findings; the procedure for balancing, weighing, and evaluating evidence; and the treatment of post-factum interpretations. Research experience suggests that these latter procedures contribute importantly to theoretically fruitful analyses.

Serendipity

Although the professional literature tends to present its results within the hypothesis-testing framework, the published report may by no means correspond to the actual research procedure. The research neophyte exposed to this literature may thus have the impression that the research worker, either through deductive reasoning or through intimate familiarity with the empirical literature, invariably emerges with an hypothesis which is then subjected to systematic test. He may thus be oriented narrowly to the data relevant to his hypotheses, averting his gaze from material which is presumably not pertinent.

Yet the history of science shows that alertness to results which were not the original concern of the investigator have yielded some of the most valuable scientific discoveries. The term *serendipity* has come to be applied to such conditions of discovery. The origin of this exotic term has been described by Cannon:

> In 1754 Horace Walpole, in a chatty letter to his friend Horace Mann, proposed adding a new word to our vocabulary, "serendipity." . . . Walpole's proposal was based upon his reading of a fairy tale, *The Three Princes of Serendip*. Serendip, I may interject, was the ancient name of Ceylon. "As their highnesses traveled," so Walpole wrote, "they were always making discoveries, by *accident* or *sagacity*, of things which they were not in quest of." When the word is mentioned in dictionaries, therefore, it is said to designate the happy faculty, or luck, of finding unforeseen evidence of one's ideas or, with surprise, coming upon new objects or relations which were not being sought.[1]

So important a role have such accidental findings played in actual research that an alertness to serendipitous findings may be considered a key element in the strategy of research. Merton's discussion of the serendipity pattern describes "the discovery, by chance or sagacity, of valid results which were not sought for."[2] Such findings, as Merton notes, may exert pressure for initiating theory or modifying theory. The procedure involves "observing the *unanticipated, anomalous,* and *strategic* datum which becomes the occasion for developing a new theory or for extending an existing theory."[3] Procedurally,

> . . . the seeming inconsistency provokes curiosity; it stimulates the investigator to "make sense of the datum," to fit it into a broader frame of knowledge. He explores further. He makes fresh observations. He draws inferences from the observations, inferences depending largely, of course, upon his general theoretic orientation. The more he is steeped in the data,

the greater the likelihood that he will hit upon a fruitful line of inquiry. In the fortunate circumstance that his new hunch proves justified, the anomalous datum leads to a new or extended theory. The curiosity stimulated by the anomalous datum is temporarily appeased.[4]

The history of science is replete with such serendipitous discoveries. According to Cannon:

In the records of scientific investigation this sort of happy use of good fortune has been conspicuous. A good example is afforded by the origin and development of our acquaintance with electrical phenomena. It is reported that some frogs' legs were hanging by a copper wire from an iron balustrade in the Galvani home in Bologna; they were seen to twitch when they were swung by the wind and happened to touch the iron. Whether the twitching was first noted by Luigi Galvani, the anatomist and physiologist, or by Lucia Galvani, his talented wife, is not clear. Certainly that fortuitous occurrence late in the eighteenth century was not neglected, for it started many researches which have preserved the Galvani name in the terms "galvanize" and "galvanism." And it also led to experiments by his contemporary, Volta, on the production of electric currents by contact of two dissimilar metals—and thus to the invention of the electric battery —experiments so fundamentally important that Volta's name is retained in the daily use of the words "volt" and "voltage." . . .[5]

Illustrations of serendipitous findings are perhaps no more rare in social than in natural science but are simply less conspicuous or dramatic. A finding which is serendipitous is rarely reported as such; characteristically, it is later encased within some theoretical framework. When the final report is written, one is rarely aware that the finding was serendipitous. It was only in a volume devoted to a commentary and elaboration of *The American Soldier* research that Stouffer reported that perhaps the most fruitful theoretical concept of the research—the concept of "relative deprivation"—was entirely serendipitous. He writes:

Often the pressure to "explain" or interpret a surprising empirical practical finding may lead to reflection which organizes a good many such findings. In the Research Branch I well remember our puzzlement, which went on for months, over the finding that Northern Negroes in Southern camps, in spite of the fact that they said they wanted to be stationed in the North and that they resented discrimination in Southern buses and by Southern police, showed as favorable or more favorable responses to items reflecting personal adjustment in the Army than did those in Northern camps. Some of our analysts were almost in despair at this discrepancy. They actually held up the report on their study for over a month while they checked and rechecked in the vain hope of finding errors in the data or analysis to explain the paradox. When, eventually, it was suggested that the Northern Negro soldier in the South had very great advantages over Negro civilians in the South and that the advantages over Negro civilians in the North were much less, a clue to the paradox appeared. After a number of such experiences, it became evident that some concept like "relative deprivation" might be useful. Armed with that concept, we would know how to anticipate such discrepancies better and to build into a study a means of checking up directly.[6]

Another analysis also turned up similar findings: although Air Force personnel had higher rates of promotion than Military Police soldiers, they were more likely to think their chances for promotion were poor.[7] The reason appeared to be that Air Force men saw others being promoted and were thus dissatisfied at their own lack of advancement, whereas Military Police soldiers observed few promotions and thus felt no dissatisfaction at their own absence of vertical mobility. Without the concept of relative deprivation generated by the earlier anomalous finding, this would have been a puzzling result indeed.

The development of dissonance theory again illustrates how unexpected results may lead to important theoretical contributions. Festinger describes the sequence as follows:

The first hunch that generated any amount of enthusiasm among us came from trying to understand some data, reported by Prasad, concerning rumors subsequent to the Indian earthquake of 1934. . . . The fact reported by Prasad which puzzled us was that following the earthquake, the vast majority of the rumors that were widely circulated predicted even worse disasters to come in the very near future. Certainly the belief that horrible disasters were about to occur is not a very pleasant belief, and we may ask why rumors that were "anxiety provoking" arose and were so widely accepted. Finally, a possible answer to this question occurred to us—an answer that held promise of having rather general application: perhaps these rumors predicting even worse disasters to come were not "anxiety provoking" at all but were rather "anxiety justifying." That is, as a result of the earthquake these people were already frightened, and the rumors served the function of giving them something to be frightened about. Perhaps these rumors provided people with information that fit with the way they already felt.

From this start, and with the help of many discussions in which we attempted to pin the idea down and to formalize it somewhat, we arrived at the concept of dissonance and the hypotheses concerning dissonance reduction. Once the formulation in terms of dissonance and the reduction of dissonance was made, numerous implications became obvious. Following these implications through soon became the major activity of the project.[8]

The history of science is in fact strewn with examples of serendipity making important contributions, if not major breakthroughs, to knowledge. The research worker who is alerted to the serendipitous potentialities of his data is likely to exploit them more fully and thereby to increase his contribution to sociological theory and knowledge.

In research, one must also be willing to play hunches and to take risks. One might, for example, conduct a study to test whether working-class people are more likely to become schizophrenic than middle-class people. If the study is properly done, one should then be in a position to confirm or disprove the hypothesis. But the sociologist would probably not stop here. While he was at it, he might also want to see whether sex, age, race, rural-urban residence, marital status, family size, nationality, religion, etc., were also associated with schizophrenia; whether they were associated with neuroses; etc. In so doing, he might be guided by certain vague hunches concerning the relevance of these factors; only when the data were in hand, however, might their true significance be revealed.

To be sure, there are certain dangers involved in this procedure, since the interpretations are necessarily post factum, but we shall see later that it is possible to cope with these problems. If one were to avoid such tentative explorations, one might abort valuable research contributions.

The Assaying of Evidence

The aim of any science is to arrive at generalizations. The historian or the journalist may be interested in the concrete event, condition, or situation, but the scientist's focus on the concrete has the sole purpose of deriving general principles or patterns.

It is useful to distinguish two types of generalizations: *descriptive* and *theoretical*. The research worker is interested in both of these, but the procedures for arriving at these generalizations are quite different. The distinction between these two types of generalizations is presented by Jahoda, Deutsch, and Cook:

> Frequently, our interest in generalizing is not merely to draw conclusions about a broader population of people or of events from a smaller number of cases but rather to draw inferences about a relationship among variables that are conceptually, rather than phenomenally, defined. We wish to know, for instance, whether there is a relationship between the volume of a gas and its temperature—independently of whether the increase in temperature is caused by heating with a coal fire, an electric stove, or by any other method of producing heat. Similarly, we may wish to know whether equal-status contact between prejudiced people and minority-group members will, under certain specified conditions, lead to a reduction of prejudice—independently of whether the equal-status contact, under the given conditions, takes place in a housing community, in the army, at work, or at college.[9]

To generalize a finding based on a smaller number of cases to a broader population would be a descriptive generalization, but to enunciate a principle which encompasses a variety of situations provides a theoretical generalization. Otherwise expressed, a descriptive generalization refers to the relationship between the concrete categories under consideration, generalized to the population on which the sample is based. In a theoretical generalization the concrete variables are seen as *indicators* or *indices* of broader concepts.

The difference may be illustrated by the following example. Let us say that a study shows that Catholics are more likely than Protestants to vote for the Democratic Party. If the sample has been properly selected, this finding may be generalized to the population on which the sample is based. One cannot replicate this finding within the same study, of course, but one can examine other studies to determine whether they too show that Catholics are more likely to vote Democratic.[10] This other research will either support or weaken this descriptive generalization.

One might, however, interpret this finding to suggest that low-status group members will tend to vote for the more "radical" political party. Guided, perhaps, by Mannheim's theory of ideology and utopia,[11] one might reason that the low-status group is subject to greater social and economic deprivation, oppression, and exploitation and thus is interested in social change, via political means, which will alleviate its lot. Conversely, the high-status group will tend to prefer the maintenance of the status quo which supports its privileges and position; it would therefore lean in the conservative direction.

The reason this is considered a theoretical generalization is that each of the concrete variables is viewed as an indicator of a broader concept. "Catholicism" is employed as an indicator of "low-status group membership," "Protestantism" as an indicator of "high-status group membership," "Democratic Party" as an indicator of "liberal or radical political ideology," and "Republican Party" as an indicator of "conservative political ideology." If, at some future time, the Catholics became the higher-status group and Protestants the lower group, then (assuming party ideology remained the same) one would expect Catholics to vote Republican and Protestants Democratic. The same would be expected if the political parties reversed their ideologies.

If this change occurred, then the *descriptive generalization* would be reversed, but the *theoretical generalization* would remain the same. One can thus see that the theoretical generalization has much greater power in uncovering the unity from the diversity of social life. There are, however, different ways of confirming these generalizations.

Let us first consider the confirmation of a descriptive generalization. Such confirmation is basically founded on the process of *replication*. Replication is "the systematic restudy of a given relationship in different contexts."[12] Such replications may be of several different types.

The first type of replication involves a comparison of one's data with that of another sample of the same or closely comparable populations. Let us say that, in a nationwide voting study, one found that 60 per cent of the Catholics and 35 per cent of the Protestants supported the Democratic Party. On statistical grounds, one could determine the range of possible error at a certain level of confidence. But errors other than probability errors enter into every survey. If four or five other nationwide polling organizations also reached the same conclusion, however, then one would have greater confidence in the accuracy of the descriptive generalization.

A somewhat different type of replication is one involving the same descriptive generalization in a number of different populations. For example, when the Surgeon General reports that in 25 out of 26 smoking studies, conducted at different times and under different conditions, a positive correlation between cigarette smoking and incidence of lung cancer appears, one's confidence that the generalization is sound is considerably enhanced.

Durkheim is an avid practitioner of this type of replication. He finds, for example, that Protestants have higher suicide rates than Catholics in France. But his basic argument rests on whether Protestants *generally* have higher suicide rates. Hence, he replicates this finding in 17 different countries or regions of Europe.[13] With this cumulative weight of evidence, the descriptive generalization achieves a power it could never attain in a single study on a single population.

These two types of replication require one to refer to data outside one's immediate sample in order to support the descriptive generalization. One cannot replicate the identical finding with the identical data. There is one form of replication, noted by Selvin, which may increase confidence in a descriptive generalization and which may be conducted within the same study. This is Stouffer's method of "matched comparisons." Here the investigator seeks to determine whether a descriptive generalization characterizing the entire sample also characterizes a wide range of subgroups in that sample. The weight of evidence is judged by the consistency with which the empirical generalization obtains in these various subgroups. In a study of American soldiers, Stouffer found that noncommissioned officers in the total sample were more likely than privates to say that they were in good spirits. The sample was then broken down "into 3 groups by Army component, . . . each of which is subdivided again into 2 groups by educational level," which is further subdivided into 6 groups by length of time in the Army.[14] Omitting those groups containing fewer than 40 cases, the results show that, in 13 comparisons, the noncoms were more likely to be in good spirits, two cases were ties, and in one comparison the privates were more likely to be in good spirits. These results lend strength to the conclusion that noncoms outstrip privates in this aspect of morale. If, on the other hand, the result for the total sample were due to the fact that this relationship appeared in a few heavily represented groups, but did not appear in a large number of other groups, the descriptive generalization would to some extent have been undermined.

It may be noted that while replication can confirm a *finding*, it cannot confirm an *interpretation*. The fact that a finding recurs in diverse samples lends no strength to the interpretation. While descriptive generalizations are, in a narrow sense, valuable for prediction, they do not necessarily lead to understanding. For this we must turn to theoretical generalizations.

If the basic procedure for confirming an empirical generalization is replication, the basic procedure for confirming a theoretical generalization is the selection of alternative indicators (or indices) of the same concept. Every concept is reflected in a range of empirical manifestations. Often it is not evident that these diverse empirical referents are dealing with the same idea, and a high level of imagination may be required of the analyst to indicate the sense in which they do.

Durkheim's analysis of suicide is an outstanding case in point. He found, for example, that Jews in nineteenth-century Europe had lower suicide rates than Christians. He reasoned that the Jews, subject to much greater discrimination and oppression, felt more tightly bound to, or integrated with, their own religious group, and that such integration was an insulator against suicide.[15] He was thus no longer treating Jews as a particular religious group but as an indicator of a group characterized by strong social solidarity. Now, in mid-twentieth-century America, the prejudice against Jews has decreased, a large measure of assimilation has occurred, and it is likely that the strong integration of the group has been reduced (evidenced, for example, by a weakening attachment to ritual and tradition). In terms of Durkheim's theoretical generalization, one would expect the Jewish suicide rate to rise to the level of that of other groups, and recent evidence supports this expectation.[16]

In sum, Durkheim's descriptive generalization (Jews have low suicide rates) may change, but his theoretical generalization (socially integrated groups have low suicide rates) may be supported.

In the study of suicide, Durkheim uses empirical materials, but he is invariably concerned with theoretical generalizations. His fundamental theme is that the high social integration of a group leads to lower suicide rates. Phrased in this general way, he examines a variety of groups characterized by high social integration. He assumes that Catholics have a higher level of integration than Protestants (who are more individuated); that Jews are more highly integrated than Christians; that married people have greater integration than single people (who are more socially isolated); that more poorly educated people have greater integration than more highly educated people; that "traditionalistic" countries (England, the Balkan countries) are more integrated than other countries; that women (on the basis of their conservatism, traditionalism, etc.) are more integrated than men; etc. In every case, he finds that the more highly integrated group has lower suicide rates.[17]

Despite some questionable aspects of this procedure (partly based on dubious assumptions but mostly based on inadequate data), Durkheim here offers a brilliant example of the marshalling of evidence. He is able to coordinate a large number of empirical generalizations into a single *theoretical generalization*—that a high level of social integration is associated with a low suicide rate. The cumulative evidence bearing upon the same proposition makes the argument particularly powerful and persuasive.

Or consider, in a study of political behavior, the association between age and acquaintanceship with political party workers: older people are more likely to know party workers.[18] As such, this is a descriptive generalization; it might be tested in other studies. However, suppose one interpreted this result to suggest that people who are more deeply integrated into the community will have a greater likelihood of being familiar with political activists. Older people might be expected to have this greater integration.

But if this interpretation were correct, then one would assume that people who would otherwise be characterized as "integrated" should also have a greater knowledge of party workers. Were they not, this would call into question the view that the older people's knowledge of party workers was due to their greater integration. One would assume that *long-term residents* are more integrated than community new-comers; that *members of community organizations* are more integrated than nonmembers; and that *professionals* (who are likely to have wide-ranging contacts) are more integrated than unskilled workers. And, in fact, the data show that each of the integrated groups—older people, long-term residents, organization members, and professionals —do have greater knowledge of political party workers.[19] The empirical generalization concerning the relationship of age to party-worker knowledge is thus enlarged to suggest a theoretical generalization concerning the relationship of community integration to party-worker knowledge; at the same time, these data strengthen the interpretation of the original relationship.

One caution must be introduced with regard to such research strategy, namely, that one may not be selective in one's test of the theoretical generalization. Within one's study, all data which bear on the theoretical proposition must be examined. If, for example, Durkheim's empirical generalization was found to hold for Catholics, Jews, married people, and women, but did not hold for traditionalistic countries and poorly educated people, it would not be legitimate to report the first four findings and to neglect the last two. All the relevant data must be considered.

There are at least four ways in which the assaying of evidence can improve understanding and interpretive power. The first is that the support of other data strengthens the original theoretical proposition, endowing it with a power and generality far exceeding the descriptive data upon which it is based. The finding that Catholics have lower suicide rates is of moderate interest. But if this finding is interpreted as signifying that *cohesive* groups have lower suicide rates, and if this interpretation is supported by the finding that a wide variety of other groups characterized as cohesive manifest similar behavior, then a proposition of great scope and power has been enunciated. The related evidence thus lends strength to the conviction that the theoretical generalization derived from the initial descriptive generalization is justified.

The examination of related evidence obviously also has the parallel function of disproving the theoretical generalization. It may afford a basis for rejecting the interpretation of the original finding and for seeking an alternative interpretation. Assume that one had interpreted the lower suicide rate of Catholics to be due to their higher level of integration. If, however, one found that the suicide rates of other highly integrated groups were *not* lower, this would call into question the original interpretation. One would be disposed to assume that some quality of Catholicism other than level of integration was responsible for the lower suicide rate.

A research study on adolescence affords an illustration of how the marshalling of evidence procedure may disconfirm a theoretical generalization. The empirical proposition with which the analysis began was a relationship between social class and self-esteem: adolescents from the higher class tended to have higher self-esteem than those from the lower class.[20] The obvious explanation—and indeed the one which formed the basis for the original hypothesis—was that those with higher prestige in the society would be held in higher regard by others and would, through the Meadian mechanism of reflected appraisals, come to regard themselves more favorably.

Social class is thus viewed as an indicator of social prestige, with its attendant interpersonal consequences. The *empirical* generalization is that, among adolescents, high social class is associated with high self-esteem; this is converted into the *theoretical* generalization, "high prestige in the society is associated with high self-esteem." The latter proposition can be tested by other data in the same study, whereas the former cannot. If the latter proposition were true, then one would expect Negroes, who are subject to the most shocking discrimination and have the lowest prestige in the society, to have strikingly low self-esteem; in fact, however, their self-esteem is not very much lower than that of whites. One would have a similar expectation of Jews, who rank low in the status hierarchy, but Jews actually have slightly *higher* self-esteem than others. Conversely, one would expect the high prestige "Old Yankees"—white Protestants of English and Welsh descent—to have unusually high self-esteem, but in fact their self-esteem level is slightly lower than average. But the most persuasive evidence is the following: if one places the various ethnic groups in the society in rank order of social prestige and also in rank order of proportion with high self-esteem, one emerges with a Spearman rank order correlation of close to zero; there is neither a positive nor negative relationship between ethnic prestige and self-esteem.[21] These data clearly disprove the theoretical proposition that, among adolescents, social group prestige level is associated with self-esteem. This makes it unlikely that the observed relationship between class and self-esteem is due to social prestige.

It is not, of course, always necessary for every item of evidence to be consistent with the theoretical generalization since special factors may operate in particular cases. Durkheim found, for example, that members of the military forces had much higher suicide rates,[22] despite the fact that the military was a highly integrated organization. This finding contradicted the generalization that a high level of integration was associated with a low suicide rate. Durkheim argued, however, that a different principle operated in this case, namely, that excessive integration produced *altruistic* suicide. This apparent exception did not weaken the generalization but suggested that a different principle was operating in this case.

A third advantage involved in the examination of the range of evidence is that it may enable one to select between alternative interpretations of the original finding. The lower suicide rate of Catholics might be interpreted as due to (1) their higher level of integration, or (2) the fear of facing eternity without the purgation of sin through confession before death. But if Jews and people in Protestant "traditionalistic" countries, who do not practice confession, have lower suicide rates, then the first interpretation appears more compelling than the second.

A fourth advantage of a theoretical generalization is that it is often possible to test it within the *same study*. Aside from "unit replication," this is impossible with a descriptive generalization. If one finds that upper-class adolescents have higher self-esteem than lower-class adolescents, there is no way to confirm this finding within the same body of data. One must either search for other studies, or seek to replicate this finding in further research, before one can consider the finding confirmed. If the empirical proposition is converted into the theoretical proposition that high social prestige is conducive to high self-esteem, however, then it is possible to test whether the same is true of other high prestige groups (for example, racial, religious, or nationality groups) in the *same* sample. A particular study may thus yield more confident theoretical generalizations than descriptive generalizations.

Assessment of the range of evidence also has certain statistical implications. Given a proper sample, the degree of confidence one can have in a descriptive generalization can be clearly specified. For example, we can say of an empirical generalization that in less than 5 out of 100 cases of random selection from a population in which no differences existed, would a difference of the observed size appear. We thus have a certain level of confidence that the sample data reflect the population data, and this confidence can be increased if we can objectively state that in only 1 out of 100 or 1 out of 1,000 cases could such a result have occurred by statistical chance.

Theoretical generalizations, on the other hand, tend to be more tentative since no objective statistical principles are available to guide one's judgment. Equally important is the inevitable uncertainty which enters into the selection of indices of concepts. Catholicism may, to be sure, reflect "social integration," but it obviously reflects many other things as well. Education may be an indicator of "cultural sophistication," but its imperfection is apparent. Thus, some element of uncertainty inevitably enters into theoretical generalizations, however supportive the evidence may be.

It may be suggested, however, that the assaying of evidence may on occasion enable one to have greater confidence on statistical grounds in the theoretical generaliaztion than in the empirical generalization. Assume, for the sake of argument, that the relationship between religion and suicide were significant at the 0.10 level (using sample rather than census data). One would have a low level of confidence in this empirical generalization since there is a real likelihood that it may have occurred by chance. One then converts the result into the theoretical generalization regarding the relationship of social integration and suicide. One then tests this proposition with other indicators of social integration, for example, among Jews, married people, women, poorly educated people, traditionalist societies, and finds that the relationship is in each case significant at about the 0.10 level. *One's confidence in each of the empirical relationships would thus be low but one's confidence in the theoretical generalization might be fairly high.* One would reason that such consistency of data must be more than mere coincidence and that the relationship between social integration and suicide is a real one, even though any one of the findings might be due to statistical artifacts.

In the above-mentioned self-image study, for example, a group of students were selected who considered their academic performance in school to be poor. Among this group, it was found that those who felt it was important to do well in school had lower self-esteem than those who considered it unimportant. This finding suggested the following theoretical generalization: self-estimates of qualities are particularly likely to affect global self-esteem *when the quality is highly valued.*

One would, however, require more than the valuation of academic performance to have confidence in the generalization. Hence, the 16 qualities most highly valued by the respondents (for example, reliability, intelligence, morality, popularity, etc.) were selected for consideration. With regard to 15 out of the 16 qualities, those who considered themselves deficient in the quality but valued it highly had lower global self-esteem than those who considered themselves *equally* deficient but did *not* value it.[23] With regard to some of these qualities, the differences were not statistically significant, but the impressive consistency of the results provided evidence that the theoretical generalization was sound. In this case, on the whole, one could have greater confidence in the theoretical generalization than in many of the descriptive generalizations on which it was based.

Assaying evidence thus makes a number of contributions to the development of theoretical generalizations. The first is that it may lend support to the interpretation of the finding, thereby producing a theoretical generalization of power and scope. Second, it may call into question a theoretical interpretation, thereby directing attention to alternative explanations which may better fit the facts. Third, if two explanations appear to be equally "plausible" or compelling, the confirmatory data may show, in a comparable empirical situation, which explanation is supported and which is weakened or disproved. Fourth, it is often susceptible of test within the *same* study. Finally, the cumulation of evidence may increase confidence in the theoretical generalization in the face of doubts about the statistical adequacy of each of the descriptive relationships.

Post-Factum Interpretations

In view of all that may be learned through elaboration, the flow of analysis, serendipity, the assaying of evidence, etc., why does hypothesis-testing continue to remain the research model in behavioral science? One important reason, we would suggest, is that it avoids a major problem of data analysis, namely, the post-factum interpretation.

Let us consider again the nature of hypothesis-testing. Ideally, on the basis of a strict logico-deductive system, the scientist arrives at a conclusion which he seeks to test in the world of reality. The evidence thus confirms or disconfirms his entire line of reasoning. The superiority of this procedure over post-factum interpretations is obvious. In hypothesis-testing, the investigator *begins* with a specific interpretation and determines whether the data are consistent with it, whereas, in the post-factum interpretation, the analyst begins with the data and seeks an interpretation consistent with it. Merton observes:

Post-factum explanations remain at the level of plausibility (low evidential value) rather than leading to "compelling evidence" (a high degree of confirmation). Plausibility, in distinction to compelling evidence, is found when an interpretation is consistent with one set of data (which typically has, indeed, given rise to the decision to utilize one, rather than another, interpretation).[24]

But why do post-factum interpretations have low evidential value compared with hypothesis-testing? There are three distinctive disadvantages of post-factum interpretations: they are *flexible, not nullifiable, and not dependent on external confirmation.*

Excessive *flexibility* is one of the most conspicuous problems of post-factum interpretations. In principle, one is free to choose or change one's interpretation at will. If, for example, one finds that professors in large universities were more likely than those in small colleges to be subject to the "McCarthy scare," one can bring to bear a number of possible interpretations of this result. If, on the other hand, the empirical result had been precisely the reverse, one could have come up with equally satisfactory explanations.

The second problem is that post-factum interpretations are *not nullifiable.* If one finds that working-class people are more radical, one might interpret this finding to be due to their resentment at their economic exploitation. But, as it stands, there is no way to prove this interpretation wrong. In hypothesis-testing, on the other hand, the theory presumably generated the data examination, and the data are thus capable of nullifying the hypothesis and the theory underpinning it.

The third issue is that of *dependence on external confirmation.* If an interpretation is offered after the data are in, there is no confirmation that the interpretation is correct. One cannot refer back to the data for confirmation; the strength of the interpretation resides solely in the logical system in which it is imbedded. In hypothesis-testing, on the other hand, the data come after the hypothesis has been formulated and thus represent external confirmation of one's line of reasoning.

Relative to hypothesis-testing, then, post-factum interpretations have the limitations of excessive flexibility, absence of nullifiability, and lack of confirmation. *These problems can be overcome, however, by various procedures we have already discussed.* Specifically, the procedures of elaboration and assaying of evidence are particularly valuable in this regard. Basically, the procedure involves drawing *inferences* from the interpretation and undertaking to *test* these inferences. The post-factum interpretation is thus not the completion of the analysis but only the first step in it. The interpretation is made *conditional* upon the presence of other evidence to support it. One reasons that *if* the interpretation one has assigned to a relationship were correct, *then* certain empirical consequences would follow. If these empirical consequences do in fact appear, then the interpretation is strengthened. If they do not appear, then a new interpretation is required, which is also subject to further empirical test.

Consider the following findings and interpretations:

1. *Finding:* Durkheim finds that highly educated people have higher suicide rates than poorly educated people.[25]

Interpretation: On deductive grounds, Durkheim interprets this relationship as misleading. Education in itself is not conducive to suicide, he argues. Both suicide and the spirit of free inquiry arise from "the weakening of traditional beliefs."[26] Essentially, the relationship is due to the fact that each variable is a separate consequence of a common cause.

This post-factum interpretation has strength, for it is founded on a clear and powerful system of reasoning based on an intimate knowledge of the phenomena under consideration. Nevertheless, it is not firmly convincing because of the issues of flexibility, nullifiability, and confirmation. It is flexible in the sense that it or another interpretation might equally well have been offered, so long as adequate theoretical support were available. The interpretation is also not nullifiable; one may dispute Durkheim's reasoning, but one cannot prove him wrong. Finally, it lacks *external confirmation.* The strength of the interpretation is vested entirely on its inner logic, not on evidence external to it.

The introduction of extraneous variables can deal with all three problems. In this case, Durkheim suggests that religious traditionalism is the extraneous variable. In principle, then, one could examine the relationship of education to suicide, *controlling* on religious tradition-alism. (Such data were not available to Durkheim.) Infinite *flexibility* is eliminated because the specific hypothesis is exposed to test. The interpretation finally selected is not then merely a matter of prefer-ence, but of systematic investigation. Second, the interpretation is *nullifiable.* If, after controlling on religious traditionalism, the relation-ship between education and suicide remains as strong as ever, then Durkheim's interpretation must be rejected. Finally, the interpretation is subject to *external confirmation.* If, after controlling on traditional-ism, the relationship vanishes entirely, then the interpretation is con-firmed. This confirmation is based on external empirical evidence, not solely on the logic of the argument.

2. *Finding:* Working-class people are more likely than middle-class people to stress "obedience" as a quality that they value in their children.[27]

Interpretation: Working-class people tend to be subject to the authority of others in the occupational realm; the occupational experience makes them view the world in terms of authority and causes them to stress this quality in their children.

This (oversimplified) interpretation is buttressed by a convincing theoretical argument,[28] but is still plagued by the issues of flexibility, nullifiability, and external confirmation. These issues are dealt with by examining the relationship between class and parental values, con-trolling on the component variable of "subjection to supervision in the occupational realm."[29] A precise interpretation is thus subjected to test. If the relationship remains after the component variable has been controlled, then the interpretation is nullified. If the relationship vanishes (which largely occurs), the interpretation receives external confirmation.

3. *Finding:* Youngsters from broken homes are more likely to become delinquent.

Interpretation: The reduction of parental authority makes the child more subject to street gang influence, and this street gang influence presses in the direction of delinquency.

This post-factum interpretation is plausible and is consistent with a good deal of empirical and theoretical work. It can, however, be put to specific test by examining the relationship between family rupture and delinquency, *controlling on the intervening variable of street gang influence*. The persistence of the relationship nullifies the interpretation; the disappearance of the relationship confirms it.

We thus see that whether the interpretation is based on an extraneous, component, or intervening variable, it can be put to specific test and can be nullified or confirmed. Such confirmation does not prove that the interpretation is correct (indeed, it is probable that no interpretation can ever be proved), but it lends strength to it. It thereby helps to overcome some of the limitations of post-factum interpretations.

4. *Finding:* Children of divorce tend to have lower self-esteem than children from intact families.[30]

Interpretation: Children of divorce have experienced particularly discordant family lives and feel stigmatized by their socially anomalous positions; these experiences have a deleterious effect upon their self-esteem.

This interpretation is subject to test through the examination of *conditional relationships*. If the relationship is a consequence of discordant family relationships and social stigma, then it would follow that in those groups in which divorce is socially most strongly condemned (that is, among Catholics and Jews), the social stigma and parental disharmony in divorced families should be greater and the effect of divorce on self-esteem should be stronger. If the relationship of parental divorce and self-esteem were the *same* among Catholics and Jews as among Protestants, this would tend to nullify the interpretation. If, on the other hand, the relationship were *stronger* among Catholics and Jews than among Protestants, the result would tend to confirm it.[31]

Another example in which a conditional relationship confirms an interpretation is presented by Durkheim. Durkheim finds that the suicide rates are higher in the summer than during the other seasons. He interprets this finding to indicate that it is the density of social interaction which is suicidogenic. It is when social life is at its peak (in the summer) that society most makes its influence felt and stimulates suicidal dispositions.[32]

But if this interpretation is correct, then certain empirical consequences should follow. Specifically, under those conditions in which social interaction is high, the relationship should be stronger; where this is less the case, it should be weaker. What might such conditions be? Durkheim comes up with an ingenious answer—the conditions of rural and urban life. In the cities—particularly Paris—there is lively social interaction throughout the year. This is much less the case in the provinces and rural areas. One would thus expect the high point of the summer to be more strongly associated with suicide in the rural than in the urban areas. And, Durkheim shows, this is precisely what occurs.[33] The interpretation that the relationship between season of year and suicide is due to intensity of social interaction is thus strikingly supported by these *conditional relationships*.

5. *Finding:* Miners are more radical than most other workers.[34]

Interpretation: Workers with extreme insecurity of income develop political militance and a tendency to think in terms of more fundamental reform.

In this case, *the assaying of evidence* may enable one to test the theoretical interpretation. The greater radicalism of miners is interpreted post-factum as indicating the effect of insecurity of income on political ideology. If this were so, however, then one would expect members of other economically insecure occupations, for example, lumbermen, sailors, longshoremen, fishermen, and commercial farmers also to be more politically radical. Since this turns out to be the case, the interpretation is supported; had it not been so, the interpretation would have been weakened.[35]

In sum, the drawbacks of post factum interpretations, relative to hypothesis-testing, reside in their excessive flexibility, lack of nullifiability, and absence of confirmation. We have seen, however, that through controlling on extraneous, component, and intervening variables, through the examination of conditional relationships, and through the assaying of evidence dealing with theoretical generalizations, these drawbacks can in large measure be overcome in survey analysis.

It may further be noted that in actual research practice the contrast between hypothesis-testing and post-factum interpretation is not so great as it may appear. Many preformulated hypotheses are based on common-sense considerations rather than derived in a strictly deductive fashion from a tight theoretical system. On the other hand, many interpretations which appear to be post-factum are not entirely so. As a general rule, the survey analyst is guided by at least some implicit hypotheses in conducting his data analyses. It is true that each hypothesis may not be derived deductively from a well-developed theoretical system, but the analyst characteristically has some idea about why he is looking at the relationship in the first place. If, for example, he examines the relationship between sex and mental health, he does so on the basis of at least certain crude notions regarding the stressful experiences undergone by men and women in society. He does not, after all, relate a person's color of hair or initials to mental health, since he can see no reason for any possible association. Admittedly, the theory guiding the hypothesis may be ill-formed, but the observed relationship often supports some hypothesis, however crude.

It is also important to consider the theoretical defense of an interpretation. The statement that post-factum interpretations are merely plausible (low evidential value) does not mean that they are all *equally* plausible. In this sense, post-factum interpretations are like hypothesis-testing; in each case the strength of the interpretation rests upon the theoretical or deductive foundations which underpin it. Just because two interpretations are post-factum, then, does not mean that they have equal evidential value. If the theoretical or logical foundation is strong, then the interpretation has great evidential value; if weak, little evidential value. Conversely, if one tests an hypothesis derived from a dubious theory, the confirmation of the hypothesis does not prove the theory.

The survey analyst is thus obliged to use post-factum interpretations, and can do so in good scientific conscience, but he must be alert to the uncertainties surrounding the use of this method and must seek to deal with them through use of some of the above-mentioned procedures.

In actual survey work, the research is guided by hypotheses but also generates hypotheses, all this involving a complex intellectual interplay. Hypothesis-testing is of course important, but survey analysis also involves the various processes of elaboration, the flow of analysis, the pursuit of an idea, the exploitation of serendipitous findings, the assaying of evidence, and the confirmation of post-factum interpretations. Hypothesis-testing, valuable though it is, is too limited a procedure to serve as the sole model for survey data analysis.

The Units of Analysis

In our discussion of the process of elaboration—test factors, conditional relationships, and conjoint influence—relationships between characteristics of *individuals* have generally been examined. This is understandable, since the survey typically is based on a randomly selected sample of individuals from a given population. The procedure of elaboration, however, is equally applicable to data based on other units of analysis. At least seven levels of sociological analysis may be distinguished—the individual, the group, the organizational, the ecological, the institutional, the cultural, and the societal levels.

Individual units of analysis

A typical sociological or social psychological study might show that working-class people are more likely to stress "obedience" in their children, that Protestants commit suicide more than Catholics, that old people say they are less happy than young people, that women vote less than men. In each case, individuals are studied; they are characterized in terms of certain dispositions or behavior (valuing obedience, committing suicide, expressing feelings of happiness, voting) and are compared in terms of properties (class, religion, age, sex). This is by far the most common mode of survey analysis.

The group level

Groups consist of people who interact with one another in accord with established patterns, identify themselves as group members and are so identified by others.[36] Relationships among group variables may be among the most productive of research results.

The well-known study of democratic, authoritarian, and laissez faire groups is a good case in point.[37] The characterization of groups in these terms was not defined by the attitudes of the group members but by the behavior of the group leader—his mode of handling the boys. When the leader left the room, or when the boys were released from class, a certain amount of group horseplay occurred. It was possible to characterize the degree of horseplay of the group. Although the horseplay consisted of the acts of the *individual* boys, the interest was in describing the amount of *group* horseplay. It turned out that the authoritarian group displayed more horseplay when shifted to a democratic or laissez faire group situation,[38] a result suggesting that the repressive atmosphere created by the authoritarian leadership created a pent-up tension which found release in horseplay. This illustrates the examination of the relationship between two *group* characteristics, without reference to individual properties.

If one has a sufficiently large number of groups available for analysis, then the analysis of the relationship between group properties can achieve full quantitative expression and elaboration. We might, for example, study a sample of groups, 50 of which were small (six or fewer members) and 150 of which were large (seven or more members). One might find that 70 per cent of the large groups were permeable (easy to enter and leave), but that this was true of only 40 per cent of the smaller groups. This result might suggest that the larger the group, the less personal difference any one member makes, thus making it easier to enter or leave large groups.

But the analyst might consider whether extraneous variables were implicated. It might be suggested that the difference in permeability is not due to size as such, but to the fact that larger groups are more likely to have formal leaders than small groups. This hypothesis could be tested by dividing the sample into groups with or without elected leaders and observing whether the relationship between group size and permeability were maintained. If the relationship continued to exist, one would conclude that the leadership factor had nothing to do with it; if the relationship vanished, one would conclude that leadership was responsible for the result.

Organizational units of analysis

It is possible to study organizations abstracted from the individuals who constitute it. Whether the organization be a factory, a government office, or a university, it possesses a structure, a stability, and a permanence which is independent of its particular members. In such organizations, people may come and go, times may change, but the organization exists as a distinctive entity.

In some cases, one can characterize the organization by some summary measure of the individuals who constitute it; for example, the morale of the organization may be judged by the "average" morale of its members.[39] At the same time, one would not infer the economic strength of a company from the economic strength of its members. Indeed, the two may vary inversely. The less the employees are paid, the greater may be the profits. There may thus be some danger in inferring a property of the organization from the properties of its members.

Beyond this, however, there are certain qualities of organizations which cannot be inferred from any cumulation of data about individuals. One may speak of the degree of bureaucratization of an organization; degree of specialization of function; "efficiency" of the organization; fineness of hierarchical discrimination; the rigidity of rules; "particularistic" or "universalistic" criteria of recruitment and advancement; patterns of "succession;" flexibility of decision; "aggressiveness" or "cautiousness" of the organization; etc. Certain of these characteristics—flexibility, aggressiveness—are applicable to individuals, but one cannot characterize the organization in these terms on the basis of any summation of these qualities of the individuals who constitute it. For example, a cautious staff with an aggressive director may well be an aggressive organization.

Data analysis of organizational properties possesses the same logic as that of other units of analysis. Lazarsfeld and Thielens, for example, show that universities of outstanding quality are more likely to report incidents involving academic freedom.[40] These two properties—"university reputation" and "ratio of incidents"—are group or organizational properties; they do not refer to characteristics of individuals. An individual level of analysis would examine the relationship between an *individual* faculty member's reputation and *his* involvement in academic freedom incidents. The results at the individual and the organizational level could be quite different, and the interpretation of the results could be radically different.

Similarly, one might examine the relationship between the efficiency of organizations and their flexibility; fineness of hierarchical discrimination and rigidity of rules; morale and profitability (a major concern of industrial sociology); bureaucratization and universalistic criteria of recruitment and promotion. Any of these relationships could also be controlled on test factors (for example, size of organization) to reveal the presence of extraneous, component, intervening, etc., factors or to demonstrate the presence of conditional relationships.

Institutional units of analysis

Institutional analysis employs the legal, political, economic, family, etc., institutions of society as the units of analysis. One can examine the relationships of elements within institutions and across institutions.

Marxist analysis is strongly concerned with the relationship between the structure of the economic institution and other institutions. When Marx and Engels discuss the relevance of the economic substructure for the political, legal, scientific, religious, artistic, etc., superstructures, they are proceeding at the institutional level of analysis, and this aspect of its underlying logic is not fundamentally different from ordinary survey analysis. In *The Division of Labor*, Durkheim shows that the advance of specialization of economic function is associated with a shift to patterns of restitutive justice in the legal system.[41] Presumably, if statistical data were available and a static relationship were deemed adequate, one might have found a result similar to that appearing in Table 9–1.

Such a result would clearly support Durkheim's contention. Expressed in these terms, however, further questions might be raised. Perhaps it is not the fact of the division of labor (persuasive though this contention may be) which is responsible for the nature of the legal system, but the fact that nations with an advanced division of labor tend to derive their legal traditions from Roman law. One might then attempt to examine the relationship in Table 9–1 among nations influenced by Roman law, among those influenced by Anglo-Saxon law, and among those influenced by other types of law. The relationship between these two institutional areas could be substantially elaborated and clarified by such a level of analysis.

The study of the relationships of variables *within* institutions is also of interest. In the area of the family, one might find that endogamy is associated with the extended family system whereas exogamy is associated with the nuclear family system. Or it may be that an authoritarian family structure is associated with the principle of primogeniture.

It is thus meaningful to examine the relationship between attributes of different institutional areas or attributes within the same institutional area. There are, to be sure, practical problems of sampling and data collection involved in such studies, but these are not always so insuperable as they may at first appear; in any case, it may often

Table 9–1

*Division of Labor and Nature of Legal System**

	Advanced Division of Labor	Simple Division of Labor
Legal system primarily restitutive in nature	100	2
Legal system primarily retributive in nature	2	100

* Hypothetical.

be worth making some compromise with the canons of scientific rigor in order to deal with problems of such importance and scope.

Spatial units of analysis

Spatial units of analysis are the subject matter of human ecology. Since ecological research predated the use of sample survey research, it has a well-established history and a substantial literature. Basically, it is concerned with characterizing the attributes of areas and examining the associations among them. A well-known example is the relationship between social integration of an area (indexed by social class composition) and rate and type of psychosis.[42] The relationship appears in Table 9–2. The data indicate that the lower-class slum areas show a disproportionate amount of schizophrenia, relative to other regions of the city.

Table 9–2

Percentage of All Cases of Mental Disorder and the Percentage of the Population in Each Fourth of the 120 Subcommunities Grouped on the Basis of the Magnitude of the Rates[*]

Quartile Grouping	Percentage of Cases in Each Quartile	Percentage of Population in Each Quartile
Fourth or upper	40.7	23.5
Third	26.2	27.0
Second	18.5	24.7
First	14.6	24.8
Total per cent	100.0	100.0

[*] Robert E. L. Faris and H. Warren Dunham, *Mental Disorders in Urban Areas* (Chicago: University of Chicago Press, 1939), p. 35, Table 5. (Reprinted by permission of Robert E. L. Faris and H. Warren Dunham.)

It should be noted that the associated variables are spatial properties—the class composition of the area (not the class of the individual) and the schizophrenic or manic-depressive *rate* of the area (not the schizophrenia or manic-depression of the individual). Of course, the authors reason from a relationship between properties of the area to the properties of individuals, but the data are strictly on the ecological level.

The fields of social disorganization and social deviance have made frequent use of spatial units of analysis. Studies have been conducted on the relationship between proportion of broken homes in an area and delinquency rate in that area; average rental and crime rate; average rental and voting rate; etc. The distinction between the individual and the spatial unit is plain. If one shows a relationship between the rental paid by an individual family and delinquency in that particular home, the individual family is the unit of analysis; if one shows the relationship between the *average* rental of a district and the delinquency *rate* of that district, the area is the unit of analysis. One cannot, of course, automatically use results based on ecological relationships to infer generalizations about individuals.[43]

The cultural level of analysis

It is a sociological axiom that while individuals are the bearers of culture, cultural elements are independent of individuals. No one has stressed this point more strongly than Durkheim, who spoke of social facts as "things." Culture, of course, refers to the norms, values, practices, traditions, technological objects, ideologies, etc., of a group of people. It is thus possible to note whether certain cultural elements are characteristically associated with one another.

Whiting and Child, for example, have shown that in a sample of societies selected from throughout the world, those societies which characteristically impose stressful conditions on children (such as teasing or the sudden withdrawal of affection) also tend to have puberty rites which are especially severe.[44] Many other examples of such relationships between norms are cited in their work.

The classic work relating cultural elements is Murdock's *Social Structure*.[45] There he examines the relationships between such cultural elements as family structure, mode of economic production, technological practices, child-rearing customs, puberty rites, marital practices, myths, magic, religion, etc. The understanding of particular cultures, and of culture in general, is substantially clarified by the analysis of the relationship of cultural elements. Typically, two-variable analysis is employed in such studies, but there is nothing inherent in the method which precludes the procedure of elaboration characteristically applied to individual data.

Societal units of analysis

Societal elements would include such characteristics as the nature of the stratification system, the degree of urbanization, the geographical features of the territorial unit, etc. Sometimes, societies are characterized by their major institutions—one may speak of a specialized society, a feudal society, an advanced technological society, an underdeveloped society, etc. On other occasions, major cultural values are at issue: one may speak of an "equalitarian" society, a "democratic" (in the nonpolitical sense) society, an "acquisitive" society,[46] an "other-directed" society,[47] etc.

Lipset, for example, has shown that countries with high indices of wealth, industrialization, education, and urbanization are more likely to be stable democracies, whereas countries with low indices tend to be unstable democracies or dictatorships.[48] The distribution of political party strength in western societies has been shown to be associated with other institutional or societal variables.

While the procedure of elaboration has overwhelmingly been applied to data using the individual as the unit of analysis, there is no necessary reason why it must be confined to this level. In principle, it is applicable to units at any of the seven levels of analysis described. It is to be expected that the increasing use of levels of analysis other than the individual will increase the power, range, and generalizability of empirically based sociological propositions.

It is perhaps evident from the foregoing that it is also possible and meaningful to examine the relationship between units at different levels of analysis, for example, the individual and group levels, the organizational and cultural levels, the individual and ecological levels, etc. Perhaps the best known of such types of analysis has come to be known as "contextual analysis."[49] In this case, an organizational variable may be related to an individual variable, or a group variable may reveal conditional relationships between individual variables, etc. This highly fruitful research approach, however, requires extended discussion and exceeds the scope of this book.

Patently, the theoretical potentialities of elaborating these diverse units of analysis have not been fully exploited. It is sometimes felt that there is a qualitative difference, an unbridgeable gap, between the theoretically oriented data analysis of a Marx or a Durkheim or a Spengler or a Comte and that of contemporary survey analysis. We would suggest that the fundamental logic of these approaches is not as different as it may appear. The main difference may, in fact, be less in the logic of procedure than in the unit of analysis. The classical theorist is more likely to use the institution, culture, or society as the unit of analysis. There are, to be sure, other logical differences between these approaches, but this difference is among the most prominent.

The contemporary survey analyst may well be critical of the work of the classical theorist on various methodological grounds—the failure to quantify the phenomena, the frequent ambiguity of concepts, the dubious indicators, the failure to take account of extraneous or intervening variables, etc. On the other hand, the charge frequently launched against survey research that its generalizations are limited and trivial, while not entirely true, are also not without foundation. There is, after all, a limit to what one can understand about societies through the study of individuals. The sociologist may thus profit from greater attention to other units of analysis—groups, organizations, institutions, cultures, and societies. The principles of survey analysis should not be abandoned but rather *applied* to these other units of analysis.

In sum, the central concern of this book has been to explicate the procedure of *elaboration*. We have attempted to point to the range of information that can be gained by introducing a third variable into a two-variable relationship. As noted above, test factors, conditional relationships, and conjoint influences have typically been examined in studies involving the individual as the unit of analysis. In principle, however, there is no reason why they cannot be employed equally well when groups, organizations, institutions, etc., are the subjects of investigation. There is good reason to believe that such practice will eventuate in that union of theoretical fruitfulness and scientific precision which is the desideratum of any science.

NOTES

1. Walter B. Cannon, *The Way of an Investigator* (New York: W. W. Norton and Co., Inc., 1945), p. 68. (Reprinted by permission of W. W. Norton and Co., Inc.)
2. Robert K. Merton, *Social Theory and Social Structure* (Glencoe, Ill.: The Free Press, 1949), p. 98.
3. *Loc. cit.*
4. *Ibid.*, pp. 98–99. (Reprinted with permission of The Macmillan Company. Copyright 1949 by The Free Press, A Corporation.)
5. Cannon, *op. cit.*, p. 69. (Reprinted by permission of W. W. Norton and Co., Inc.)
6. Samuel A. Stouffer, "Some Afterthoughts of a Contributor to 'The American Soldier,'" in R. K. Merton and P. F. Lazarsfeld, eds., *Continuities in Social Research: Studies in the Scope and Method of "The American Soldier"* (Glencoe, Ill.: The Free Press, 1950). (Reprinted with permission of The Macmillan Company. Copyright 1950 by The Free Press, A Corporation.)
7. Samuel A. Stouffer et al., *The American Soldier: Adjustment During Army Life* (Princeton, N.J.: Princeton University Press, 1949), p. 252.
8. Leon Festinger, *A Theory of Cognitive Dissonance* (Evanston, Ill.: Row, Peterson, 1957), pp. vi–vii. (Reprinted by permission of Leon Festinger.)
9. Marie Jahoda, Morton Deutsch, and Stuart W. Cook, *Research Methods in Social Relations* (New York: Dryden Press, 1951), p. 87. (Reprinted by permission of Holt, Rinehart and Winston, Inc., Publishers. Copyright 1951 by Holt, Rinehart and Winston, Inc., Publishers.)
10. See, for example, Bernard R. Berelson, Paul F. Lazarsfeld, and William N. McPhee, *Voting* (Chicago: University of Chicago Press, 1954), p. 333.
11. Karl Mannheim, *Ideology and Utopia*, trans. Louis Wirth and Edward Shils (New York: Harcourt, Brace and World, Inc., 1936).
12. Hanan C. Selvin, "Durkheim's *Suicide* and Problems of Empirical Research," *American Journal of Sociology*, LXIII (May 1958), 612.
13. Emile Durkheim, *Suicide*, trans. John A. Spaulding and George Simpson (Glencoe, Ill.: The Free Press, 1951). Cited in Selvin, *op. cit.*, p. 614.
14. Stouffer et al., *The American Soldier*, *op. cit.*, p. 92. Cited in Selvin, *op. cit.*, p. 614.
15. Durkheim, *op. cit.*, pp. 155–160.
16. James M. Weiss, "Suicide: An Epidemiological Analysis," *Psychiatric Quarterly*, XXVIII (1954), 225–252.

17. Durkheim, *op. cit.*, Book II, chaps. 2–3.
18. Bernard R. Berelson, Paul F. Lazarsfeld, and William N. McPhee, *Voting* (Chicago: University of Chicago Press, 1954), p. 170.
19. *Loc. cit.*
20. Morris Rosenberg, *Society and the Adolescent Self-Image* (Princeton, N.J.: Princeton University Press, 1965), p. 40.
21. *Ibid.*, pp. 56–58.
22. Durkheim, *op. cit.*, p. 228.
23. Rosenberg, *op. cit.*, p. 248.
24. Merton, *op. cit.*, p. 90. (Reprinted with permission of The Free Press.)
25. Durkheim, *op. cit.*, pp. 164–168.
26. *Ibid.*, p. 168.
27. Leonard I. Pearlin and Melvin L. Kohn, "Social Class, Occupation, and Parental Values: A Cross-National Study," *American Sociological Review*, XXXI (August 1966), 466–479.
28. Melvin L. Kohn, "Social Class and Parent-Child Relationships: An Interpretation," *American Journal of Sociology*, LXVIII (January 1963), 471–480.
29. Pearlin and Kohn, *op. cit.*
30. Rosenberg, *op. cit.*, p. 86.
31. *Ibid.*, p. 89.
32. Durkheim, *op. cit.*, pp. 119–122.
33. *Ibid.*, p. 120.
34. Seymour Martin Lipset et al., "The Psychology of Voting: An Analysis of Political Behavior," in Gardner Lindzey, ed., *Handbook of Social Psychology*, (Reading, Mass.: Addison-Wesley, 1954), Vol. II, 1136–1138.
35. *Loc. cit.*
36. Robert K. Merton, *Social Theory and Social Structure* (revised and enlarged ed., Glencoe, Ill.: The Free Press, 1957), pp. 285–286.
37. Ronald Lippitt and Ralph K. White, "An Experimental Study of Leadership and Group Life," in T. M. Newcomb and E. L. Hartley, eds., *Readings in Social Psychology* (New York: Holt, Rinehart & Winston, Inc., 1947), pp. 315–330.
38. *Ibid.*, pp. 323–324.
39. Paul F. Lazarsfeld, "Problems in Methodology," in R. K. Merton, L. Broom, and L. S. Cottrell, Jr., eds., *Sociology Today* (New York: Basic Books, Inc., 1959), p. 58.
40. Paul F. Lazarsfeld and Wagner Thielens, *The Academic Mind* (Glencoe, Ill.: The Free Press, 1958), p. 167.
41. Emile Durkheim, *The Division of Labor in Society*, trans. George Simpson (Glencoe, Ill.: The Free Press, 1949).
42. Robert E. L. Faris and H. Warren Dunham, *Mental Disorders in Urban Areas* (Chicago: University of Chicago Press, 1939).
43. Some dangers involved in generalizing from ecological relationships to relationships among individuals are vividly described in William Robinson's discussion of the "ecological fallacy" in "Ecological Correlations and the Behavior of Individuals," *American Sociological Review*, XV (1950), 351–357. This problem is clarified by the consideration of the "fallacy of division" and the "fallacy of composition" in Morris R. Cohen and Ernest Nagel, *An Introduction to Logic and Scientific Method* (New York: Harcourt, Brace, and World, Inc., 1934), p. 377.

44. John W. M. Whiting and Irvin L. Child, *Child Training and Personality: A Cross-Cultural Study* (New Haven: Yale University Press, 1953).
45. George P. Murdock, *Social Structure* (New York: The Macmillan Company, 1949).
46. R. H. Tawney, *The Acquisitive Society* (New York: Harcourt, Brace, and World, Inc., 1920).
47. David Riessman, *The Lonely Crowd* (New Haven: Yale University Press, 1950).
48. Seymour Martin Lipset, *Political Man* (Garden City, N.Y.: Doubleday and Company, Inc., Anchor Books, 1963), chap. 2.
49. A methodological discussion of contextual analysis appears in Lazarsfeld, "Problems in Methodology," *op. cit.*, pp. 69–73. Some illustrations of the procedure appear in Alan B. Wilson, "Residential Segregation of Social Classes and Aspirations of High School Boys," *American Sociological Review,* XXIV (1959), 836–845; Leonard I. Pearlin and Morris Rosenberg, "Nurse-Patient Social Distance and the Structural Context of a Mental Hospital," *American Sociological Review,* XXVII (1962), 56–65; and Philip H. Ennis, "The Contextual Dimension in Voting," in William McPhee and William A. Glaser, eds., *Public Opinion and Congressional Elections* (New York: The Free Press of Glencoe, 1962), pp. 180–211.

APPENDIX A

Basic
Principles
of
Table
Reading

by Roberta G. Simmons

Although this volume is intended as an exposition of the logic of survey analysis, rather than as a manual, a cookbook discussion of table reading may be useful for the less experienced student. Characteristically, the analyst begins with a two-variable table, which is the most basic and the simplest to read. Table A–1 is a typical two-variable table, adapted from Lenski's *The Religious Factor*.[1] In this table religious group is seen as the independent variable, political party preference as the dependent variable.[2] The analyst asks whether people's religious background affects their party preference.

Table A–1 presents numbers of cases, not percentages; for example, 235 Protestants are Democrats. It is obvious that one cannot compare the actual numerical frequencies in the various table-cells. The fact that only 32 Jews are Democrats in comparison to 235 Protestants does not mean that Protestants are more likely to vote Democratic

Table A–1

Socio-Religious Group	Party Preference			Totals (Marginals) (N's)
	Democrat	Republican	Other	
White Protestants	(235)	(249)	(140)	(624)
White Catholics	(274)	(92)	(113)	(479)
Jews	(32)	(1)	(15)	(48)

than are Jews. The total, or "marginal," column indicates that the sample contains far fewer Jews than Protestants (48 as compared to 624); and, therefore, there are fewer Jews available to vote for either of the political parties. To control for this inequality of "N's,"[3] it is necessary to compute percentages. If there is reason to believe that one variable is the independent variable (that is, the determinant of the other variable), then the usual practice is to use the total number of cases for each category of this independent variable as a base for percentaging. Here, 624 Protestants represent 100 per cent of the Protestants, and we wish to see what per cent of these 624 people vote Democrat, Republican, or other; similarly, 479 Catholics and 48 Jews form 100 per cent of their respective groups. In Table A–2, the percentages across each row add up to 100 per cent.

The first task in reading another investigator's table is to determine in which direction the percentaging has been done. Has the percentaging been computed across the rows, down the columns, on the basis of the whole table; or is the table an abbreviated one in which the percentages as presented cannot add up to 100 per cent? The direction is determined by observing where the investigator has inserted his 100 per cent or total cases. In Table A–2, the percentages have

Table A–2

Socio-Religious Group		Party Preference			Totals (Marginals) (N's)
		Democrat	Republican	Other	
White Protestants	No.	(235)	(249)	(140)	(624)
	%	37.7	39.9	22.4	100.0
White Catholics	No.	(274)	(92)	(113)	(479)
	%	57.2	19.2	23.6	100.0
Jews	No.	(32)	(1)	(15)	(48)
	%	66.7	2.1	31.2	100.0

been computed across the rows. One can now observe that 66.7 per cent of Jews prefer the Democratic Party in contrast to only 37.7 per cent of Protestants. Jews are more, not less, likely to vote Democratic.

Note the manner in which this comparison is made. If the percentages have been computed *across* the rows (as in Table A–2), then we compare percentages *down* the columns. The proportion of Protestants who vote Democratic is compared to the proportion of Catholics and Jews who vote Democratic (37.7 to 57.2 to 66.7 per cent). The proportions of each of the religious groups who vote Republican can also be examined (39.9 compared to 19.2 compared to 2.1 per cent). Catholics and Jews appear to be more likely than Protestants to prefer the Democrats and less likely to prefer the Republicans.

The analyst does not usually begin by comparing the cells in the same direction in which the percentages have been computed. The fact that 37.7 per cent of Protestants prefer the Democratic Party as compared to 39.9 per cent of Protestants who choose the Republican Party may indicate that Protestants are almost as likely to vote Democratic as Republican; but, with this information only, we have not determined whether religion affects voting preference. We do not know whether Protestants are more or less likely to vote Democratic than other religious groups. In general, one wishes to compare the different proportions of people in the various independent variable groupings who select a given response-category of the dependent variable.

Whether one places the independent variable along the rows or columns is a matter of taste. It would be perfectly possible to reverse the above table (see Table A–3). Here the percentaging is computed

Table A–3

| | Socio-Religious Group | | | | | |
| | White Protestants | | White Catholics | | Jews | |
Party Preference	No.	%	No.	%	No.	%
Democrat	(235)	37.7	(274)	57.2	(32)	66.7
Republican	(249)	39.9	(92)	19.2	(1)	2.1
Other	(140)	22.4	(113)	23.6	(15)	31.2
Total	(624)	100.0	(479)	100.0	(48)	100.0

down the columns, and the percentages are compared in the opposite direction—this time along the rows (for example, 37.7 per cent is compared to 57.2 and 66.7 per cent, just as before).

Often, for the sake of simplicity, a table is abbreviated. Only part of the table is presented. Table A–4, for example, shows the proportion of each group who vote Democratic. The reader understands that the remainder of each group has voted Republican or "other." It is crucial to realize that the three percentages in this table do not add

Table A–4

Socio-Religious Group	Percentage of Each Group Preferring the Democratic Party	
White Protestants	37.7	(N = 624)
White Catholics	57.2	(N = 479)
Jews	66.7	(N = 48)

up to 100 per cent—that is, they are not based on the total number of people voting Democratic. These three percentages are to be compared directly to one another, for they represent the different proportions of subjects in the three independent variable groupings who have selected *one* response-category of the dependent variable.

The Three-Variable Table

When the investigator decides to explore further the link between his original independent and dependent variables, the three-variable table often appears. Once a third variable is introduced, it is possible to examine the relationship of the independent and dependent variables under each condition of the third variable. The three-variable table is actually a series of two-variable tables: for each category or condition of the third variable, the investigator presents a two-variable table containing the independent and dependent variables. In Table A–5, Lenski has added social class as the third variable, dividing

Table A-5

Party Preference by Class and Socio-Religious Group for the
1957 and 1958 Surveys Combined*

		MIDDLE CLASS				WORKING CLASS			
		Democrat	Republican	Other	Total	Democrat	Republican	Other	Total
White Protestants	No.	(60)	(139)	(60)	(259)	(175)	(110)	(80)	(365)
	%	23	54	23	100	48	30	22	100
White Catholics	No.	(68)	(52)	(52)	(172)	(206)	(40)	(61)	(307)
	%	40	30	30	100	67	13	20	100
Jews	No.	(23)	(1)	(12)	(36)	(9)	(0)	(3)	(12)
	%	64	3	33	100	75	0	25	100
Total	No.	(151)	(192)	(124)	(467)	(390)	(150)	(144)	(684)
	%	32	41	27	100	57	22	21	100

* Gerhard Lenski, *The Religious Factor* (Garden City, N.Y.: Doubleday and Co., 1961), p. 125, Table 15 (adapted). (Copyright 1961 by Gerhard Lenski. Reprinted by permission of Doubleday and Company, Inc.)

social class into two categories: working class and middle class. As a result, one now has, in effect, two relationships: (1) a relationship between religion and party preference in the middle class, and (2) a relationship between religion and party preference in the working class.

The total relationship between the independent and dependent variables, that is, between religion and voting behavior, has been subdivided into two partial (or contingent) relationships. We are now able to ask: Is this relationship between religion and voting preference maintained, reduced, increased, or changed when we introduce the third variable?[4] For middle-class subjects, the relationship is maintained (that is, within the middle class as within the total sample, Protestants are the least likely of the three religious groups to vote Democratic, Jews the most likely). Table A–5 shows that only 23 per cent of middle-class Protestants choose the Democratic Party as compared to 40 per cent of middle-class Catholics and 64 per cent of middle-class Jews. Similarly, the relationship is maintained for working-class subjects: 48 per cent of working-class Protestants as compared to 67 per cent of working-class Catholics and 75 per cent of working-class Jews select the Democratic Party.

Here, the original two-variable relationship is maintained. However, if the original relationship had disappeared within each of the subtables when we controlled for the third variable, then we would conclude that this original relationship was due to the third variable. For example, let us say that, among middle-class subjects, approximately 30 per cent of each religious group had chosen the Democratic Party and, among working-class subjects, about 60 per cent of each religious group had selected the Democrats. Then, since within each of the two classes the same proportion of each religious group had voted Democratic, we could conclude that the original relationship between religion and voting preference was accounted for by social class factors and was not really due to differences in religious affiliation. In this hypothetical case, we might say that the fact that Catholics were more likely to belong to the working class than Protestants, combined with the fact that working-class people were more likely to prefer the Democrats, accounted for the Catholics' apparent preference for the Democratic Party in the total sample. In the total sample, it would be the Catholics' working-class status, not their religion, that was determining their voting preference. The manner in which a third variable can account for a relationship between two other variables is discussed in detail in the text and therefore is touched on only briefly here (see Chapters 2 to 4).

Such an examination of the contingent or partial relations in a three-variable table will often suffice for purposes of analysis. But the reader must recognize that a large amount of information is contained in a three-variable table. Essentially, it is based on three two-variable relationships. First, there is the overall relationship between religion and party preference for the total sample (the original relationship); secondly, there is the overall relationship between social class and party preference; and finally, there is the relationship between social class and religion for the total sample.

These relationships are called marginal relationships since the figures on which they are based can be found outside the body of the table in the margins. They are thus distinguished from the contingent or partial relationships found inside the table. If we look at the bottom row-margins of each of the subtables in Table A–5, we see that social class is related to party preference. Only 32 per cent of the middle class, compared to 57 per cent of the working-class, subjects prefer the Democratic Party; on the other hand, 41 per cent of the middle-class subjects, as compared to only 22 per cent of the working-class subjects, choose the Republican Party. Lower social class status is thus related to a preference for the Democratic Party.

In order to see whether social class is related to religious background, we can use the marginal columns from each of the subtables[5] to create a new two-variable table, Table A–6. This table shows that

Table A–6

| Socio-Religious Group | | SOCIAL CLASS | | |
		Middle Class	Working Class	Total
White Protestants	No.	(259)	(365)	(624)
	%	42	58	100.0
White Catholics	No.	(172)	(307)	(479)
	%	36	64	100.0
Jews	No.	(36)	(12)	(48)
	%	75	25	100.0

religion and social class are related. Of all three religious groups, the Jews are least likely to be working class and the Catholics most likely. Only 25 per cent of Jews compared to 58 per cent of Protestants and 64 per cent of Catholics are in the working class.

These observations deal with the basic way of looking at a three-variable table. But there are also other ways of analyzing such a table, depending on one's perspective. One such way would be in terms of the "conditional relationship": for instance, we might be interested in whether the relationship between religion and voting is stronger for the middle class than for the working class. Another issue to consider would be "conjoint influence": for instance, we might want to investigate the combined influence of both religion and social class upon party preference. Since these matters are considered more fully in the text, they will not be discussed in detail at this point.

NOTES

1. Gerhard Lenski, *The Religious Factor* (Garden City, N.Y., Anchor Books: 1963). All the tables in this Appendix are derived from Table 15, p. 139. The basic data appear in Table A–5.
2. This is an example of a property-disposition relationship. See Chapter 1.
3. The numbers in the total column are also referred to as marginals and as N's (numbers).
4. The exact question asked depends on the reason the third variable was added in the first place. The rationale for introducing third variables is covered fully in the text and will not be discussed here.
5. The middle-class marginal table tells us that in the middle-class sample, there are 259 Protestants, 172 Catholics, and 36 Jews; the working-class marginal table tells us that in the working-class sample, there are 365 Protestants, 307 Catholics, and 12 Jews.

The
Arithmetic
of
Controls

The inexperienced researcher may be bewildered at the fact that the introduction of a test factor may have such strange consequences for the original relationship: it may cause the relationship to disappear, to emerge, or to reverse direction. Such changes are neither mysteries nor miracles; they derive directly from the distribution of the marginal frequencies. This arithmetic phenomenon underpins the logic of survey analysis.

In every two-variable relationship, there are currents and cross-currents at work which eventuate in the observed relationship. A relationship involves, in effect, a sum of meanings. Each correlation consists of a number of subcorrelations which, when combined, constitute the total correlation. These subcorrelations are called "partial associations" or "contingent associations." An understanding of the total association can only be derived from a knowledge of the complex set of associations which constitute it.

Assume, for example, that one examined the association between occupational role and powerlessness. Not only is there a relationship between these two variables for the total sample, but there is also one relationship between occupational role and powerlessness among men and another among women; there is a separate relationship for Irish, Polish, Germans, Jews, etc.; for whites and Negroes; for upper-, middle-, and lower-class people; for farm, village, small town, etc., dwellers. The total relationship is the "sum"of these various contingent relationships, which combine in various ways.

Proper analysis thus requires one to get "inside" a two-variable relationship, to learn about the contingent associations which constitute it, and to understand how these contingent associations recombine to constitute the total. One cannot predict the contingent associations from the total association, or vice versa.

Relationships among independent variable, dependent variable, and test factor

We have indicated that if the test factor is to account for the relationship between the independent and the dependent variable, then it must be statistically associated *both* with the independent *and* the dependent variable. This means that if the test factor accounts for the relationship, then three relationships must exist: (1) between the independent and the dependent variable, (2) between the test factor and the independent variable, and (3) between the test factor and the dependent variable. These relationships are shown in Table B-1, which deals with the association between broken homes and anxiety level. Part II is the total association; Part I shows two contingent associations—one for upper-class families, the other for lower-class families.

In Part II, we see, people from broken families are more likely than those from intact families to have high anxiety levels (53 per cent to 43 per cent). Part I shows that those from upper-class families are less likely than those from lower-class families to come from broken homes. This can be seen from an examination of the total cases (marginals) at the base of the table. Only 5 out of a total of 50 upper-class people (10 per cent) come from broken homes, compared with 110 out of 200 lower-class families (55 per cent). The test factor (class) is thus related to the independent variable (broken home).

Table B-1
Broken Home Background and Anxiety Level: I. Relationship Controlled on Social Class and II. Original Relationship*

	Part I						Part II		
	Contingent Associations						Total Association		
	UPPER CLASS			LOWER CLASS			TOTAL SAMPLE		
Anxiety level	Broken Family	Intact Family	Number	Broken Family	Intact Family	Number	Broken Family	Intact Family	Number
High	20%	20%	(10)	55%	54%	(109)	53%	43%	(119)
Medium	20	20	(10)	18	18	(36)	18	19	(46)
Low	60	60	(30)	27	28	(55)	29	39	(85)
Total per cent	100	100		100	100		100	100	
Number	(5)	(45)	(50)	(110)	(90)	(200)	(115)	(135)	(250)

* Hypothetical.

Finally, an examination of the horizontal totals shows that only 10 out of 50 upper-class people (20 per cent) have high anxiety levels, compared with 109 out of 200 lower-class people (55 per cent). The test factor (class) is thus also associated with the dependent variable (anxiety).

There is thus a positive relationship between the independent and the dependent variables, between the test factor and the independent variable, and between the test factor and the dependent variable. If these three relationships did not obtain, it would be inappropriate to introduce an extraneous, component, or intervening test factor.

Now let us note the impact of the test factor on the original relationship. In Table B-1, Part II, as noted above, those from broken homes are more likely than those from intact homes to have high anxiety (53 per cent to 43 per cent). When one controls on class, however, this difference disappears: in the upper class, the anxiety levels of those from broken or intact homes is the same (20 per cent each), and the same is true in the working class (55 per cent and 54 per cent). And yet the upper class and the lower class, when combined, equal the total sample; for the total sample, definite differences do exist.

Consider the following facts: in the upper class, 20 per cent of those from broken families have high anxiety; in the lower class, 55 per cent of those from broken families have high anxiety. When these two groups are combined to form the total sample of broken families, we find that 53 per cent have high anxiety. In some manner, the 20 per cent and 55 per cent "add" to 53 per cent.

Similarly, in the upper class, 20 per cent of those from intact families have high anxiety; in the lower class, the corresponding figure is 54 per cent. When these two groups are combined to form the total sample, we find that 43 per cent of intact families have high anxiety. In some way the 20 per cent and the 54 per cent "add" to 43 per cent.

The total relationship, which is positive, thus consists of two contingent relationships, each of which is virtually zero. It is therefore necessary to understand how the combined percentages of the contingent associations unite to produce the percentage for the total. How, among broken families, do the 20 per cent and 54 per cent combine to produce a total of 43 per cent? Certainly, there is nothing in the percentages themselves which would suggest such results. The answer, we shall see, must be found in the marginal totals.

Marginal totals

The marginal totals refer to the *number of cases* which appear at the base or at the right side of each association. Consider the marginals in the upper class in Table B-1, Part I. We see that there are 5 people from broken families and 45 from intact families, constituting the 50 members of the upper class. These are the vertical totals. Similarly, there are 10 people who have high anxiety, 10 who have medium anxiety, and 30 who have low anxiety, constituting the 50 people in the upper class. These are the horizontal marginals. It is these horizontal and vertical marginals which explain the phenomenon we are examining.

Let us first consider the importance of the vertical marginals. How is it that if 20 per cent of the broken families in the upper class have high anxiety and 55 per cent of the broken families in the lower class have high anxiety, this results in 53 per cent of the broken families in the total sample having high anxiety? The calculation is simple. If 20 per cent of the 5 broken families in the upper class have high anxiety, this means that one person in this group has high anxiety, this means that one person in this group has high anxiety. If 55 per cent of the 110 broken families in the lower class have high anxiety, this means that 61 people in the lower class have high anxiety. There is thus a total of 62 people in the broken families in both classes who have high anxiety. The total number of people from broken families in the entire sample is 115 (5 from the upper class and 110 from the lower class). The proportion of people with high anxiety among broken families in the entire sample is $62/115$, which equals 53 per cent. This is how the 20 per cent in the upper class and the 55 per cent in the lower class combine to produce a total of 53 per cent.

Similarly, we find that combining that 20 per cent of the intact upper-class families who are high in anxiety with the 54 per cent of the intact lower-class families results in 43 per cent of the intact families in the total sample with high anxiety. The reason is that 20 per cent of the 45 upper-class intact families represents 9 people, and that 54 per cent of the 90 lower-class intact families represents 49 people, thus producing a total of 58 people among the intact families of the entire sample who have high anxiety. Since there is a total of 135 members of intact families in the total sample (45 in the upper class and 90 in the lower class), there are thus 58 out of 135 members of intact families who have high anxiety, or 43 per cent.

It is, therefore, not simply the percentages in each group, but also the total number of cases in each column, which influences the total percentage. It is this factor which makes it possible to begin with a relationship between two variables, to stratify the sample by the test factor categories, and to find: (1) that there is no longer a relationship between the original two variables in each of the contingent associations; (2) that the size of the relationship in each of the contingent associations is *greater* than that in the original relationship; or (3) that the direction of the relationship in each of the contingent associations is the *reverse* of that in the original relationship.

Unequal marginals

In Table B-1, it will be noted that the marginal totals within each class are unequal. In the middle class, for example, only 5 people come from broken homes and 45 people come from intact homes. In the working class, on the other hand, 110 people come from broken homes and 90 come from intact homes. It is these unequal totals which largely account for the divergence between the contingent associations and the total association. If, in the upper class, the number of people from broken and intact families were the same and if, in the lower class, the number of people from broken and intact families were the same, then the effect that we have observed would not appear. In fact, if the *ratio* between broken and intact families were the same in both classes, then the effect would not appear. It will only appear if the marginals within each contingent association differ or, rather, if the proportions differ.

But what if the proportions do not differ? The answer is that they *must* differ if the test factor is related to the independent variable; this is inherent in the idea of a relationship. We noted earlier that the test factor must be related to the independent variable (and to the dependent variable) if it is to be used as a test factor.[1] In Table B-1, it is obviously so related. In the upper class, 20 per cent (5 out of 50) come from broken homes, whereas in the lower class, 55 per cent (110 out of 200) come from broken homes. Unequal totals thus help to explain the divergence between the contingent associations and the total association. But this inequality is required, in the sense that it must always exist if the test factor is associated with the independent variable.

To recapitulate: We begin with a relationship between broken home and anxiety (53 per cent of those from broken homes, but 43 per cent of those from intact families, have high anxiety). We then control on social class and find that, within each social class, there is no longer any relationship between broken home and anxiety. We then say that the relationship between broken home and anxiety is "due to" social class.

Let us attempt to spell out what this statement means. It means that the reason people from broken homes have higher anxiety is that they are more likely to come from the lower class (out of 115 broken families, 110 are in the lower class, whereas out of 135 intact families, only 90 are in the lower class), and that lower-class people are more likely than upper-class people to have high anxiety (109 out of 200 lower-class people are high in anxiety compared with only 10 out of 50 upper-class people). This is the particular sense in which the relationship between broken home and anxiety is said to be "due to" class.

Suppressor and distorter variables

In the foregoing discussion, we have attempted to show how a relationship between two variables may, when stratified according to the several test-factor categories, become noncorrelations (or weakened correlations) in the contingent associations. When this occurs, the test factor will be either an extraneous variable, a component variable, or an intervening variable.

When one deals with a suppressor variable, the matter is reversed. Here one begins with a noncorrelation between the independent and dependent variables; when one stratifies according to the test factor categories, a relationship *emerges* in each of the contingent associations. The suppressor variable is thus the exact opposite of the extraneous, component, or intervening variable. The extraneous variable causes an *existing* relationship to *disappear* when it is introduced; a suppressor variable causes a noncorrelation to *become* a correlation when it is introduced.

It should be stressed that, in dealing with suppressor variables, we are describing a situation in which each of the contingent associations has the same sign— positive or negative— even though the total association is near zero. What is the arithmetic that makes this anomalous situation possible?

Consider the example drawn from Arnold Rose, dealing with the relationship between length of time in the union and "tolerance" regarding Jewish union officers. (In this context, we are defining "tolerance" as indicating indifference to whether Jews are union officers; respondents neither favor nor oppose the idea.) For the total sample, we noted, there was no difference in tolerance between those who had been in the union four or more years and those who had been in less than four years. When we examined this relationship within three separate age groups, however, we found that, in each group, those who had been in the union longer were more tolerant than those who had been in the union less time. How is it possible that when one combines these three positive relationships, the total relationship is virtually zero? The answer, once again, is to be found in the marginals.

First, let us consider the relationships among the independent variable, the dependent variable, and the test factor (Table B-2). For the total association, there is a zero association between the independent variable (years in union) and the dependent variable (tolerance); but, within each age group, those who have been in the union longer are more tolerant.

Consider now the relationship between the test factor (age) and the independent variable (years in union). Among the younger men, 78 men out of a total of 129, that is, 60 per cent, have been in the

Table B-2

Length of Time in Union and Attitudes Toward Jews on Union Staff: I. Controlled on Age and II. Total Relationship*

Jews on Union Staff	Contingent Associations I — Age									Total Association II		
	29 YEARS OR LESS			30–49 YEARS Years in Union			50 + YEARS			TOTAL SAMPLE Years in Union		
	4 −	4 +	Number	4 −	4 +	Number	4 −	4 +	Number	4 −	4 +	Number
Per cent "tolerant"†	56	63	(76)	37	48	(69)	38	46	(46)	49	50	(191)
Other	44	37	(53)	63	52	(82)	62	54	(56)	51	50	(191)
Total per cent	100	100		100	100		100	100		100	100	
Number	(78)	(51)	(129)	(35)	(116)	(151)	(13)	(89)	(102)	(126)	(256)	(382)

* Arnold M. Rose, *Union Solidarity* (Minneapolis: University of Minnesota Press, 1952), p. 128, Table 42 (abridged and adapted). Reprinted with permission of the University of Minnesota Press.)
† In this table, the percentages are rounded for simplicity of presentation. The number of cases is, however, based on the percentages carried to one place beyond the decimal point, as shown in Table 4–6 of the text.

union a short time. Among the medium aged group, only 35 out of a total of 151, that is, 23 per cent, have been in a short time. Finally, in the older age group, only 13 out of 102, that is, 13 per cent, have been in a short time. There is thus a strong relationship between the test factor and the independent variable. The younger the man, the greater the likelihood that he has been a union member for less than four years.

Now consider the relationship between the test factor and the dependent variable. In the younger age group, 76 men out of a total of 129, that is, 59 per cent, are tolerant; in the medium age group, 69 out of 151, or 46 per cent, are tolerant; and in the older group, only 46 out of 102, or 45 per cent, are tolerant. We thus see that the younger men are more likely to be tolerant than the older.

Among men who have been in a short time, 56, 37, and 38 per cent, respectively, are tolerant. How do these three combine to produce a total of 49 per cent? It is based on the fact that the younger men, who are the most tolerant, represent a large proportion of the newcomers; out of a total of 126 newcomers, 78 (62 per cent) are younger. Therefore, their high level of tolerance will tend to raise the general level of tolerance of the newcomers substantially. Conversely, the relatively tolerant young men are less likely to be old-timers in the union; among the 256 old-timers in the union, only 51 (20 per cent) are young. Therefore, the high level of tolerance of the young men will have only a small effect on the total tolerance levels of the union members. When the 63, 48, and 36 per cent of the tolerant veterans are combined, they produce a total of 50 per cent tolerant among the veterans in the sample as a whole. As a result, for the total sample, 49 per cent of the newcomers and 50 per cent of the veterans are tolerant—virtually no difference.

We can thus see how the suppressor phenomenon operates. It appears by virtue of the fact that the test factor bears a "positive" relationship to the independent variable and a "negative" relationship to the dependent variable. (How one defines "positive" or "negative" in data of this sort makes no difference, so long as consistency is maintained; the point is that the relationship of the test factor to the independent and dependent variables must be in opposite directions, must have opposite signs.) Thus, the younger the person, the less likely he is to be a union veteran, but the more likely he is to be tolerant.

To summarize Table B-2, we would say that there "really" is a relationship between length of time in the union and tolerance, as is evident from an examination of the contingent associations. The reason this relationship does not appear in the total association is that younger men are more tolerant, but younger men tend to be in the union a shorter time. Eliminating the effect of age (by controlling on it), length of time in the union *is* conducive to tolerance.

It is only a simple extension of this principle to enable us to understand the operation of distorter variables. If, as in the suppressor variable situation, a zero correlation can become a relationship of a certain direction, it is obviously possible for a relationship in one direction to become a relationship in the opposite direction. A simple illustration appears in the hypothetical example, cited earlier, showing that working-class people are more pro-civil rights than middle-class people. When one controls on race, however, the results are reversed; it is the middle-class people who are more pro-civil rights. The reason is plain: working-class people are more pro-civil rights because they are more likely to be Negro, and Negroes are much more pro-civil rights. Another way of saying this is that, in this sample, working-class people are actually less pro-civil rights; but because so many of the workers are Negroes, and because Negroes are more pro-civil rights, the net result is that the sum total of workers is more pro-civil rights.

It is interesting to see how the arithmetic demonstrates this point. Table B-3 shows that there is an equal number of white-collar and manual workers in the sample. Seventy per cent of the 20 white-collar Negroes (14 people) and 30 per cent of the 100 white-collar whites (30 people) are pro-civil rights, for a total of 44 people out of 120 white-collar workers (37 per cent). Fifty per cent of the 100 manual Negroes (50 people) and 20 per cent of the 20 manual whites (4 people) are pro-civil rights, for a total of 54 out of 120 manual workers (45 per cent). For the total sample, then, manual workers are more pro-civil rights, but within each racial group, white-collar workers are more pro-civil rights. It is obvious that changes in the marginal totals would completely alter the results.

Table B-3
Occupational Group and Approval of Civil Rights: I. Controlled on Race and II. Total Relationship*

Civil rights score	Contingent Associations								Total Association TOTAL SAMPLE			
	NEGROES				WHITES							
	White Collar	Number	Manual	Number	White Collar	Number	Manual	Number	White Collar	Number	Manual	Number
Pro-civil rights	70%	(14)	50%	(50)	30%	(30)	20%	(4)	37%	(44)	45%	(54)
Anti-civil rights	30	(6)	50	(50)	70	(70)	80	(16)	63	(76)	55	(66)
Total per cent Number	100	(20)	100	(100)	100	(100)	100	(20)	100	(120)	100	(120)

* Hypothetical.

We have attempted to indicate how it is that a positive relationship, when stratified by a test factor, may disappear in the contingent associations; how a noncorrelation, when stratified by a test factor, may show a positive correlation in the contingent associations; and how a positive correlation, when stratified, may produce a correlation of an opposite sign. The general procedure employed is known as "subgroup classification." This is not the only technique for controlling on test factors. Standardization and partial correlation also perform this task; but, whichever procedure is used, the logic of analysis which we have been discussing remains the same. The purpose of the present discussion has been to expose the statistical mystery of controls; it is probable that a more precise understanding of the arithmetic involved will enhance one's understanding of the meaning of the tables.

NOTE

1. Even if it were not, however, it might be used for the study of conditional relationships or conjoint influence, discussed in chapters 5 to 7.

Index

DATE DUE

DEC 2 9 1995	

BRODART, INC.   Cat. No. 23-221